THE WIND SPIRIT

MICHEL TOURNIER

Translated by Arthur Goldhammer

BEACON PRESS · BOSTON

Beacon Press
25 Beacon Street
Boston, Massachusetts 02108

Beacon Press books
are published under the auspices of
the Unitarian Universalist Association
of Congregations.

95 94 93 92 91 90 89 88   1 2 3 4 5 6 7 8

Text design by Linda Koegel

Library of Congress Cataloging-in-Publication Data
Tournier, Michel.
[Vent paraclet. English]
The wind spirit : an autobiography / Michel Tournier ;
translated by Arthur Goldhammer.
p.   cm.
Translation of : Le vent paraclet
Bibliography: p.
ISBN 0-8070-7040-8
1. Tournier, Michel—Biography.   2. Novelists, French—20th
century—Biography.   I. Title.
PQ2680.083Z52713 1988
843'.914—dc19   88-47660

CONTENTS

TRANSLATOR'S
NOTE

Normally I think it best for a translator to stand aside and let his work speak for itself. To explain is to admit defeat. But as in Michel Tournier's fiction, in this literary autobiography no detail is insignificant. Every image is mirrored somewhere else in the text. The first section is entitled, in French, "L'Enfant Coiffé." Now, this is a figure of speech for a child born with a caul, and in France as in England and North America it is a sign of good luck. Hence translating, as I have done, as "Born Under a Lucky Star" captures the sense but not the concrete image. This is a shame for two reasons. First, it obscures the connection between the title of the first section and the epigraph from Saint-John Perse's *Eloge* XVII: "When you stop grooming me / I'll stop hating you" (in French, "Quand vous aurez fini de me *coiffer,* / j'aurai fini de vous haïr"). And second, the explicit image of the amnion adhering to the child's head is important because it is echoed in an image that occurs later in the work, that of the placenta as metaphor for the author of a philosophical system. Perhaps this single example will suffice to give the reader some idea of the difficulty of translating Tournier, for under the seeming simplicity and concreteness of his prose lies a complexity born of cunning.

The two quotations from *The Ogre* are taken from Barbara Bray's excellent translation, which oddly enough has been published under two titles, being known in England as *The Erl-King*. A rapid comparison turned up only one difference between the two, however: in the translation of the epigraph from Flaubert.

I have added a number of translator's notes to those already provided by the author in the Folio edition of *Le Vent Paraclet*. Many are intended simply to identify French names and institutions that may be unfamiliar to English-speaking readers.

1

BORN UNDER A LUCKY STAR

When you stop grooming me
I'll stop hating you.
—Saint-John Perse

My grandfather on my mother's side was six years old when the Prussians entered his native village of Bligny-sur-Ouche. The year was 1871. More than once I heard him tell the story of the "music stand." For, you see, he *was* the music stand. The leader of the military band lined up in the village square had chosen him from among the children in the first row of onlookers to carry his score. Little Edouard used both hands to hold up the large book that rested on his forehead. So no one could see him, but everyone could hear him because he was screaming, and his loud sobs mingled with the blare of the Prussian fanfare. A child in tears hidden by the book he is carrying:

this image, a family tradition, makes a fitting frontispiece to this essay.

Edouard's brother Gustave, five years older, weathered the occupation more easily. He became friendly with the band's flutist, whom he persuaded to give him lessons in German and music. There began two traditions to which my family has remained faithful to this day: the flute and *Germanistik*.[1]

Twenty years later, in the same town of Bligny, Edouard Fournier opened a pharmacy that still exists today. He remained its proprietor for nearly a half a century, until 1938. An old-fashioned apothecary, he made everything himself: pills, syrups, tablets, creams, suppositories. He was a botanist, a mycologist, and a connoisseur of wine (Burgundy, of course, there being no other). Like his elder brother he played the flute, and he also wrote little poems that appeared on Sundays in the *Fireside Friend*. For a long time he served as the photographer who took pictures of draftees, newlyweds, newborns, and children at First Communion. When he retired, I was too young to take an interest in his photographic archives, which have since been scattered or destroyed. Today I wish I still had those countless negatives, which bore witness to an era, to the faces of a generation. Each generation, I think, has a face unlike any other, because in some mysterious way it reflects the world that it confronts. Who can deny that movies, television, and jet travel have changed the features and expressions of our contemporaries?

Edouard Fournier had his pew in church and carried a banner in the processions of the Confraternity of Saint Sebastian. He detested Flaubert, guilty of having portrayed Monsieur Homais as both a pharmacist and an anticlerical.[2] He was a jovial, irascible man with a thunderous voice, but strength of character was not his most notable quality. He paid the price. Rarely has a man whose life was on the whole rather unhappy begun with so many advantages: an iron constitution, a highly sensual nature, blind faith, and a respected profession in one of France's finest provinces, prosperous and sophisticated Burgundy, with its dry climate, icy winters, and scorching summers. But that is another story.

From my earliest childhood his dispensary was my holiday stamping ground. (I can still hear him correcting my mistake in a tone of mild shock: "A pharmacy is not a shop. It's a dispensary.") Its prim, formal appearance hid an alchemist's lair. The facade was ordinary enough, rectangular in shape and all done in dark wood, but the floor had been tiled by a team of Piedmontese who had insisted upon working without witnesses. And in the window were two large glass urns filled with colored liquid—green on the right, red on the left—illuminated from behind by electric lights. Rows of porcelain jars whose gilt inscriptions told of such inoffensive medicines as licorice, jujubes, gumballs, and vetiver flanked a redoubtable locked cabinet, the key to which never left the druggist's watch chain: there the poisons and narcotics were kept. And there was also an alcove filled with bottles, bags, demijohns, and barrels. One day I removed the stopper from a carboy and sniffed at its mouth. Feeling as though I had been hit in the face, I staggered backwards. It was only ammonia, but there were fifty liters of it. In any case the place was magical primarily because of its odors, or perhaps I should say because of its odor, in the singular, for there was a characteristic, homogeneous, and unforgettable smell whose complexity must have resulted from the mingling of the most various and offensive chemical and medicinal musts, all somehow amalgamated, attenuated, and refined by long years of concoction.

Yet the pharmacy's greatest contribution to my development came in the form of words. Words were everywhere, on labels, jars, and bottles, and it was there that I truly learned to read. And what words they were, at once mysterious and extremely precise, mystery and precision being the two essential attributes of poetry. The label on one tall, slender-necked vial sticks in my mind because of its enchanting melody: spirit of colocynth. Only later did I learn that this exquisitely musical appellation designates the harshest and bitterest of purgatives.

Under the roof, in the mansard whose walls and wainscotting were entirely covered with illustrations from a mail-order catalog known as *The Illustrated Department Store,* there was also a dusty library consisting primarily of medical works, from which I imbibed terrifying, delicious knowledge that made me laugh with pity at my classmates, who had no choice but to turn to the dictionary to discover the secrets of love. This attic, furnished with but a single, dusty sofa, was an ideal place for private reverie. When it rained, the various parts of the roof with its runners and gutters combined to form a complex, mournful symphony to which one could listen as the night fell.

Sometimes, assuming an air of innocence, I used to question my grandfather. I can see him still, his broad back bent over an analytical balance that he had carefully removed from its glass cage, his cap pushed down around his neck, his glasses balanced on the end of his nose. Gently with his right hand he tapped his left, which held a piece of paper folded in two. Down the crease minute quantities of a white powder tumbled into a small cup.

"Tell me, grandpa, what does this mean: DI-U-RE-TIC?"

Unflinchingly he replied, "You drink one glass and you piss two."

There was also an inner courtyard above which towered the town hall belfry, whose bell, rung twice on the hour and once on the quarter- and half-hour, made for a never-ending concert. The courtyard was connected to the street by a portico long enough to serve as a garage for the angular, high-slung silhouette of a Citroën B12, purchased for 25,000 francs in 1924, a formidable sum that has since been enshrined in the family folklore. Edouard, who would never have dared to look under the hood, missed no opportunity to praise the elegance of the car's crystal flower vase or the quality of its pure wool upholstery and rugs. At the other end of the courtyard loomed the high doors of the barn, in which slumbered firewood, potatoes, and summer bicycles. This was a dark, cool place that smelled of old potatoes, dried mushrooms, and wine and served as a refuge for cats, owls, mice, and bats. We never set foot there at night.

Three times a day the little train that ran from Arnay to Beaune drawn by a cute, fire-breathing locomotive passed in front of the house with much commotion. The last train ran late enough that we were in bed by the time it heralded its arrival in town with a blast of its whistle. Listening to the din, we also enjoyed the fantastic light show that its searchlights created on the ceiling of our room as their beams passed through the slats of the shutters.

Cross the street and you were in another world. Opposite the pharmacy stood the handsome house of the village physician, Dr. Gabriel Roy. He was a small man, whose spiritual air, blue eyes, and blond beard went well with a somewhat mystical cast of mind. It is impossible to conceive of a family more utterly medical than his. There were three brothers and four sisters. Of the latter, three were pharmacists and the fourth a stomatologist. As for the men, in addition to Gabriel the general practitioner there were Jean the surgeon and Joseph, a celebrated homeopath.

Dr. Gabriel Roy had eight children, and they were our playmates. My favorite, Geneviève, was as sweet and blonde as her name would suggest. In fate's surprise-packet she found a fairy tale of sorts. Needing a governess for his children Alexander and Christina, Aristotle Onassis made inquiries at the Swiss nursing college where Geneviève was a student, and she was chosen. Thus the country girl from Bligny-sur-Ouche suddenly became part of the family of the man of whom Maria Callas said, "He was as handsome as Croesus." She had to get used to the ever-present gorillas with bulging pockets who stood guard over her too-precious charges. Much of her life was spent aboard the *Christina,* the most beautiful yacht in the world—so much, in fact, that when the children were grown and she regained her liberty, she married the captain. A naturalized citizen of Greece, she has since lived in Athens. Another marriage brought us closer together. Her uncle, the celebrated homeopath Joseph Roy, became my uncle by marrying the pharmacist's youngest daughter, my aunt Marie-Louise.

Insurmountable anxiety kept me away from the gatherings of this medical clan, which to me seemed like a family of ogres. For my familiarity with the pharmacy by no means drew me closer to the world of medicine—quite the contrary. Today I understand the meaning of the apprenticeship that I was undergoing. I had been learning to heal myself so that I might avoid the ministrations of the feared medical fraternity. That hope has not been disappointed. As I write these lines, the last doctor I saw has vanished into the mists of a past so distant that all memory of him has been effaced from my mind. In fact, I live on a dozen drugs that I discovered on my own, some of which surely act solely as placebos. I use these medications parsimoniously and with complete satisfaction.

The reason for my fear is that at the dawn of my little personal prehistory there was the Aggression, the Attack, a crime that bloodied my childhood and from whose horror I have never recovered.

I was four years old, an extremely nervous child, subject to convulsions, hypersensitive, and perpetually ill, not only with the usual childhood diseases but also with many quite unusual ones, most no doubt partly psychosomatic. One morning, two people I had never seen before burst into my room, wearing white coats, white caps, and with shiny laryngoscopes on their foreheads. It was like something out of science fiction or a horror film. They hurled themselves upon me, wrapped me in my sheets, and then tried to remove my jaw from its socket with a screw-operated separator. Then the pincers came into play, because the tonsils are not cut out but pulled, like teeth. I was literally drenched in my own blood.

That vicious attack left me gasping and limp, and I have no idea how they revived me. Forty-five years later I still bear traces of the operation, and I remain incapable of describing the scene dispassionately. During the last war prepubescent girls were raped by soldiers. I maintain that they were less traumatized than I was by having my throat slit at the age of four, and hence that an inebriated trooper armed to the teeth and drunk with power is less dangerous to humanity than certain surgeons—medical school professors, no less. It is tragic that a brutish imbecile like my surgeon was not forever banished from a profession he was so obviously incapable of practicing from the moment of his first crime. That butcher's name was Bourgeois. A well-known physician, he was the only man in the world whom I have ever hated without reservation, because he did me incalculable harm, having branded my heart at the most tender age with an incurable distrust of my fellow human beings, even those nearest and dearest to me.

I never heard of him again until the day when news of his death mysteriously reached me. There are people in the world to whom we are bound by love or hate and whose fate we secretly track, even if we never see them. On that day I breathed more easily. It is sweet to think that he died in horrible, interminable agony.

I have never stopped ruminating on that bloody mishap that left my childhood spattered as though it had bathed in a huge red sun, and from it I have drawn all sorts of questions, ideas, and hypotheses. Childhood is given to us as ardent confusion, and the rest of life is not time enough to make sense of it or explain to ourselves what happened.

I believe that I recovered fairly quickly from my ordeal and that my tormenters were able to congratulate themselves on their nice piece of work. The family had to stop taking me along on shopping expeditions, however: the sight of the butcher's bloodstained apron sent me into convulsions. One of the most paradoxical things about children is their curious mixture of fragility and ruggedness. They are at once infinitely vulnerable and utterly indefatigable. No doubt both qualities are necessary, for while a child must be tender enough to register every impression that it receives, still it must not die from its wounds.

Initiation. The word comes to my pen enhanced by all that I have learned about the subject from my study of anthropology. A child's initiation is a twofold phenomenon, consisting of entry into society (primarily a male bastion) combined with exit from the maternal orbit. It is, in short, a transition from a biological state to a social status. And it is never completed without tears and wails. Burns, bites, mutilations, removal of teeth—the list of tortures inflicted on children in so-called primitive societies as the price of their being granted the status of adult male is endless. In extreme cases the candidate may even be put to death—symbolically—only to be reborn afterward, ready to begin his life *ab initio,* this time with a man for mother: the witch doctor.[3]

Should the plucking out of my tonsils be interpreted as an unconscious—and thus still savage—vestige of an initiatory rite? This did not occur to me until one day a pediatrician confessed that the operation has no therapeutic or preventive value whatsoever. The hypothesis is confirmed, I think, by the, to say the least, peculiar fact that this butchery is inflicted far more often on boys than on girls, who are traditionally exempt from initiatory rituals. I then thought of another, far more remarkable instance of aggression by adult males against small boys, namely, circumcision. This mutilation, too, is camouflaged by religious or hygienic pretexts. Yet in fact it is an antierotic mutilation, a symbolic castration, which seriously and irremediably reduces genital sensitivity as a result of keratinization of the epidermis of the glans. Fellatio becomes impossible, or at least so laborious that it loses all its charm. The prepuce is like the lid of an eye, and the glans of a circumcised male resembles an eye whose lid has been torn off. When exposed to the harsh elements, crystalline matter sometimes becomes dry, thick, and vitreous and loses its transparency; similarly, the vision of such a lidless eye would be crude, rough, and approximate.

Statistics on the subject might prove quite revealing. If the figures showed that circumcised males were subjected to markedly fewer tonsillectomies than uncircumcised males, then it would be obvious that both forms of aggression were vestigial rites of initiation, the two operations having nothing else in common and hence there being no other reason why it should be possible to substitute one for the other.

As for exiting the maternal orbit, that was an experience I was not to undergo for two more years. By then I was six, a child with an enormous head upon a sparrowlike body, and I neither slept nor ate. It was obvious that I would not long survive the Paris climate. It was probably at about this time that I became aware of my deep-seated dislike of my native city. To love Paris and to sing about Montmartre and Pigalle you have to be an American like Josephine Baker or an Italian like Yves Montand or a Dane like Georg Ulmer. But when you're born on rue de la Victoire in the Ninth Arrondissement, when you've learned to walk in Louis XVI Square on the ashes of the victims of the Terror and in the shadow of the sinister Memorial, you don't sing, you vomit. Sure, a tiny portion of the city can boast of superb monuments and noble views, but people don't live in monuments or views, and I know of no city more completely alien, more fundamentally hostile to well-being, or in which the tree has been more stupidly sacrificed to the automobile, than Paris. Having been born there, I consider myself to have been born nowhere, to have fallen from the sky like a meteorite. The same can be said, incidentally, of Parisians in general, for there is no such thing as a true Parisian. My father came originally from northern France, from the town of Dorignies, not far from Douai, and my mother from Burgundy. Paris is thus filled with provincials, who spend their careers there and flee as soon as they can. Marseilles, Lyons, and Bordeaux no doubt have genuinely indigenous populations, which date back several generations and possess their own peculiar characters, traditions, culinary specialties, and slang. But Paris is like a huge pump, which alternately sucks up and spews out provincials. Albert Thibaudet long ago pointed out how few great writers were born in Paris, surely less than the one in ten that one would expect from simple demographics and not even allowing for the qualitative and cultural factors that one would expect to give the capital an edge.

People say that Hitler in 1944 ordered his troops to set fire to Paris before evacuating it. Upon learning of the Liberation he is supposed to have asked, "Is Paris burning?" The question became the title of a well-known film. I have my doubts. Burn Paris? How could so clever an idea have originated in so wicked a mind? But if the story is true despite my doubts, for once I am sorry that Hitler was not obeyed, since for once he made a wise decision.

In any event, I arrived one night in November 1931 in Gstaad, Switzerland, where I had been sent to live in a home for sickly children born with silver spoons, the Chalet Flora. A raging torrent nearby made my first night there almost a metaphysical experience. For I was astonished by the noise and questioned everyone about its nature and origin. They in turn were astonished by my astonishment. Being a newcomer, I was the only one who heard it. Obviously that did not last, and eventually I, too, became accustomed to the sound, but on that occasion, having left my family for the first time, I came close to what must be the ordinary state of certain mystics, who alone among men hear the voices of angels or perceive the presence of something or Someone.

I shall have nothing bad to say about Swiss education, which is surely traditional in some ways, innovative in others. At the risk of dismaying educators, I must say that I am only too convinced of the inability of adults to bridge the abyss that separates them from the individual child and still more from communities of children, which are more closed and secretive than any conspiratorial society. Yet on one point I must protest against the methods of the Swiss, who claimed to be more enlightened than most. Why did our schoolmasters contrive so ingeniously to make us suffer from thirst? For I was desperately thirsty throughout my childhood, and I would like someone to tell me why. Someone must have told the adults in charge of our upbringing that liquids and solids had been assigned moral coefficients, liquids being marked minus and solids plus, and that, unlike eating to relieve hunger, drinking to relieve thirst had something in common with the more unmentionable forms of pleasure. For a boy to drink when he was hot was to risk death, or so we were told. (But when we were cold, naturally we weren't thirsty.) It isn't good to "drown the stomach." To control thirst is a sign of character. In short, solid is virtuous, liquid vicious. At the Chalet Flora this alimentary morality was applied in all its strictness. At table the drinks were doled out to each child in proportion to the amount of dry matter he was willing to chew or swallow. But I was never hungry, always thirsty!

The bedrooms contained two beds, each "little" pupil being placed under the protection of a "big" one. My roommate, whose name was Niño, was "big" by virtue not only of his eleven years but also of having been born a Spanish grandee. As for his protection, from the first day he was a despot and I his slave, besides which I was subjected to a variety of tortures, for the most part inflicted with the help of a small rope. While still very young I discovered all the uses to which such a seemingly inoffensive object can be put by a child sadist.

Gstaad was my first journey, my first exile, an experience which, though rather harsh, was nevertheless, all things considered, tolerably rewarding and to which my extraordinary thirst and Niño's tortures lent a needed air of profundity and seriousness. Take a sickly, sensitive child raised in his mother's skirts, pluck him out of the gray drizzle of a Paris November and suddenly transport him to a cosmopolitan setting in the Swiss mountains. What will he experience? The snow; the roof festooned with sta-lactites toward which an equal number of stalagmites rose from the ground in rows, like candles; the skiing; the skat-ing; the rides in sleighs drawn by jingling horses; the howling of the torrent muted by the ice; the naps during which I lay wrapped in blankets on the great terrace, op-posite mountain peaks over whose black-and-white fir caps flew mournful squadrons of jackdaws; solitude; pas-sion; sorrow; and last but not least this cruel but salutary lesson: in a couple the one who loves more is always the weaker, the clumsier, the more vulnerable, the less happy of the two. (That he was also the richer, the more alive, and the more creative, and that the future belonged to him, he would not find out until much later.) All these discoveries will cause the boy's heart to burst, and he will remember them as a painful moment of birth.

Yes, the first years of man's offspring are a time of wrenching loss. Stripped from his mother's womb like a fox cub from its lair, the child finds tenuous and tempo-rary shelter in his mother's arms, nourished by capricious and parsimonious breasts. Subsequently he must abandon this refuge as well, after which he will be allowed only a few minutes a day in that last haven, his mother's bed, a vast ship, white and shadowy, in which for the briefest of intervals his body again clings to the body from which it sprang. Then comes the final expulsion. Grown "too big," the child can no longer "decently" lie in its parents' bed. Thereupon begins a long trek across a vast and terrifying desert.

For me, that expulsion, the beginning of that trek, that desert's first grains of sand were called Gstaad. And the first cactus in whose thorny arms I half-maimed myself was named Niño. Was this inevitable? Was it on the whole beneficial? Is there no better way to produce a healthy, well-balanced adult, blessed with a diversity of interests and numerous friends? I am not unaware of the literary advantage to be derived from one's wounds and bruises— I am the first to admit it. But not everyone is fortunate enough to practice a profession that allows him to set his tears to music. I wonder what justifies such a desert, and what its cost may be. Once the child has been expelled from his mother's bed, he finds himself deprived of all physical contact for some fifteen years, that is, throughout his childhood and adolescence. When access to another person's body is finally restored—at sixteen, eighteen, twenty-five years of age, sometimes even later—when the child can once again nestle his face in the hollow of a shoulder or sense the pressure of breast against breast, sex against sex, then, in a moment of immense relief, of released anxiety, of feverish joy in the great rediscovery of the other, he will be vaguely aware of a reminiscence, of an infinitely remote and disturbing memory of the last physical embrace accorded him in the immemorial time of mama's bed.

Again, why? Why must the most tender and then the most ardent years of human life unfold in an aridity artificially created and maintained by society? In my novel *Gemini* I described a pair of twins who lived through this period of their lives joined together as they had been in their mother's womb. But I have read studies of twin psychology[4] and listened to the confessions of twins both male and female, so I know that not all of them, alas, escape the effects of a stupid and peevish puritanism that keeps children and adolescents in a systematic state of emotional distress. Quite often physical intimacy between twins is taboo even in their own eyes, and if forced to share a bed for a night they will imagine an invisible line dividing the mattress in two, the crossing of which constitutes a grave sin. Why? Because society keeps children and adolescents in a triple-walled prison designed to prevent all physical contact. First, they are kept under constant surveillance, particularly in boarding schools. Who has not heard of that ominous dictum, *Nunquam duo* (never two), the operative rule in all seminaries and boarding-school dormitories? Second, constant moral pressure obliges each child to internalize the prohibition and thus to become his own persecutor. In order to violate the physical taboo, one must therefore elude the vigilance of proctors, overcome one's own inhibitions, and finally vanquish the inhibitions of one's partner—a threefold victory that demands both exceptional strength of character and extraordinary circumstances.

When I speak of physical contact, I mean of course something far more vast and more primitive than erotic games and sexual relations, which are merely a special case. Freudian psychoanalysis has long persisted in viewing the need for physical contact simply as a libidinal impulse given concrete form by the desire of the newborn for its mother's breast or, later, by genital sexuality. But recently several psychologists have more or less simultaneously proposed a new idea, which, though seemingly of modest import, nevertheless profoundly alters the very foundations of psychoanalysis, namely, the idea of *attachment* as a primary and irreducible drive. According to this view, the infant's attachment to its mother is not a consequence of oral gratification but a primitive and fundamental bond, which may later diversify and seek other partners. For Freud, "it is libido, the sexual drive, that gradually leads to love, which in the final analysis is only a means of obtaining pleasure. The new view is that for the higher animals and man love is primary, prior to sexuality, and that it is this love, the foundation of trust and security, that prepares the way for sexuality with all its preliminaries, games, and consummations as well as for loves of a new order."[5] One considerable advantage of this new view is that it is applicable to the higher animals as well as to human beings, whereas the classical Freudian schema is obviously valid only for man. In fact the young chimpanzee does exhibit a primary attachment to its mother, an attachment prior to the young animal's normal dependence on its mother for nourishment.

Everyone says that young children like to play with dolls and teddy bears, and sometimes they are permitted to play with small animals. It is also commonly said, however, that dogs like bones. The truth is that dogs gnaw on bones when they have nothing else, but you can take my word for it, they would prefer a good cut of steak or a nice veal cutlet. As for children, it is quite simply a dreadful thing that we toss them dolls and animals in order to assuage their need for a warm, loving body. Of course sailors on long voyages sometimes avail themselves of inflatable rubber females, and lonely shepherds in the mountains have been known to mount a lamb or goat. But children are neither sailors nor shepherds and do not lack for human company. Their distress is the invention of a fiercely antiphysical society, of a mutilating, castrating culture, and there is no question that many character disorders, violent outbursts, and cases of juvenile drug addiction are consequences of the physical desert into which the child and adolescent are customarily banished in our society.

Before discussing influences—records and books—I want to speak of certain objects, certain occupations—I hardly dare call them toys or games—whose common denominator seems to have been a high degree of solitude. But before discussing any of these things I must quote the philosopher Leibniz, for reasons which will become obvious.

Leibniz's *Monadology* (1714) was never for me a bitter tonic like certain other great works of philosophy, particularly Kant's, the study of which "edified" me (that is, constructed my intellect and instructed my moral understanding) all the more for having repelled me at first sight. With Leibniz I immediately felt that I was dealing with someone who understood me; I felt that my convictions and habits of mind were not only accepted but almost honored.

Leibniz is the baroque thinker par excellence. His system—or, rather, the series of scale models of a system that he offers in lieu of a vast and comprehensive exposé—is reminiscent of those graceful Swabian and Austrian churches decorated with friezes of blue, white, and pink stucco, in which wreaths of laughing angels with chubby cheeks and buttocks surround saints male and female, their faces radiant with intelligent goodness and their supple bodies twisting and dancing as though wafted heavenward by the wind of the spirit. The *Monadology* describes a universe devoid of coercion, friction, or contact of any kind; everything owes its beginning and end to a series of correspondences, harmonies, and concordances. The creation of the world, for example, is not the result of a sudden and arbitrary decision, reeking of the sulfurous volcano and apocalypse of Genesis, but more like a gentle, steady rain-fall or snowfall, an accompaniment to certain reflections within the mind of God: "God calculates and the world is made." There is an immense number of possible worlds, each of which presses toward existence to the degree that there is goodness in it, goodness propelling the possible toward the real like a ballast of lead. The real world, there-fore, is nothing other than that compound of compatible possible worlds containing the maximum total sum of goodness. It is in this sense that the real world is "the best of all possible worlds," and not by dint of some foolish optimism of the sort that Voltaire, with dismaying frivol-ity, chose to attack in *Candide*. Implicit in Leibniz's account of the creation of the world is a version of the ontological argument delightful for its simplicity and clarity. Of all the possible worlds that press toward existence—the vast ma-jority of which are eliminated by incompatibility with the ultimate outcome—the possible-God is the first to be re-alized, the highest priority, since it possesses an unsurpass-able quantity of goodness. Hence no problem of compat-ibility arises for it, and therefore if God is possible, God exists. Q.E.D.

The monad is a closed microcosm containing in more or less distinct form every detail of the entire world. *In more or less distinct form:* the crux of the matter lies in this "more or less," for when two monads represent the same detail with unequal distinctness, the more distinct repre-sentation is called the *cause* and the less distinct represen-tation is called the *effect*. Consider two examples, one the ultimate in sublimity, the other more mundane. God, being the most distinct of all monads, must be considered to be the creator of the world. On the other hand, if a billiard ball *A* strikes a billiard ball *B*, *A* stops and *B* begins to move, but it is false to conclude that the two balls have touched and that the momentum in *A* has passed to *B*. In fact, the balls have not touched; *nothing ever touches anything else*. *A* has come infinitesimally close to *B*. *A* did not stop. Its momentum spontaneously decreased to an infinitesimal amount. *B* did not begin moving, since it was moving already, but at an infinitesimal speed. Spontaneously its motion accelerated and thus became perceptible. My interpretation of this entire interaction depends upon my point of view, and since to my eyes the motion of *A* is made intelligible by the motion of the cue and the action of the billiard player, and since for me the reasons for *B*'s motion remain obscure, I say that *A* is the cause and *B* the effect. But this is merely a manner of speaking, nothing more.

From these tiny, closed cells, devoid of material contact and conspiring together to create a harmonious, hierarchical order, there emanates a pure, tranquil light, which is none other than the sovereignty of intelligence, possessing no power but that of persuasion. The monadology describes an ideal society in which the laws of nature might be called politeness, courtesy, and affability. To reiterate, I know no other philosophy of such charming persuasiveness.

No one is immune to Leibniz's charm, but I have reason to believe that I was more susceptible than most. If I were to declare myself in favor of any philosophy, this is surely the one I would choose. I shall mention just two early memories in which I see a Leibnizian predestination.

As a child, first of all, I had a strong predilection for certain objects that were in fact nothing other than transparent, self-contained little worlds. I am thinking in particular of those little celluloid spheres half-filled with water, upon the surface of which float two ducks. In my bed I hid an entire lake composed of these atoms, and I liked to expose my ducks to the vagaries of the weather, to tempest as well as calm. In *Gemini* I imputed my fondness for these objects to the twins Jean and Paul. They in turn saw the little plastic spheres as symbols of the twin cell with its dual inhabitants, hermetically sealed against perturbations emanating from the world of "individuals."

I was also fascinated by another object more obviously connected with meteorology. This was a sort of globe or paperweight, in which by shaking one could cause snow to fall around a miniature replica of the Eiffel Tower or Mont Saint-Michel.

In my mind these objects undoubtedly anticipated Leibniz's hermetic monad, without "doors or windows through which one could enter or leave"[6] yet in whose inner sanctum the external world was reproduced in its entirety, including even its inclement weather.

Still more Leibnizian were certain games that I thought up before I could read or write—the significance of this detail will emerge presently. For hours on end, for instance, I compared two maps of France, whose format, colors, and scales were of course different. The less the two maps were alike, the more I liked to compare them, for the whole point of the game was to note identities in spite of differences, to identify a particular gulf or bend in a river but above all to discover the names of cities, towns, bodies of water, and the like, even though they were printed in different fonts on each map. For the child not yet fully initiated into the mysteries of reading and writing, these coincidences of signs seemed miraculous.

Now, as it happens, this game corresponds quite closely to Leibniz's notion of "preestablished harmony," since the two maps were similar not by virtue of a direct influence of one upon the other but because they shared a common model, a formidable and formidably inaccessible reality, France itself.

Because my father's profession required him to maintain regular contacts with companies that manufactured phonograph records, he periodically brought home from the office bundles of recordings sent out by the companies for publicity. He would play them once on the phonograph in the living room and then forget about them, and sooner or later the cast-off records would end up in my room.

For my favorite toy was a phonograph. Actually I called it a "phono," the more august term *phonograph* being reserved for the massive oak object in the living room, whose resonator was equipped with two small doors. The problem was that at first, when I was three or four, I was still too small to turn the crank, and I spent my days begging everyone who passed my door to rewind the machine. Today I wonder why my parents never thought of hiring an additional servant (they could have afforded it) whose only job would have been to rewind my phono. I should add that I sorely tried everyone's patience by indefatigably replaying the same record, with my child's taste for the same old saws and catchy tunes repeated ad nauseam, rather like a drug. It is really quite remarkable that the virtues of "suspense" are apparent only to adults. For the child there is additional pleasure in knowing in advance every episode of a story, every reply in a dialogue, and every note in a song, and that pleasure increases with each repetition. The child subscribes to an "antisuspense" aesthetic. It is the same with the professional storytellers who make the rounds of rural towns and who begin by giving a brief summary of the story they are about to recount, as

if to kill all untoward curiosity in the audience and to prepare them for voluptuous immersion in a vast sea of detail
and digression.

To what records did I listen so immoderately, then,
given that it would be impossible to overestimate the influence of such large doses of music on such a young listener?
No doubt the best and the worst were both represented,
but I have distinct memories of such classical works
as Beethoven's *Pastoral* Symphony, Bizet's *L'Arlésienne*,
Saint-Saëns' *Algerian Suite* and *Danse Macabre*, Ravel's
Bolero, and von Suppé's *Charge of the Light Brigade* and
of such popular songs of the period as *Constantinople*,
Hallelujah, *Aie-aie-aie*, *Blanche de Castille*, *La Mousmée*, *Le
Siffleur et son chien*, *Le saxophone qui rit*, and *Jalousie*. My
favorites, though, were talking records, and the two primary ones, both packaged in thick boxes, stand for opposite extremes of the genre: *A Performance by Grock the
Clown* and Jean Cocteau's *La Voix humaine* read by Berthe
Bovy. With hindsight the coupling of these two names is
not without a certain savor, but I was oblivious to the contrast. *La Voix humaine!* With horrified fascination I witnessed the spectacle, repeated a thousand times—over a
period of years—of the aging woman, writhing in damp
sheets, her makeup undone, wailing and begging the male
deserter—how well we understand him!—with one hand
on her heart, the other on a bottle of phenobarbitol. The
jilted woman's mating cry, which wailed in my young ears
day after day, impressed upon me a certain image of the
fair sex, which later experiences covered over without entirely obliterating. We do not choose our emotional initia-
tions. I long believed that in order to write this dreadful
piece Cocteau must have harbored a boundless hatred and
contempt for women, until one day I saw a performance
of *Le Bel Indifférent*, which is in a sense the decoded ver-

sion, the translation into plain text, of *La Voix humaine*.
Only then did I understand that the author without question identified with the sniveling, clinging creature in the
bed and that the play was the cruelest bit of masochism
imaginable.

Fortunately there was also Grock, whom I never saw in
the circus but whose unique brand of comedy made a deep
impression on me at an important moment in my life. The
clown's big problem is that he belongs to a class of actors
for whom no one writes, so that he is obliged to create his
own repertoire. He has no choice but to join the age-old
fraternity of actor-writers, the tradition not just of Sacha
Guitry but also of Shakespeare and Molière, and that is
obviously a great deal to ask. Grock devoted his life to
perfecting his act, which ultimately ran some two hours
long. The clown's art carries with it certain obligations,
some positive, others negative. A great clown owes it to
himself to make use of all the traditional resources of the
trade, most notably acrobatics and music. He must also
employ artifices of makeup and costume, at times going
to grotesque extremes in the use of "special effects" such
as revolving wigs, squirting tears, skulls that explode
when struck, and so on. Yet he is not permitted to be
either handsome or tragic—not to the ultimate degree, at
any rate. Ugliness and ridiculousness are inevitably a part
of his equipment. As for Grock, his triumph was the culmination of an evolutionary process, which, though it
lasted barely a century and a half, is most instructive for
anyone interested in the aesthetics of the theater.

In the beginning the white clown appeared alone. To a
rough audience of rustics or workers he represented elegance, distinction, and intelligence. While his spectators
had dark or ruddy faces, his white face was that of the
high-society salon. His right eyebrow rose audaciously to

the middle of his forehead in an expression of surprise coupled with perspicacity. A clever aristocrat, he directed his sallies at the most oafish of his spectators, causing the others to laugh at the scapegoat he had chosen. In his banter there was an edge of cruelty, even a whiff of sadism, yet the cooperation of the victim's peers was easily obtained.

Most likely he had the idea one night of hiding a confederate in the audience, a victim truer than life, and of directing his jibes exclusively at this prearranged target, even bringing him down into the ring by his side. This was an unfortunate idea, for from it was born Augustus, whose success grew steadily to the point where eventually the white clown was relegated to the role of second fiddle. But the evolutionary process was not complete until Grock, a genius of the genre, arrived on the scene, combining remarkable skills of physical contortion with a sharp wit. He wore his sleeves bunched up but with white gloves and starched cuffs. When he pushed a piano, it was to move it closer to the stool, and when he opened a box the size of a coffin, it was to extract from it a tiny violin.

Grock's white partner was never sufficiently docile, unobtrusive, and servile for his taste, and his whole career was marked by quarrels with his straight men until the day he decided to do his act by himself. But the white clown is immortal, for a comedian is forever faced with a simple alternative: to make people laugh at himself (the red clown) or to make them laugh at someone else (the white clown). In any case, even as the red clown with Grock's cardboard head was taking over the big top, the white clown, metamorphosed and intellectualized, was simultaneously being raised to new heights by Sacha Guitry. Guitry's talent was to make people laugh at someone else, at a designated victim, while himself remaining in the back-

ground. The best illustration of this is *Le Diable boiteux*
("The Limping Devil"), his film about the life of Talleyrand. Immaculately dressed and wearing the powdered
wig of the prince of the Périgord, his silk-stockinged
bowed calves made famous by a crude joke, Sacha gave
free rein to his sharp tongue. Without hesitation he cast
Napoleon in the role of red clown, for which one must
forgive him, as the subject lent itself to such treatment.
After all, was not Augustus also the name of a great emperor?

The child "plays the clown" with such gusto that one
wonders if it isn't perhaps the clown's natural function to
"play the child." As the white clown's immaculate, measured, verbal world is destroyed by a combination of prat-
falls, buffoonery, and outrageous travesty, the child discovers a model for his struggle against the oppressive
regimentation of adult society. Fighting with his back
to the wall, the "ill-bred" child, like the clown, relies on
grimace and contortion, employing all the resources of his
body to combat the discipline of speech and writing. The
red clown attacks the polite world in the two areas that the
child finds most oppressive: the dinner table (and table
manners) and the school. He is the humiliated and rebellious brother of that other childhood hero, the wild man,
in his twin guises as Mowgli and Tarzan.

To play the clown: throughout my educational "career"
this was my only outlet, my refuge, my drug—and the
results are not difficult to imagine. Yes, I was an execrable
student, and rarely did I finish a school year in the same
institution in which I began. I have often wondered about
the inevitability of all this, which weighed so heavily upon
my childhood. An additional fact sheds some light on the

subject: I was as good a student in college as I was a poor student in high school. In this, perhaps, an answer lies. For no one is a good student who cannot and does not like to work *alone*. The college student must learn to work independently of his teachers and devote himself to individual research. At this I excelled. But the younger pupil is incapable of such solitary work. His progress comes under the close scrutiny of his teachers and depends upon establishing a good rapport with them. To receive knowledge from a flesh-and-blood human being who waved his arms in front of me and obsessed me with his tics and odors was more than I could do. I had dozens of teachers, both male and female. I retained little of what they taught, but with hallucinatory precision I can still see their features, almost always ugly or ridiculous. I have no wish to cause distress to any member of the teaching profession—which in any case was to have been my calling—but it seems to me that it includes more than its share of eccentrics, lunatics, derelicts, and grotesques. Perhaps this line of work is more destructive than others to those who practice it. It has been said that power induces madness and absolute power induces absolute madness. It is possible that the teacher's authority over a class of children in the long run saps his character and personality. If so, then the relaxation of discipline typical of modern education should have a beneficial effect on the mental health of teachers. In any case I hope that today's schoolchildren need never make the acquaintance of the incredibile imbeciles with whom I had to cope. One of them served as headmaster in one of the many schools through which I passed. He was given to appearing in person in the classroom to read the grades on compositions, which he naturally coupled with adverse comments on our work. These became a sort of refrain. He always began with the same line, uttered in the same reproachful tones: "I don't see many of you among the top ten." Originally, perhaps, this absurdity was intended to be witty, but it had become a habit and the words fell from his lips mechanically, absolutely devoid of humor. (Such is the punishment meted out to those who would be wits but who neglect the first rule of the genre, which is inventiveness and creativity. I have a friend who for months made fun of his gardener's southern accent. His imitations had an irresistible effect on his family and guests. Then the gardener quit, but the accent—much moderated, it is true—remained, and my friend was never able to rid himself of it entirely. He had allowed himself to be *possessed,* in the most religious sense of the word.) I'm no longer sure whether it was this headmaster or some other whom I surprised one day on the playground. Noticing a piece of paper on the ground, he bent down to pick it up and then walked over to a trash barrel to dispose of it. But this first mechanical action was soon followed by another: taking a pen from his pocket, he signed the paper before tossing it into the receptacle.

Among the many teachers whom I remember only for their tics two stand out as exceptions, and in passing I want to honor them with an affectionate tip of the hat. René Letréguilly was my sixth-grade teacher. I don't know whether he was simply lucky or chose me deliberately. Had the French university system not stood in the way of my vocation, the sixth grade is the class I would have liked to have taught, Marcel Jouhandeau notwithstanding.[7] The pupils are then in the adult stage of childhood, when the child's individuality is fully developed but before it has been overwhelmed by puberty. (People die, of course, at all ages, but statistics tell us that eleven-year-olds are least likely to pass away.) René Letréguilly, a small, mild, timid man, knew how to establish a wonderful rapport with his students, the first beneficiary of which was the Latin grammar. I have never known a teacher less authoritarian or more completely obeyed. But he sometimes came up with rather dotty ideas. A case in point was Luigini's *Egyptian Ballet,* which he took it into his head to have us perform for the school's anniversary celebration. On the blackboard he had drawn robes and tiaras that we copied down and had our mothers reproduce. He had also invented an "Egyptian step," remarkably priestly in conception, which made us look as though we had stepped out of a bas-relief from Aswan. Alas, after listening and relistening to Luigini's ballet music, we had to yield to the evidence: the celebrated "step" turned out to be totally incompatible with the ancient rhythm of the supposedly "Egyptian" ballet. After a brief period of disarray, I stepped forward and saved the day, a fact of which I am still proud forty years later. One day I showed up at school with that year's great hit recording, *The Dance of the Japanese Lanterns* by the German-Japanese composer Yoshitomo, in my knapsack. It was played on the classroom phonograph, while the whole class listened in religious silence. Then we danced. And a miracle occurred: the Breton Letréguilly's "Egyptian step" was wonderfully well suited to the Japanese rhythm of the German Yoshitomo. Our performance was a success, but few people had any idea of the musical miscellany from which it had been concocted.

I heard from Letréguilly again some thirty-five years later. He had written to me after reading about a literary prize I had won. Retired from teaching, he and his wife kept a small bookshop in Gréoux-les-Bains. He sent me a photo of myself at age eleven and spoke of "our" sixth-grade class with a wealth of detail that astonished me. I had not been a very remarkable pupil, so far as I was aware, so where had he dug up this treasure trove of memories? "You have no special place in my memory," he wrote. "But I have a fairly clear image of the some twelve hundred students whom I taught in my career." And he added that of that horde of graduates only two had had their pictures in the newspapers. The other "celebrity" was Jacques Fesch, who was executed in 1957 after being convicted of a bloody robbery. He had corresponded with his former teacher from the depths of his prison cell.

Two years later the eighth grade yielded me another friend in Laurent de Gouvion Saint-Cyr, a swaggering musketeer of a man, as adventurous and ebullient as Letréguilly was timid and unobtrusive. He was twenty-three years old; we were thirteen. We felt very close to him, all the more so because, with hindsight, I suspect that at the time he knew little more French, Latin, and Greek (the subjects he taught) than his pupils. It was plain enough that he had devoted all his time until then to horsemanship and fencing, noble occupations in any case and all but obligatory when one is descended on one's father's side from a marshal of the Empire and on one's mother's side from Count Joseph de Maistre. As for French, Latin, and Greek, he was perfectly capable of plumbing their mysteries along with us, one day at a time. Seriously, I think there is no better method. His extraordinary influence over us and the undeniable efficacy of his teaching derived partly from the freshness and vivacity of his knowledge, which he communicated to us in its nascent state. Naturally the official curriculum bored him, and we galloped through the *chansons de geste* and Corneille only to linger over Cocteau, Giono, and Giraudoux. I am optimistic enough to believe that those in the upper reaches of the Ministry of Education have finally grasped the fact that the closer a writer is in time to the student, the more likely he is to attract his attention and add something to his life. All literary education must begin with contemporaries. At the time, however, the schools were organized on diametrically opposed principles, and they succeeded in killing forever their students' taste for poetry and fiction by inflicting upon their unprepared minds the lays of Marie de France and the tales of Chrétien de Troyes. Gouvion Saint-Cyr did wonders for us by ignoring (in both senses of the word) the classics of the official curriculum he was supposed to teach.

He, too, has remained in my visual memory, so much so that in the slender and supple silhouette of Uncle Alexander in *Gemini,* in his physical courage and fondness for the sword, in his impulsive, instinctive, and spontaneous nature, there is a great deal of Gouvion Saint-Cyr. As to sexuality, it is true, they differ completely, as my former teacher is still possessed by so ardent a love for the opposite sex that he is always ready to commit the most juvenile of follies on its behalf.

But one swallow does not make a spring, nor even two swallows, and despite these exemplary teachers my scholastic life was on the whole chaotic. It was disrupted in particular by an absolute, instinctive, and definitive rejection of mathematics. I learned addition, subtraction, multiplication, and the method of checking known as "casting out nines." But when it came to division I distinctly heard the sound of mental locks snapping shut: my intelligence had forever closed itself to the truths of mathematics. Ever since I have carried this repudiation of a form of language and reasoning with me as a kind of infirmity, and it took miracles to ensure that it didn't prevent me from graduating and attending university. Educational psychologists ought to look into phobias of this kind, which are strangely similar to neurotic inhibitions. My case is particularly odd in that my mind, perforce subjected to a rather debilitating course of purely literary studies, was suddenly aroused and filled with ardor by its first contact with philosophy and devoured chapters of metaphysics generally regarded as particularly gristly. When faced with a difficult metaphysical problem, my intelligence gauged the effort required (I don't know why I use the past tense—this remains the case today) and gathered its forces for the attack. Or else—as often happened—deemed the problem beyond its powers and attempted to measure the amount of study needed to overcome the difficulty. And then my mind plunged into its studies hour after hour, day after day, so deep was its obsession with mastery, its cerebral will to power.

So what was the problem with math? I see several possible explanations for my refusal to come to terms with the subject. First, abstraction. Mathematics is abstract. Indeed, it is the height of abstraction. When a child is told for the first time that 3 + 6 = 9, he immediately wants to know whether it is nine sheep or nine apples. Normally we play along and say nine sheep, one just like the next, standing in a field, or nine apples dropping into a basket. But beware of telling the child that it doesn't matter whether it's sheep or apples, for something may snap. By contrast, the essence of metaphysics is always to go straight to the heart of the concrete, which is the reason for the subject's peculiar difficulty. If I say that God exists because by definition his essence includes his existence (the ontological argument of Saint Anselm), I may not make myself understood right away, but at least no one will ask me whether I'm talking about sheep or apples. In fact, I am performing the quintessential metaphysical act, combining a logical operation with a mystical intuition. The logical operation posits existence as one attribute of God's essence, a paradoxical notion that has given rise to innumerable polemics and to philosophical research of extraordinary fecundity. But at the same time I acquire a direct, immediate vision of God's inner being, for as Jean Guitton has written,

> the ontological argument is a profound definition of God. It is located in the deepest depth of the most high, within the mystery of God's existence, that is, within the reality of the necessary being, independent of the existence of the world. And this thought of God as God, without his creation, is absolutely necessary if we are to conceive of God truly. Here we begin with perfection. We identify perfection with necessity. We are at the heart of ontology. We truly love God, because we perceive him as he is, in himself and independent of all his creatures, hence independent of the one who prays to him. We truly adopt the standpoint of divine solitude. Then we ask whether this perfect and necessary God can be defined by love and, if so, what act is most worthy of a love so absolute, from which the creation follows as a contingent consequence.

This idea may seem difficult, but certainly not because of excessive abstraction. If a difficulty exists at all, surely it comes from an overabundance of concrete presence. The great joy of metaphysics is the warm and powerful conviction that by force of intellect one can proceed straight to the root of the most palpable of things, to the fragrance and texture of the world. Anyone who has never experienced this has no idea what metaphysics is. Whereas $ax^2 + bx + c = 0$ is nothing but a heap of marbles, meaningless but for some tacit convention.[8]

So mathematics is conventional, and it may be that the mind is most repelled by unavowed infirmity. Its rebellion stems, no doubt, from the feeling that it is being forced to accept an arbitrary system as if it were real. Is $3 + 6 = 9$ an absolute, unconditional truth that one must accept without a murmur? It is as such that it is served up to the schoolchild. It would be educationally more sound, I think, to tell the student that mathematics is a game whose rules are as much a matter of convention as those of chess or lotto—and not only educationally more sound but also closer to the truth. No doubt 3 + 6 does equal 9, but under very strict conditions. Not, for instance, if we're talking about three toms and six female cats, for in six weeks each female will have given birth to four kittens, so that the equation becomes 3 + 6 = 9 (adult cats) + 24 (kittens) = 33. Or if we are talking about blocks of ice left out in the warm sun: 3 + 6 = 0. It is easy enough to come up with examples demonstrating any result you please.

I read little and late. This was but one aspect of an immaturity—if that is the word for the opposite of precocity—which I think remains a basic element of my character. For many years my father cited this fact as proof of my mental retardation. Of all my children's books I remain unforgettably fond of the picture books of Benjamin Rabier. Gédéon the duck, Aglaé the goat, Chabernac the ape, and above all the beautiful, lovely, lush surroundings in which these characters lived—what an extraordinary tableau that teeming barnyard made! Animal books were not as outrageously unrealistic as fairy tales, nor were they vile caricatures like the Pieds Nicklés or Bibi Fricotin or the books in the "Bécassine" series.[9] They were reality, ever so slightly transfigured and humanized, and seen with a kindly, comprehending eye. Perhaps the best word to describe the spirit of Rabier's work is that handsome epithet, *classic*. His vision of animals and trees comes close to that of Louis Pergaud[10] for lucidity, tranquillity, and sympathy. Leafing through a selection of run-of-the-mill children's books, you would think they were written for brutes impervious to all but the most gut-twisting trash. Fantasy, cruelty, and ugliness join together in an unrelenting assault on the senses. Rabier's serenity stands in sharp contrast to the outrages purveyed by these little shops of horror.

But the first true and great book of my childhood was *The Wonderful Adventure of Nils* written by Selma Lagerlöf in 1906 or 1907. Admittedly there is fantasy in this book, since the story begins with the urchin Nils' being slapped by a *tomte,* a sort of midget magician whom he has caught with a butterfly net. This slap transforms the boy into a midget himself, no taller than the back of a hand. Yet the metamorphosis does not take us into the fake and arbitrary world of the fairy tale. In fact, the great thing about the book is that what takes place is just the opposite. Simply by virtue of having been reduced to a minuscule gnome, Nils comes to see and understand reality better than when he was human-sized. His dwarf stature becomes a means of escape and an instrument of heightened understanding. I profited from this lesson in my short story, "The Red Dwarf." [11]

Early in the tale is the magnificent episode of the wild geese. It is springtime. Migratory birds fly over Nils' farm in triangular formations, hastening northward with raucous cries. The domestic geese are moved by the calls of their wild brethren. They run about wildly, beating their wings in a hilarious yet moving spectacle. The great voyage of initiation is not for these fat white fowl, destined to end their days in a pot! One young male, however, is bold enough to try. Straining hard, he rises into the air. But not without being spotted by Nils, who rushes toward him and grabs onto his feathers. The farmyard gander hastens after the wild geese, carrying the midget child with him. At first the gander has a hard time keeping up, but he works at it with all his might, encouraged by Nils and mocked by the wild geese. Freedom's apprenticeship is hard.

We are led on a tour of Sweden, through woodland, steppe, and fjord as far north as Lapland and the land of the midnight sun. Every night, Nils places his wooden shoes next to his gander's webbed feet and slips beneath his soft, white wings as though crawling into an immense, living bed. The tale is one of geography transfigured, of tenderness and animal warmth.

One of the finest episodes has for its hero Gorgo the eagle, imprisoned in a cage. Having long since abandoned all hope of escape, he stands motionless, a sullen ball of feathers on his perch. Nils decides to set him free. To do so he must file through the bars of the cage, a long and arduous task. Little Nils labors through the night. But at the first glimmer of dawn, when the hole is finished, he realizes that his work is not yet done. The eagle suddenly turns on him: "Leave me alone. Let me be. I am flying, soaring at a tremendous altitude."

Gorgo, carried away by his dream and oblivious to real life, does not wish to leave his cage. This is the reverse of the story of the barnyard gander who abandons his home to follow the gray goose.

The book is a superb study of discovery and liberation, a treatise on initiation. Initiation: I use this important word a second time. And I shall soon be using it again. In my opinion it sums up the whole problem of childhood. In any case, it is certainly the theme whose presence in a work of literature most urgently commands my attention and enlists my sensibility.

To take another example, let me mention Hans Christian Andersen's masterpiece *The Snow Queen,* whose distant memory continues to glow, like an unobtrusive but

inextinguishable night light. Why? Because little Kay of
Amsterdam is obliged to undergo two trials of initiation,
both of evil inspiration and apt to turn him into a diabolical creature.

First comes the story of the devil's mirror. The devil
has made a mirror—a distorting mirror, naturally. Even
worse: an inverting mirror. Whatever beauty is reflected in
it becomes hideous. Anything wicked seen in it becomes
irresistibly attractive. For a time the devil amuses himself
with this terrifying toy, until at length the most diabolical
of ideas comes into his head: to place this wretched mirror
before the face of God himself! He carries the mirror up
to heaven, but the closer he comes to the Supreme Being,
the more the mirror writhes, bends, and twists, until finally it breaks, shattering into thousands upon thousands
of pieces. This accident is a terrible misfortune for mankind, for the entire earth is spangled with glass shards,
pellets, and particles which distort the appearance of every
object and living thing. Some pieces are large enough to
be picked up and made into windows—but woe unto the
inhabitants of the house in which they are used—while an
even greater number are big enough to be made into eye-
glasses—but woe unto those who wear such glasses.

At the moment the mirror explodes, little Kay and
Gerda are absorbed in a book filled with pictures of flowers and birds. The church bells are striking five when suddenly Kay shudders with pain. Something has stuck in his
eye, and the hurt radiates to the depths of his heart. A
second later he no longer feels anything, but with disgust
he pushes away both the book, which now seems filled
with vile filth, and the little girl, who to him looks uglier
than a witch. A speck from the devil's pulverized mirror
has lodged in Kay's eye. From that day on, people are
struck by the child's intelligence and penetration, yet they

also fear him for his wickedness and for his unfortunate habit of seeing only the foolishness and ugliness in other people.

Some years later, Kay is subjected to still another trial of initiation. It is wintertime. Amsterdam is covered with snow. Kay and some other rowdy boys are having a good time hitching their little sleds to the sleighs of the peasants and townspeople and riding back and forth across the town. A splendid blue and gold sleigh drawn by white horses and attended by liveried footmen comes within sight. Intimidated, the children hesitate. Kay jumps out, hitches his sled to the back of the great vehicle, and off he goes. The team picks up speed, and Kay, excited by the breakneck pace at which he finds himself traveling in his jolting and skidding sled, scarcely notices the last houses of the town and the beginnings of the vast white plain. The speed picks up even more. Kay tries to unhitch his sled but cannot. He shouts, but no one hears. He wants to recite the Lord's Prayer, but only the multiplication table comes to his lips.

Suddenly, in the middle of the forest, the magnificent sleigh comes to a halt. An enormous coachman gets down. He lifts Kay as though he were a feather and with a hearty laugh tosses him into the sleigh as though he were a bundle of merchandise. There, a very beautiful lady with translucent, angular features takes him into her arms. The Snow Queen—for it is she—wraps him in the cold, immaculate furs in which she herself is muffled. She gives him a kiss that sends a chill through his mouth and heart to the very marrow of his bone. Whereupon the horses resume their gallop, while the child cries out, "My sled! My sled!" For his little sled, which is all that attaches him to life, is still fastened to the magnificent sleigh drawn by the team of white horses.

I could not resist retelling the beginning of this tale. I wrote from memory and hope that in some way I have been unfaithful to Andersen, for there is no other work that I am as sorry not to have written myself. No other story I know so felicitously marries the most familiar details with the most grandiose fantasy.

Finally, let me also cite from memory, with all the uncertainties inherent in the re-creation of things past, from the work of the American James Oliver Curwood (1878–1927). He, too, knew how to set the most fantastic tales in the humblest and most quotidian of surroundings. His world was the Canadian Far North, with its black forests, frozen lakes, wolf packs, and half-Indian, half-Eskimo population. In my novel *The Ogre* I cited excerpts from the only book of his still in my possession, *The Golden Snare*. Its hero is a hermit, a savage, living alone among the wolves. His lair is a hidden, abandoned gold mine, and in all simplicity he uses its gold, the only metal he has, to make traps, utensils, and bullets. He can kill men with impunity, for the witness becomes his accomplice upon recovering the bullet.

Still more charming is a story told in another book now impossible to find, *The River's End*. It centers on a man who, having committed a murder, attempts to elude capture by heading north. A policeman follows his trail. Soon the mutual obsession with the chase creates a strange bond between the two men. Without ever setting eyes on each other, they live *together* in the great white wilderness as on a desert island. One day, however, the criminal becomes certain that he is no longer being followed. An instinct tells him that the policeman is no longer there. Paradoxically, he is seized with anxiety. He even turns around, backtracking along the very trail that the policeman has stopped following. At length he finds his pursuer snug inside his regulation tent, but ill—very ill, in fact dying.

What strikes both men the moment they set eyes on each other for the first time is how similar they are. Because of the long, obsessive chase? They have become like twin brothers. The criminal does everything he can for the other man, but in the end he dies. Not, however, before imparting to the man he had wanted to arrest all his secrets and all his memories—in short, the whole of his life. With the barrel of his revolver heated red-hot in the fire he even brands the criminal's cheek with a mark that resembles a scar at the same spot on his own face. Afterwards, the criminal becomes a new man. Wearing the policeman's uniform, he insinuates himself into the man's life and returns to town carrying his own remains as proof that his mission is accomplished. Everything appears to go smoothly. Nobody recognizes him. Nobody, that is, except the neighborhood's Chinese grocer, who calls him by his real name.

Some day perhaps the computer will make it possible to measure the exact influence of yesterday's authors on today's. The works of our great forebears would have to be "stored" in such a way as to reveal not only their vocabulary but also their use of pairs and groups of words and of certain characteristic rhythms. There can be no doubt, for instance, that the famous opening sentence of Flaubert's *Salammbô*—"It was in Megara, a suburb of Carthage, in the gardens of Hamilcar"—consciously or unconsciously remembered by so many writers, has had an impact on thousands of subsequent works of every type and description. To stick with Flaubert, the description of Nestor's bicycle in *The Ogre* was inspired by Flaubert's description of the wedding-cake ornament created by the baker of Yvetot in *Madame Bovary*.

Reminiscence often enough becomes so clear that it

takes the form of more or less literal citation, a kind of furtive homage to the "master" with a wink of the eye to the reader alert enough or well-enough read to understand. In *The Ogre,* for instance, the reader will find Heredia's "muffled footfall of marching legions," while *Gemini* contains Paul Valéry's line "Hail to the gods through pink and salt." The latter book also imputes to Alexander a judgment of female homosexuality as seen by a male homosexual, a judgment for which I have been castigated by certain lesbians but which is taken word for word from Colette's *Ces plaisirs:* "Enormous, intact, eternal, Sodom contemplates from on high its squalid counterfeit." [12]

These are mere diversions. More serious is the situation in which a writer's admiration for certain masterpieces is heightened by intense feelings of frustration. Is the culprit jealousy or envy, perhaps? No. The writer's frustration stems—more creditably—from a dispiriting illusion. He feels about a particular story or page or episode or poem that he and he alone should have written it, that he was for all eternity its predestined author. But by a stroke of ill fortune so-and-so was born first and beat him to it. Having arrived too late on the scene, he is stripped of his possession, disinherited of what was rightfully his. And of course the author thus dispossessed feels that by virtue of his vocation he would have tapped this particular vein more thoroughly than its actual author did, that he would have produced something even finer than his predecessor. But now that the wrong has been done, what can he do?

Common sense says, "Think of something else." But stubbornness says, "Do it anyway." Do it anyway? And expose oneself to the charge of plagiarism? Yes, provided one has the strength to invert the chronological order by substituting for it another order of a more profound, more essential kind.

I shall mention only one instance of such violent reversal of chronology. At the beginning of *The Ogre* there is a scene set in the playground of Saint Christopher's School that no doubt caused many readers to think, I've already read this somewhere. The pupils engage in a rather brutal game: "The lighter boys perched on the shoulders of the stronger ones, and the pairs thus formed—horsemen and their mounts—faced one another for the sole purpose of unseating their rivals. . . . There were some hard falls onto the cinders." As it happens, this scene was imagined, visualized, and described by Alain-Fournier fifty-seven years before *The Ogre* in his novel *Le Grand Meaulnes*. People did not refrain from pointing this out to me. My answer is that this episode is more properly my possession than Alain-Fournier's, because in *Le Grand Meaulnes* it is a mere anecdote, whereas in *The Ogre* it foreshadows the entire sequel of the story, being an example of the novel's sole subject, what I call *phoria*. It seems to me that Alain-Fournier's priority in time does not stand up in the face of such a well-justified thematic priority, and that if one of us—Fournier or Tournier—is to be accused of plagiarism, justice demands that Fournier be found guilty.

But these are the problems of the adult, and the adult writer. To return to childhood reading, I think that what a person reads as a child forms an intangible foundation, an impregnable base upon which to erect not only literary cultivation and judgment but also a personal sensibility and mythology—intangible and impregnable because we can no more deny our earliest admirations than we can reject the influence of heredity. I cannot, for instance, bear to hear anyone condemn or ridicule the Parnassian poets for the simple reason that for me at age eleven Heredia and Leconte de Lisle *were* poetry, and none other. And how could I have been wrong? Such tender and total commitment assumes a kind of infallibility. I continue to like and respect those poets (whom I associate with a luminous lineage perpetuated by Paul Valéry and Saint-John Perse) not out of some foolish attachment to the past but because I believe that in this case it is the child who is right, as Raimu said in *Marius*. The truth is that the child is always right.

Rereading my little stories and examining the thoughts they inspired as I wrote them, I wonder if perhaps we ought not to reconsider our ideas of education, initiation, and upbringing, to trace their historical ancestry and see where we end up. I am thinking in particular of a place in *Thoughts about Education* in which the philosopher Alain (1868–1951) contrasts the school and the family. The two, he says, are qualitatively different, not to say antagonistic, environments, the one biological, the other social:

> The school contrasts sharply with the family, and this contrast awakens the child from his biological slumbers, forces him to seek beyond the self-sufficient family instinct. In school there is equality of age, and biological ties are weak. . . . Perhaps the child is delivered from love by the school bell and the heartless teacher. For the teacher is indeed unmoved by affection, which in school does not count. He should be insensitive, and he is. Here the child catches his first glimpse of truth and justice, but tailored to his age. Here the joy of existence is erased. At first everything is external and strange. The human reveals itself in the restrained language, chanted recitations, and standard exercises of the classroom, and even in mischief which, because it is ritualized, poses no danger to the soul. In the classroom one finds a certain indifference. . . . The eye measures and counts; it does not hope or fear. . . . Work displays its chilling visage, indifferent to pain and even to pleasure. . . . By contrast, the family does a bad job of teaching and even of

upbringing. Shared blood fosters matchless but undisciplined affections. For you see, we trust in those affections. Hence everyone is a tyrant with all his heart. It smacks of savagery.

Were things always like this, or was the school's "chilling visage" the result of centuries of evolution? Education in the broad sense of the word prepares a child to enter society and to occupy his place in it. In all times and places it appears to come in two forms, one moral, emotional, indeed magical, the other purely intellectual and rational. The first is called initiation, the second instruction. We have this equation:

$$education = initiation + instruction.$$

Of course these two components of education assume many guises, and their importance varies. My view is quite simply that, historically, the relative importance of initiation has been diminishing compared with that of instruction and that for some time now this has passed the point of being harmful.

In most primitive societies, from Tierra del Fuego to the frozen Arctic, children seem to enjoy a freedom and immunity that travelers and anthropologists have found both surprising and admirable. We must not be too hasty to mark this fact of society down to the credit of the "noble savage," to extol him as an ideal educator capable of sparing his children the obligations and punishments with which we encumber our own. The truth is simpler and more radical: namely, that the primitive child is not yet part of the body social, that he has yet to make his entry into society. As an absolute outsider, he is not subject to the taboos and ritual obligations that hold the social organism together. In such a society, initiation—a magical procedure whereby new members instantly become part of the group—takes on its fullest and starkest significance. For to judge by the difficulty and cruelty of the trials to which the child is subjected, it seems almost as though the intention is to make him pay once and for all for the carefree years of freedom that he has just enjoyed.

Let us now imagine ourselves transported into the midst of eighteenth-century French society. We witness a peculiar metamorphosis. The aristocracy is gradually receding, giving up land, wealth, and power to the rising bourgeoisie. Bourgeois ideology, first embodied in the *Encyclopedia,* has not yet reached the great turning point that we call Romanticism, but from Diderot it is only a short step to Rousseau, who himself anticipates Chateaubriand. We see the leading proponents of the new ideology attack the form of education to which they have been subjected: the classical, aristocratic education dispensed primarily by the Jesuit schools. What criticisms do they offer? That their education was irrelevant, useless, and disinterested. That it was good only for training "clerks," meaning lawyers, physicians, and clergymen. Commerce, navigation, technology, scientific research—all things that were becoming increasingly important in the eighteenth century—were *terra incognita* to the young Diafoirus brought up by the good fathers. Fleury waxed indignant at the thought of the student

> who spends his life studying Latin or Greek, who knows the history, mores, and laws of the Ancient Romans, but who does not know how France is governed or how people live today. . . . Accustomed to conversing exclusively with Greeks and Romans, he will be quite disconcerted when he is obliged to speak with men wearing hats and wigs or to deal with the interests of France and Germany, where there are no tribunes or comitia or consuls.

Charles Nodier carried the attack still further: "The name of Rome was the first to strike my ears, so that I was re-

mote from Paris, a stranger to its walls, and I lived in
Rome. . . . In later years it took me a long time to reac-
quire citizenship in my own country." And Voltaire wrote:
"I did not know whether Francis I had been taken prisoner
at Pavia or where Pavia was. The very country in which I
was born I knew not. I was unfamiliar with the principal
laws and interests of my fatherland. . . . All that I knew
about my country was what Caesar and Tacitus had said
about it." La Chalotais was particularly critical of the mo-
nastic aspect of contemporary education:

> If one were to explain the details of this instruction to a for-
> eigner, he would imagine that France was bent on populat-
> ing its seminaries. . . . Everything bears the imprint of the
> monastic mind. . . . The most common and ordinary affairs
> are neglected, those that have to do with the maintenance of
> life and the foundations of civil society. Most young people
> know nothing about the world in which they live or the land
> that feeds them or the men who fill their daily needs.[13]

Behind these indictments (echoes of which can still be
heard today in strictures against the teaching of Latin and
Greek) lies a lack of understanding that comes close to bad
faith. The critics pretend that the Jesuits' instruction was
intended to equip the child with the knowledge needed to
become a merchant, manufacturer, sailor, or government
official. Had that been its purpose, it would indeed have
fallen far short of its goal! But to begin with, the Jesuits
were educating young aristocrats, who did not need to become scholars in order to succeed. High birth was enough.
But they were also supposed to be human beings, and the
education they were offered was supposed to help them
toward that end. Here we touch on the crux of the mis-
understanding that arose in this period between the "ancients" and the "moderns." For the aristocrat, the child
was not a full-fledged human being. He was a little animal,
dirty, vicious, and stupid, on the whole rather contempt-

ible. Education was supposed to make him presentable.
The Jesuits were concerned not with enriching the child's
mind and preparing him for a career but with shaping his
moral being. Toward that end they caused him to live in a
wholly unreal world in which people spoke only Latin and
all the inhabitants were called Socrates, Nestor, Alexander,
Cincinnatus, and Demosthenes. Associated with these
names were various edifying anecdotes: the hemlock, the
Gordian knot, the little fox hidden beneath the Spartan
child's toga, Diogenes' lantern burning in broad daylight.
In other words, initiation was much more important than
instruction in this version of education. But the moderns
had no notion what this initiation was all about, and they
actively opposed it. For them, the child was not wicked
but simply uninformed. His mind was a blank page upon
which knowledge had to be inscribed. Whereas the only
ambition of earlier educators was to conduct the child
from an animal state to a human one, the moderns wished
to enrich his mind with science and technology, tools with
which to make his fortune and that of his family.

This crisis, which began in the eighteenth century, appears to have been a turning point in the history of education, as moral initiation gradually lost out to practical
instruction. Since that time, the initiatory function of education has steadily diminished, and we are now witnessing
the elimination of the few vestiges that remain. First to go
was corporal punishment, which established a sadomaso-
chistic bond between teachers and pupils, followed by religious instruction and confession, which established a
similar bond at a spiritual level. More recently, Greek,
Latin, philosophy, and literature have been stricken from
the curriculum as obviously superfluous nonsense. All
traces of humanity must be eliminated from the classroom
so that the "heartless teacher" advocated by Alain can in-

oculate his students exclusively with knowledge deemed to be of practical use. Only rarely and with a feeling of illicitness do students have the sense of confronting a human being, a person like the two teachers I described earlier.

I alluded a moment ago to religious instruction, and surely it was no accident that both of the teachers I admired were employed by a religious school, Saint Erembert's in Saint-Germain-en-Laye, which I attended for three years as a day student. After that I spent a year as a boarding student at Saint Francis's School in Alençon. These two Catholic schools occupy a special place among the dozen or so schools I attended in the course of my chaotic scholastic career, probably because religious schools in the period just before the war were more successful than their lay counterparts in preserving the initiatory aspects of education. The Catholic religion, with its rituals, holy days, theology, and mythology, served as a marvelous emotional counterweight to mathematics and the natural sciences, a counterweight without which the child or adolescent is afflicted by a sense of dryness and aridity. In any case, I cannot separate my memory of theology—the only subject apart from German in which I excelled—from the sumptuousness of ritual. Dunce that I was, I found in religious history and catechism an anticipation of what I later discovered in metaphysics: concrete speculation inextricably intertwined with powerful and brilliant imagery. For metaphysics is nothing other than the rigor of mathematics wedded to the richness of poetry. I had little use for the bludgeon of dogma or for the zombie-like obedience and faith of the humble. From earliest childhood I had a yen for the constructs of the mind, for subtle proofs, for a rare and technical vocabulary, and nothing enchanted me more than the infinite nuances of grace, that "mysterious adornment of regenerate souls," which could be habitual and sanctifying, present and temporary, effective or sufficient—*distinguos* which have divided Thomists from Molinists, congruists, Pelagians, semi-Pelagians, Calvinists, Socinians, and Jansenists. My only assurance of God's existence has always come from Saint Anselm's ontological argument, that excrescence of the idea of divinity which causes existence itself to leap forth from the myriad obligatory attributes of God.

In the ostentation of ritual these spiritual riches found their sensible sign. Gold, incense, and the music of the organ respond to the need for jubilation that is in our hearts, just as theology satisfies the fervor for understanding that is in our brains. As I cast about for a way to illustrate these two aspects of the ideal Church, an image came to mind, that of the Corpus Christi procession. Is not the ontological argument symbolized by the monstrance, that mystical sun carried in cortege along a carpet of petals to its temporary altar of flowers and leaves, the culmination of a verdant, baroque apotheosis?

In those days the Church responded fully to its calling, which was to initiate the child by way of the spirit as well as the senses. There can be no doubt that for centuries it was through the priest—the monk or curate—and in the church that the peasant and artisan as well as the noble discovered philosophy, poetry, music, painting, sculpture, and architecture.

But the institutionalized clergy also has another face, hideous, hypocritical, and hateful. Having lost its temporal power, the Church signed on as handmaiden to the most constricted, conservative element of the bourgeoisie, whose interests and ideas it ardently adopted as its own. It continued to draw its teachings from the Gospel, but from the words of the Pharisees rather than those of Jesus. In

other words, it began to preach respect for social hierar-
chies, money, and power as well as hatred of sexuality. The
depths to which the Church could fall are measured by the
tragedy of Lamennais.[14]

Make no mistake. Because the Church teaches a false
morality, conservative and anti-erotic, it cannot teach the
true one, not even in a subsidiary way. The mask in this
instance does not cover the face but takes its place. Pru-
dishness, which was nowhere more successful than in late
nineteenth-century England, enabled the Victorians to establish a social order in the midst of a foul swamp of crime
and injustice. The very same England was replete with
children's prisons and made war on China in order to force
the repeal of laws limiting the import of opium, the
scourge of the Chinese people, because that opium was
produced in India under British license.

Along with my classmates I endured the oppressive
presence of this wan and morbid face of the Church during
my year as a boarder at Alençon. There was an army base
in the town, and the students who received the most favorable treatment were the sons of bluebloods who had
made a career in the military. My disgraceful background
provided three reasons for treating me with contempt: I
was a Parisian, a civilian, and a nonaristocrat. But none of
this would have mattered had it not been for the absolutely
apolitical and antisexual pseudomorality that hung about
our necks like a lead weight. Everyone was obsessed with
the fear of sex. In the days of the Popular Front, the Spanish Civil War, and the rise of Nazism, our teachers were
interested only in masturbation. Fear of the flesh has made
the crucifix—a corpse nailed to two pieces of wood—the
center of Catholic worship in preference to all other Christian symbols, such as the radiant Christ of the Transfigu-
ration. The Church has resolutely set its face against the

dogma of resurrection in the flesh and attempts to ignore the fact that whenever Jesus encountered sexuality—even in the antisocial forms of prostitution and adultery—he defended it against the wrath of the Pharisees. Despised, ridiculed, scorned, and condemned to the gutter of pornography, sex takes on the sinister visage of its persecutors. Prudes are ugly and impute their own ugliness to love, but when they spit on it, they spit on themselves. Loved and celebrated in those we love, the flesh is as radiant as that of Jesus on Mount Tabor.

Sumptuous, subtle, and erotic—such is the initiatory Church of which I dream when I think back on how my childhood might have been. I thank my stars that the Church that actually raised me only partially betrayed that ideal.

But those days are now remote, and since then it seems that Alain, that most secular of teachers, has triumphed totally. The revolution begun by the men of the Enlightenment is now complete. Emotional bonds, personal and possibly erotic relationships, pose no further danger of polluting the aseptic atmosphere of the classroom. Education, cleansed of every last vestige of initiation, has been reduced to nothing more than a dispenser of useful and saleable knowledge. Already computers are taking the place of teachers, and in this we should rejoice, as we should whenever a man is relieved of a purely mechanical task by a machine.

But what about initiation? What about that other obscure, warm, magical half of education? Banished from the official curriculum, it has assumed other guises, secret and often monstrous. Sometimes, as in the case of cruel and harmful surgical operations, these are deadly; other times, as in the case of affectionate, perhaps vaguely erotic relations between two children or between a child and an adult, they are beneficial. Beneath a heavy cloak the heart beats and the flesh quivers.

There is, of course, still the public sort of initiation: the motley lessons dispensed by films, radio, records, and television. And above all there are books. But these are one-way relationships, sources that nourish the emotions but offer no return outlet. They cannot replace moral and physical contact between the child and his initiator.

2

THE OGRE

Germany, mother of us all.
—Gérard de Nerval

My father and mother met at the Sorbonne when he was studying for a doctorate in German and she for a master's. From the inception, therefore, the family lived under the sign of *Germanistik*. As fate would have it, neither was ever to teach. My father picked an excellent date for his qualifying examination: August 1914. From the first day of the war Germany had more difficult tests in store for him than translating to and from the language, and the armistice found him convalescing from serious facial wounds at the Val-de-Grâce Military Hospital. The war had sapped his enthusiasm for German studies, but my mother kept faith with her family tradition, and we grew up with one foot in Germany, a circumstance abetted by the fact that my father's business took him all over Europe, including the part of the continent that lay just across the Rhine.

I suffered somewhat at school because I was unable to explain to my classmates in a single word what my father did. They were the sons of doctors, grocers, or architects; nothing could have been more clear. But my father was the founder and director of something called the BIEM, a mysterious set of initials whose existence was nevertheless attested by a stamp on every record sold commercially. In reality, the Bureau International des Editions Musico-Mécaniques orchestrated the complexities of rights and contracts pertaining to recorded music sold outside the rights-holder's country of origin and made sure that as much as possible of the money that flowed from place to place wound up in the right pockets. The task was at once simple and complex. A national affiliate more or less subordinate to the BIEM had to be set up in each member country. Each of these affiliates had its own name, style, and director, and since much of my father's time was taken up in dealings with them, we were bathed in a rather mysterious, cosmopolitan atmosphere not without a certain charm. Among the affiliates were AEPI in Greece, STAGMA in Germany, Mechanlizenz in Switzerland, ZAIKS in Poland, OSA in Czechoslovakia, Austromecana in Austria, and Britico in England. The directors of these various entities paraded through the house with their accents and presents for the children, who feasted one day on Spanish *touron,* the next on German marzipan, and the next on English pudding or Italian pannetone or big black olives from Greece. We had our likes and our dislikes, but none of these officials was as popular with us as the head of Germany's STAGMA, a position for which my disabled veteran father, in a decision that bordered on an act of provocation, had chosen a true blue Frenchman with the impressive name Pierre Crétin. A defrocked priest, Crétin was a red-bearded giant of a man with a formidable appetite and the memory of an elephant, who somehow managed to spend nearly forty years in Berlin while continuing to make an abominable hash of Goethe's tongue. It took nothing less than the Red Army to flush him out of the ruins of his office and force him to return to France, where he experienced difficulties of adjustment, compounded by the fact that he brought with him a wife and children, apparently having forgotten that he already possessed the equivalent in Paris. We loved his motorcycle, backpack, lederhosen, disarming bluntness, and astonishing erudition. He knew Central Europe and its museums like the back of his hand, and he liked revisiting places he had been before and hearing the guide repeat some historical howler that he had told him on a previous visit.

On my mother's side the interest in Germany can be traced back to my grandfather's brother, Gustave Fournier, a priest who taught German at Saint Francis's School in Dijon. He, too, possessed a powerful personality and encyclopedic knowledge, but his imagination was less fanciful than Pierre Crétin's. After 1918 he made the immense sacrifice of never setting foot in Germany. Too many of his former pupils had died in battle. In many respects my grandfather Edouard was a muted copy of his older brother Gustave. Both men were herbalists, flutists, and historians of art, but the younger brother, as was only fitting, trailed somewhat behind the elder. I have even heard it said that Edouard would have liked to have followed Gustave to the seminary and donned the cassock. But the parents felt that one priest in the family was enough and sent Edouard to pharmacy school. I owe my existence to this thwarted vocation, apparently endured without undue suffering.

In 1910 the priest took his niece—my mother—to Germany for the first time. They stayed at the Albertus Burse in Freiburg-im-Breisgau, a home for Catholic students run by a group of nuns. On occasion, when academic vacations left the bedrooms and dining room unoccupied, the sisters took in foreign visitors—with appropriate recommendations, to be sure. Since that first visit Ralphine has returned to the Albertus Burse every year—except, of course, when France and Germany were at war. Over more than sixty years she has known generations of nuns and a dozen mothers superior, and she can address the most recent superior with the authority of an old hand speaking to a newcomer. Naturally she took her children with her just as soon as they were presentable, and the muffled and polished atmosphere of the place, the night-lights in the corridors, the food—which our Parisian noses deemed rather rudimentary—and the old house are among the most venerable items in our family's archaeological museum. Other souvenirs include the pig kept by Ambrosius, handyman to this city of women; the poor children who filed through the lobby to be served their bowl of soup, a task in which I joined; and, on Easter Sunday, the paschal lamb, which was served in a pastry crust sprinkled with confectioner's sugar, and which held between its front paws a small stick capped by a pious oriflamme of gilded paper. In the sisters' iconography this took the place of the dubious Easter bunny with its basket full of chocolates, a legacy of pagan German mythology.

Wreathed in this very special and very powerful atmosphere, my earliest memories date from the time when Nazism was engulfing Germany. The streets were the scene of unending political and military celebrations. At any hour of the day or night we might be lured into the street by the blare of a marching band, the flicker of a torchlight procession, or the clank of tank treads on pavement. But all this commotion ended at the doorstep of the Albertus Burse, where, eyes and ears filled with fireworks and violence, we returned to the murmur of prayer and the ringing of bells.

Five minutes from the Albertus was the railway station of Freiburg, the starting point of our excursions to the Feldberg, the highest point in the Black Forest. A little train with wooden cars took us as far as Bärental (Bear Valley), climbing along a route dotted with tiny stations whose poetic and baroque names amused us no end. The series of stations began beautifully with a village answering to the sweet name Ahah. We crowded into the window of the car to watch the stationmaster stroll in his dignified way up and down the platform, shouting Ahah! every ten paces, and we imitated him with expressions on our faces that ranged from surprise to threat to illumination. Two tunnels preceded the station of Hirschsprung (Deer's Leap). Between them you had to rush to the windows— on the right side of the train on the way up, the left side on the way down—in order to catch a glimpse of the life-sized statue of a stag perched on a cliff overlooking the tracks. Then came Höllental (Hell's Valley), Himmelreich (Kingdom of Heaven), Notschrei (Cry of Distress), and Titisee (Lake Titi), continuing the hilarious litany that we learned by heart. Drawn to more arduous altitudes, we had no use for Lake Titi, a dignified little body of water festooned with luxury hotels. At Bärental we left the train and continued on foot, by car, or, in wintertime, by sled up to the top of the Feldberg, the slopes of which were dotted with chalets of dark wood with elaborately carved window boxes, often set against a black stand of virgin fir through which the wind whistled. The summit, known as the Herzogenhorn (Duke's Horn), was no more than 5,000 feet high. Mountain climbers of course disdained this cow pasture of a hill, and those who like their countryside trim and pretty would surely find the area dull and monotonous. But on those metallic lakes set like jewels in forest hollows, on those smooth peaks where the tall grasses undulate endlessly in the wind beneath the vaults of evergreen cathedrals, the wind has a fragrance and a voice unlike any other place on earth, which I recognize the moment I arrive.

I last visited one glorious autumn day not very long ago. A light breeze barely stirred the black woods, which we skirted along paths lined with crocus and gentian. We knocked at the door of the Grafenmatt Inn, surrounded by huckleberry bushes, where before the war we used to stay regularly. It was closed. We then continued our climb along footpaths gullied by the melting snows all the way up to the wooden cross at the Herzogenhorn. Inevitably our thoughts dwelt in the past, as we sang hiking songs and conjured up images of the dead. With summer on the wane the mountain was superb and funereal, and it exerted a powerful, if morbid, Baudelairean charm. Bygone years decked out in old-fashioned costume looked down from heaven's balconies, and, from the depths of the Black Lake, Smiling Sorrow rose before our eyes.

We were living then in Saint-Germain-en-Laye, a well-to-do and reactionary garrison town, whose rather Maurrassian[1] upper crust took a dim view of a family that kept such bad company. In particular there was a certain Colonel R., a wounded veteran and the father of seven children, all of whom were either career officers or married to career officers, and who in some sense embodied the national consciousness of Saint-Germain. He may not have been a member of the Croix-de-Feu,[2] but he could have been. Every day he traveled to Paris on the same train as my father. They avoided each other.

Then came the dark year of our defeat. The onslaught of the German army with its spanking new equipment, its gleam made even brighter by the rapidity of the rout and the sunshine of June, was a startling revelation for many Frenchmen, who, having seen Germany until then only through smoked lenses provided by France's inept and ignorant propaganda machine, had only the most abstract idea of it. Now they saw a nation on the march, singing in chorus and sweeping all resistance before it. We knew better. Having witnessed the birth of Nazism, we had been vaccinated against its blandishments. We knew what it whispered in private and mistrusted its intentions. The three German families we visited most frequently were anti-Nazi, in all three cases for religious reasons. As for the German army, I as a twelve-year-old knew more about its strength than the entire French general staff. I knew, in particular, that not a single army in the world was powerful enough to withstand an all-out attack, and that everything would depend on how much territory the defending forces had at their backs. France would hold out for three weeks. England was supposed to have been occupied in two, and the United States would resist for two months. In fact, the Soviets were saved only by the trackless wastes to their rear, made even more formidable by winter. As an inveterate Radical-Socialist,[3] my father felt no fondness for the new German government and often made sarcastic comments when the family gathered in the evenings around the "wireless" to listen to the news in German and the speeches of the Führer.

Had we entertained the slightest thought of collaborating, the Germans themselves would soon have disabused us. Our large house in Saint-Germain housed twenty-two German soldiers who lived a very high life indeed, raising geese on the fourth floor and causing the walls to shake with the din from their revels and orgies. Except for myself, the family lived crowded into cramped quarters on the ground floor. I was fifteen at the time and lived in a small attic room among the soldiers. I will never forget the smell of the Wehrmacht, a compound of tobacco and boot polish. For me, this was the fragrance of happiness. I had hoped for war with all my heart as a way of ending my troubles at school. Like many adolescents, I had been consumed by a desire for disorder and disaster. My wish was granted in September, when Poland was invaded by the German-Soviet allies. And to cap it all off came the debacle of June 1940, which I experienced as a vast picnic. To have our proper and orderly home life suddenly disrupted by German troops was an unexpected bonus, something in the nature of Charles Maurras's "divine surprise" but in its nasty schoolboy's version.

My parents saw things differently. One whole section of their life had suddenly crumbled. One night on the little train, Ralph, exhausted with sorrow and humiliation, had the surprise of his life. I can see him now, returning home and, before even closing the door, shouting out: "I rode home with Colonel R.! You'll never guess what he said. I was speechless. He came up to me, held out his hand, and said in a voice loud enough to be heard by other people in the car: 'Well, Tournier, I am beginning to understand you. *Your* Germans are quite something, I think. Because now that they're here, it's all over. No more Popular Front, no more Communists, no more Jews, no more homosexuals, no more surrealists, no more cubists. The end.

Now we all march in lockstep. One, two, one two. And anyway, they beat us. If they beat the French army that quickly, they must be invincible. So what next?'" *Your* Germans! It was that possessive that most flabbergasted my poor father.

Our cohabitation lasted one year. Many soldiers passed through the house (for we had the further misfortune of having been declared a "transient depot"), and all of them tirelessly repeated the refrain that peace was just around the corner, that the Germans were on the verge of victory and would be clearing out at any moment. In the spring of 1941 my parents, at their wits' end, abandoned the house and rented an apartment in Neuilly. I detested Paris, I loved Saint-Germain, and I had had no problem at all adjusting to the Occupation. But when I suggested the insane idea of remaining alone in the house at Saint-Germain while they moved to Neuilly with the rest of the family, my parents were adamant. I had no choice but to leave.

I did have one consolation, however. We had a vacation house at Villers-sur-Mer. The coast was of course fortified and off limits, but our identity cards had been renewed during the winter of 1939–40, which we had spent in Villers. Hence I was able to persuade the Germans that I was a native of the coastal region. In those days I lived on my bicycle. All the same, the 125 miles from Paris to Villers was a difficult ride, especially in a period of restricted rations and with a loaded bicycle. I covered the distance in a day, arriving that night exhausted but ecstatic, only to discover a fantastic coastline bristling with tank traps and mines, a whole country transfigured by the anticipation of apocalyptic events. Our summer house, as luck would have it, was occupied by German troops. Much to my surprise, I found our chicken coop being used as a stockade for soldiers who had broken regulations, and I slipped them cigarettes and matches through holes in the chicken-wire. Sometimes I ate with the troops and, protected by my air of being a schoolboy on vacation, I engaged in overt psychological warfare. I explained that the only war Germany could have won was a blitzkrieg, and that all was lost because they had been unable to vanquish England at the same time as France. Scattered all over Europe, the Wehrmacht would be unable to prevent a landing. From Villers you could see the coast around Le Havre, which was often obscured by fog that hung about the estuary of the Seine. I persuaded those Swabian and Pomeranian peasants, many of whom were seeing the ocean for the first time, that that bit of coastline was England and that an invasion was not far off. (I had no idea how close I was to the truth. Arromanches is only a few miles from Villers-sur-Mer.)

Our withdrawal to Neuilly unfortunately did not put an end to my family's tribulations, for all that we were steeped in Goethe and Schiller. Not that any of us were tempted by the Resistance. Perhaps I should pause a moment to explain for the benefit of readers who did not live through it exactly what the Resistance was all about. First, there were those whom the Germans persecuted not for their actions or opinions but for what they were, namely, the Jews and, later, French youths who were rounded up and sent to Germany to do war work in the factories under a program known as the STO (for Service du Travail Obligatoire: Compulsory Labor Service). Jews had no choice but to flee abroad or to vanish somewhere in France under a false identity. Young men could "take to the bush," provided by clandestine organizations with food and other supplies that made possible a precarious existence in the hinterland. Given that there are some 400,000 boys of any given age in France, and that the Germans were free to draw on young men spanning a three- or four-year age range, it is not difficult to imagine just how precarious life in the bush must have been in a starving, occupied country whose people were huddled in fear and concerned about their own survival. Shortly before the Liberation I was examined by a medical board for service with the STO. Naturally I was found to be "fit." I would certainly have done everything in my power to avoid going. Would I have been successful? No telling. Especially since the Germans were known to take reprisals against the families of those who were referred to in the jargon of the time as "recalcitrants."

Not all Jews and "recalcitrants" joined the Resistance, however. It was one thing to be hunted but quite another to become a hunter. The truth is that the Resistance became a nationwide force only after the Germans had left. During the Occupation the fight was waged by a tiny but heroic minority, whose courage got them massacred and whose civic spirit kept them from joining the race for postwar position and power. Active participation in the Resistance was one thing, and claiming participation for self-interested reasons after the war was another; the two required different, not to say incompatible, psychological complexions. Many true freedom-fighters found themselves disgusted by the grandiose proportions assumed by the Resistance myth in the postwar years, when it was made to seem that people had signed up for Resistance duty between 1940 and 1944 as routinely as they would have signed up for military service. Here we have a fine example of a country being carried away by a mythical reconstruction of a not very glorious period in its history. In the past few years books and films such as *The Sorrow and the Pity* have aimed to get a little closer to the truth about France during the Occupation. Yet there is one awfully revealing statistic which as far as I know has not previously been unearthed. True, it does cast the state of mind of the French bourgeoisie of that period in an especially harsh light. Simply compare the proportion of high-school freshmen who chose to study English rather than German before the war and during the Occupation. I confess I do not know the precise figures. But I have a vivid memory of having been one of a tiny minority of students to have studied German before the war, only to see that minority swell to include the vast majority after 1940. There is no question but that the average Frenchman in those dark years believed that England and the United States were done for. The future lay with victorious Germany, and for a long time to come. Yet all of this has fallen victim to a profound amnesia.

Obviously the Italians are much better at the tricky business of reinventing the past, because on the basis of a single film, Rossellini's *Open City,* they persuaded the entire world that Mussolini, fascism, the declaration of war on an already defeated France in 1940, and Il Duce's appeals to Hitler after the armistice that Italy be rewarded for its "victory" by the addition of Nice, Savoy, Corsica, Morocco, Algeria, and Tunisia to its territory—that all this recent and still warm history was nothing but idle nonsense and empty dreams, and that the hapless peninsula had done nothing but struggle heroically against its German occupiers. One can only tip one's hat to the dear Italians for such an enormous if ingenious fabrication, just as one must fall on one's knees and worship them for having added to the annals of war one priceless anecdote: the death at Tobruk in 1940 of Air Marshal Italo Balbo, the ace of Italian aviators, killed, as they say, in the line of duty—by his own anti-aircraft fire. Never have the ignoble glory of the military and the stupid prestige of the uniform been so cruelly mocked.

As for the Resistance, it was not until March 30, 1944, that we discovered its existence and consequences in the most painful way. For us Neuilly meant hunger and cold. My mother's thoughts turned to the tiny village of Lusigny (population 70) just over a mile from the town of Bligny-sur-Ouche in which she was born. The village council agreed to rent us a presbytery that had fallen into disuse when Bligny's priest had assumed responsibility for services in Lusigny as well. It was a large, squat house with faintly ochre limestone walls, all of whose rooms, including those on the second floor and in the attic, had been ineptly tiled. The amenities were of the most rudimentary kind, but the old priest's garden, a mossy, bushy place in which the two sources of the Ouche, the Latin Fountain and the Closed Fountain, flowed together, had all the charm and vivacity suggested by the well-known words of Maurice Leblanc.[4] Ralphine moved there for the duration with the two youngest children, Jean-Loup and Gérard, who were respectively seven and eleven years old in 1940. Ralph and Janine rarely left Neuilly. I traveled constantly back and forth between Neuilly and Lusigny, dividing my time equally between the two. To complete the portrait, I should add that my grandparents, Edouard and Jeanne, having sold the pharmacy in Bligny, had retired to Dijon, where my grandfather ran the pharmacy of the lunatic asylum maintained by the Carthusian monks of Champmol. He showed me around the asylum and introduced me to the patients and doctors and to the problems of mental illness, an experience that had a great influence on me later on. After our tours we used to stroll through the town's botanical gardens, and with the tip of his cane my grandfather would point out the *Chrysosplenium alternifolium, Anchusa sempervirens,* and *Stachys heraclea,* whose names he pronounced with his Burgundian accent.

At Lusigny the food was adequate provided one made the rounds constantly by bicycle, trailer in tow. Hogs were bred, slaughtered, and preserved with salt. Enough fallen wood could be gathered in the forest to fuel both the wood stove in the common room and the cooking stove. In our little village we experienced rural life with all the hardships of ages past, revived by rationing, fear, and the hatred born of war. Living in the country means rubbing your nose in every human frailty, since everyone knows everyone else; one sees all the drunkenness, madness, incest, suicide, and murder that remains decorously veiled in our anonymous cities. It was all part of an environment that could at times be oppressive and brutal but that was also quite lovely, mingling the odor of birch logs drying on the hearth with the fragrance of the stable, as warm as a bed, the sight of stars glimmering in the frozen night sky, and the night air alive with familiar sounds: the clank of a chain, the plaintive howl of a pup, or the grotesque trumpeting of an ass. How searing, dry, and cold that wartime Burgundy was! During the summer I was obliged to "lend my youthful arms to the earth," as the bureaucratic phraseology would have it. I worked on the small farm of a wonderful family, the Fourniers, headed by a man who looked like a Celtic warrior with his blue eyes and long blonde mustache. Tending horses, flaying the skin of one's hands on the handle of the pitchfork, carrying immense armloads of golden grass in which thistle mixed treacherously with bluets and poppies, and above all standing by through the terrible and glorious days when the thresher filled the barnyard with panting sounds and silvery dust: these were simple but important things, and I am glad I experienced them before they disappeared forever.[5]

On March 30, 1944, Easter vacation should have taken me back to Lusigny. I do not know why I was still in Neuilly. Early that morning, elements of a Ukrainian regiment under the command of German noncoms surrounded Lusigny and began a search that bore all the earmarks of a punitive reprisal. For hours the soldiers went from house to house, breaking and smashing whatever got in the way. For Ralphine alone with the two children, it was the longest day of her life. All males above the age of fifteen were locked in the church. Later they were led out into the forest. They believed that they were about to be shot. In fact, however, they were ordered to bury nine Resistance fighters killed in a skirmish, which was the cause of all the trouble. Finally, fourteen people were loaded into trucks and dispatched to an unknown distination. Our neighbor Fournier was one of those taken, along with his son of fifteen and two eldest daughters, all accused of having given food to the "Resistance." They were "my" family. I might have gone to Buchenwald with them. That sinister name was still unfamiliar when it began to be spoken in the village later on, and people asked my mother, who had traveled in Germany, if she knew the town. I used the episode in *Gemini*. Buchenwald? No, she had never heard of it. The name did not appear on any map of Germany. My mother told them it meant "beech forest." Wasn't that reassuring? Our deportees were being sent to work as loggers.

Not all of them came back, and of those who did some, like old Fournier, somehow were never again right. When people talk about the victims of the camps, they generally count only those who died in them. But some who clung to life in hope of liberation also deserve mention, for when liberation came they found it impossible, because of what they had seen, to live as other men lived, and sank slowly into death like clocks that had run down. Their numbers are alarmingly high.

I was also in Lusigny when the Liberation arrived, in the person of troops that had marched north from Marseilles under the command of de Lattre de Tassigny. After the events of March 30 only women, children, and old men remained in the village, and I, in my nineteenth spring-time, was the only quarry likely to interest the hunters in green. Thus it was with the caution and quickness of a hare that I watched the events unfold. I had prepared a combination camp and observation post in the wooded hillside overlooking the village, not far from a bronze ma-donna known as the Black Virgin. From there I watched the roads leading to Lusigny, National Highway 70 from Beaune and the smaller County Highway 17 that led rather steeply down from Cussy-la-Colonne. Unexpectedly the retreating Germans arrived via the latter road. I was hav-ing lunch in the presbytery, windows open and ears pricked, when I heard the frightening clank of a column of tanks. While the villagers barricaded themselves inside their homes, I galloped up to my eagle's nest. The men of that German armored division retreating toward Dijon still had a proud look about them. But the parade contin-ued for three days and three nights, and gradually the in-evitable dishevelment of a defeated army became apparent to the eye. The tanks were followed by trucks—dustier and dustier—and then by horse-drawn wagons, whose brakes, squealing in concert as they descended toward the village, filled the valley with a deafening wail. Bringing up the rear were the foot soldiers, each more tattered than the last. Some pushed their packs before them in baby car-riages. The troops entered a few houses in search of bi-cycles. Among those seized was my sturdy veteran of the trips to Villers-sur-Mer and the food-hunting expeditions, commandeered by the retreating Germans despite its hav-ing been shod for some time with bandages of cork.

Meanwhile the roadsides filled with weapons, mines, ammunition, and supplies. Broken-down cars were abandoned, and unshod horses wandered off into the fields.

At length the flood subsided. But the village was not yet empty of soldiers. Indeed, it was full of them, but this was a new kind of occupation, an army of the gaunt and disabled, the dead tired and the hungry, the lame, the reeling, and the whining. The hare Tournier, from his lofty observation post, realized that he could now venture into town with his head held high and even with his chest swelled out. The first soldier I saw immediately asked me where he should go to surrender. Had I had the slightest ambition, the least thought of a political career or public office, I could have made those men *my* prisoners, pretending to have captured them in order to turn them over as living tribute to the French troops expected the next day. Some who did no more than this were shortly thereafter rewarded with the power to send their neighbors and rivals to prison or to the firing squad and later became prefects and ministers. I simply explained to those lost soldiers the wonderfully unstable, ephemeral, and transitory situation in which we all found ourselves, caught between the retreating German army and the advancing First French Army, in a *Niemandsland* in which all men are equal and equally without law, and which was like a limbo standing between the heaven of peace and the hell of war.

Back at Neuilly, the excitement of the Liberation gone, I left to others the joys, sorrows, and thrills of pursuing the enemy across the Rhine. People were lining up in front of the recruitment offices, and the revitalized French army wanted equipment and instructors more than young recruits. I had better and more pressing things to do, or so I thought: to perfect my Greek and delve deeper into Plato's *Parmenides,* especially the second part, that marvel of ontological subtlety before which I had seen all scholarly commentators surrender.[6] I plunged into a thesis on Platonic ideas, which not even the Wehrmacht's Christmas offensive in the Ardennes and the specter of a renewed Occupation were able to disturb.[7] I nevertheless devoted several hours a week to military training, attending classes in "logistical support" in which I learned to drive and repair twenty-ton trucks. In later years I refreshed these memories while writing *A6,* a screenplay for television on which I based my story, "L'Aire du muguet" ("The Lily of the Valley Lay-by").[8] In any case the family had already sacrificed a daughter to the fatherland: my sister Janine had joined the Women's Army Auxiliary and been assigned as an interpreter to de Lattre de Tassigny's staff. She was therefore the only member of the family, and probably one of the few Frenchwomen, to return to Germany right behind the tanks and in khaki uniform, valiantly carrying on the family tradition of *Germanistik.* In the meantime I patiently studied my Plato, possessed, comforted, and excited by my absolute conviction that Germany rightfully belonged to me, and that in due course it would be laid at my feet, free of its Wehrmacht and its Nazis.

In any case the trials of certain journalists at that time inspired in me some very firm ideas about the relationship between the writer and his country, ideas that have changed very little since. The moment one decides to write French for a living, one enters, I think, into an enduring, intimate, and tempestuous love affair with the language—a marriage, in short, of a sort that no other profession and no other art can create, and which confers upon the writer an incomparable measure of "Frenchness." This represents a considerable handicap. A French musician, dentist, or farmer would surely suffer less from being forced to emigrate than would a French writer. For a

French writer, to leave France is rather like what it would be for a river to lose its source, its direction, and its outlet, for the émigré writer loses his inspiration, his fluency, and his audience, which is to say, everything he has.[9] Yet this infirmity of the writer is justly compensated by certain privileges, in particular that of being more French than his countrymen, French squared, as it were, so that a French writer cannot do or write anything that dilutes his Frenchness to the level of his nonwriting compatriots. Ergo, for ordinary Frenchmen to pass judgment on a French writer, to convict him of anti-French activities and writings, is an infamy of the most abject kind. Ergo, the indictment leading to the death sentence and execution of Robert Brasillach—who, by the way, was a mediocre writer and first-class traitor—was nothing but an obscenity coughed up by a bunch of filthy foreigners. I, as a French writer and by virtue of my superior Frenchness, enjoy the privilege of heaping upon France the harshest of criticisms and foulest of insults as I see fit; but to you who read me, unless you are yourselves French writers, I grant only the right to listen while standing at attention with your hats off, as if you were listening to *La Marseillaise*.[10]

In June of 1946 I defended my thesis on Plato before Raymond Bayer at the Sorbonne. I was supposed to take the *agrégation*[11] the following year, but it never happened. Germany was still smoldering from the war that had only just ended, but with Nazism driven out or buried it could once again be visited. I would have died of chagrin or nostalgia had I not set out at the earliest opportunity, especially since my desire to know, to understand, and to construct was now driving me in the direction of German philosophy: Fichte, Schelling, Hegel, Husserl, and Heidegger.

But to travel to and stay in Germany in those days was no mean feat. A French citizen had to have a "military mission order" to cross the Rhine and had to be affiliated in some way or other with the occupying forces. In a fever of excitement I moved heaven and earth, calling every contact I had. Eventually I heard about a group of thirty-odd French students, all Germanists, who had been invited to spend three weeks at the University of Tübingen by its "caretaker," Lieutenant René Cheval. But the list was closed, and in any case I was a philosophy student, not a German specialist. I begged a friend of my father's, the composer Maurice Vandair, who exercised some measure of political influence thanks to his position in the Communist Party hierarchy. He got me accepted.

On July 26, a splendid day, I arrived in the small college town of Tübingen after a twenty-four-hour journey by train. A wildly romantic town somehow miraculously spared by the war, Tübingen enchanted me. French and German students stared at one another incredulously, dazzled by the sight. Was it possible that the nightmare had come to an end? Had we truly reached the end of the tunnel? We were twenty. Had fate really given us this incredible gift, to live and work together on tasks requiring delicacy and intelligence, to create freely without fear of the stupidity of war? We belonged to ourselves at last. The world belonged to us. If ever I knew the headiness of youth, it was surely in that summer of '46 on the banks of the Neckar, whose waters reflected the steeple of Stiftkirche where on Sunday mornings a small wind ensemble gathered to regale the whole town with aubades and chorales, the austere silhouette of the Stift where Hegel and Schelling had studied, and the carpenter Zimmer's low tower where Hölderlin spent thirty-five years in the darkness of insanity.

When the three weeks were up, René Cheval called us all together and informed us that it would be possible for those who wished to continue our studies at the University of Tübingen to stay on in the most comfortable of circumstances. Because I was not a German specialist, this offer did not apply to me. But there was only one application: mine. I had gone for three weeks; I remained for four years. In a town that was half-academic, half-agricultural—with pigs and chickens roaming the streets in the Spitalkirche district—the poverty of the immediate postwar period and Germany's political disarray combined to create an atmosphere rather like that of an eighteenth-century principality. There was a sovereign who lived in a little castle on the heights of the Osterberg overlooking the city: the French governor, Guillaume Widmer, a banker in civilian life, was the veritable king of Wurtemberg. He lived in high style, assisted by a sort of chamberlain and major-domo in charge of ceremonies, balls, hunts, horse races, and other amusements, one Philippe Withechurch (whence the name of his favorite mare, Blanchéglise, which means "white church"), who was as tall and blond as his sovereign Widmer was rotund and dark. In orbit around these two lords were two bitterly antagonistic aristocracies: a nobility of the robe, as it were, consisting of bureaucrats, and a nobility of the sword, made up of officers of the occupying forces. The German population, for its part, formed a mass of serfs, subject to taxation and compulsory labor at the whim of the monarch. It goes without saying that the occupiers were as supremely ignorant of the occupied population as they were of the blacks and Arabs in the colonies from which many of them hailed. For the combat troops had been supplanted by specialists in occupation, many of whom were stupid, greedy, and chauvinistic. Widmer, however, ran his kingdom with elegance and generosity, and I often hear him remembered in Tübingen with affection and gratitude. An avid hunter, he counted among his most notable successes his efforts to protect the forests of the territory, the splendid Schönbuch National Park foremost among them, from destruction by the many people in that time of scarcity who went hunting for venison and firewood.

As the months passed, other French students joined me, and we formed a small group of rather ill-defined status in the French Occupied Zone. Administratively we were part of the French colony, if only by virtue of our always temporary, periodically renewed "mission orders," but we moved almost exclusively in German—mainly academic—circles, where we had no desire to be taken for foreigners, much less occupiers.

Presiding over our table was an elder statesman whose vast culture we adored. He knew Baroque German and Austrian better than anyone else. We also loved his gentleness, his suave, priestlike delivery and orotund episcopal manner, which went rather well with the chubby body of a witty and sophisticated sensualist. An industrialist in civilian life, Jacques Vanuxem for a brief period experienced what was surely the most exciting adventure that an admirer of prestigious and venerable objects could ever enjoy. It is largely thanks to his efforts that the crown-reliquary of Saint Louis now resides in the Louvre.

The history of that gem is recounted by Prince Ernst Heinrich of Saxony in his memoirs. Saint Louis, wishing to demonstrate his gratitude to his tutor, a monk in the Benedictine abbey at Liège, made him a gift of the crown in a solemn ceremony in the Sainte Chapelle prior to departing on the Seventh Crusade in 1248. The crown remained among the precious possessions of the abbey of Liège until 1794. In that year the monks decided to flee the

advancing armies of revolutionary France into that part of
the Low Countries that would eventually become Belgium. The crown thereupon began a long odyssey that
took it from Aix-la-Chapelle to Cologne, from there to
Leipzig, and finally to Dresden, where the former prior of
Liège offered it to Princess Caroline, the wife of Prince
Maximilian of Saxony, who, having been born the princess of Bourbon-Parma, was a descendant of Saint Louis.
On February 13, 1945, a sadly famous attack by the RAF
reduced Dresden to ashes, killing more people than the
bomb dropped on Hiroshima. Because the attack came on
the eve of Mardi Gras, countless children were pulled from
the rubble dressed as Pierrot, Harlequin, or Columbine.
The crown was discovered intact amid the ruins of the pal-
ace of the prince-electors of Saxony. Ernst Heinrich of
Saxony took refuge in the residence of his relative, the
prince of Sigmaringen, taking the crown with him in a
cardboard hatbox. In the spring of 1947 we listened daily
to Jacques Vanuxem's account of the whole affair. He and
Henri-Paul Eydoux, chief of police of the military government of Wurtemberg, were responsible for making the
initial contacts with the prince to arrange for the return of
the crown. Pierre Verlet, head conservator of the Louvre,
then went to Sigmaringen to sign an agreement with the
prince.

At the last minute an unforeseen obstacle arose. The
head of the Saxon dynasty, Prince Friedrich Christian,
margrave of Meissen and husband of the margrave of Tour
and Taxis, was afraid that he would be committing the
crime of simony if he sold this crown full of relics. A con-
ference had to be arranged in Paris among the margrave,
his wife, the future Prince Marie Emmanuel, and Cardinal
Suhard, archbishop of Paris, who granted them all prior
absolution.

Some days thereafter, on August 25, 1947, the feast day

of Saint Louis, a ceremony was held in the Sainte Chapelle, during which the crown was solemnly surrendered to Georges Salles, director of the French museum system, in the presence of the margrave, his wife, Prince Marie Emmanuel, and Monsignor Brot, auxiliary of the archbishop of Paris.

The crown, which now sits in the Gallery of Apollo alongside those of Louis XV and Napoleon I, is supposed to be returned each year on August 25 to the Sainte Chapelle. That, at any rate, was the express wish of the prince, who now lives in Ireland, where he was able to purchase a farm.

Among the Germanists who constituted the French "intelligentsia" of Tübingen, I would have been the only philosopher, had it not been for the much-noticed arrival of Claude Lanzmann,[12] who was writing a dissertation on Leibniz and who was proud to have found an apartment on Hegelstrasse. He became a popular figure in our small community not only for his wit and redoubtable lucidity but even more for his personality: he was the wandering Jew, combative, cynical, deliberately gauche, and always concocting theories concerning the three major problems in his life, namely, health, money, and women. Hungry for success with the latter, he invariably got what he wanted by provoking in his "victim" a bizarre mixture of fear, laughter, and pity. Two years later, none other than Simone de Beauvoir fell for the charm of this potent combination, as she relates in her memoirs. Claude introduced me to his brother Jacques and his brother-in-law Rezvani,[13] both painters at the time and without the least idea that it would be as novelists that they would make their mark.

Evelyne Lanzmann, who enjoyed a career in the theater

under the name Evelyne Rey, was more than a friend to
me. Loveable for her generosity, grace, and wit, she was
possessed by aspirations incompatible with her nature,
which ultimately led her to suicide. Her acute feeling
for intelligence and phobic horror of stupidity or even
mere mediocrity led her to associate with men of great
intellect but with little liking of or feeling for women.
Lou Andreas-Salomé, the friend of Nietzsche, Rilke, and
Freud, was a purely cerebral woman with an inflexible nature and very probably frigid. To live in certain climates,
in a certain rarefied atmosphere of ideas, requires nothing
less. Evelyne lacked even the small amount of virility
needed to survive in the very liberated circles that were the
only ones in which she cared to move. She was all femi-
ninity, and her fragility was incompatible with her idea of
happiness.

On the German side, two imposing figures of comparable authority, spirit, and ability to speak French, en-
livened our evening gatherings. Friedrich Sieburg was
known for his celebrated essay, "Is God French?" published in 1929 when he was the Paris correspondent for a
Frankfurt newspaper. He fought bitterly against the hostility he incurred as a result of his wartime role. The Nazi
authorities in Paris had naturally made use of him in attempting to win French intellectuals over to the cause of
Kollaboration. I know nothing of how he went about this
dubious mission, but what charm he exerted after the war
in his efforts to bury the past! Postwar France nevertheless
gave him the cold shoulder, and to all who would listen he
complained, "I married France for love, and now she rejects me." Pursuing themes developed in his famous essay,
he argued that the French, by attempting to hide their *real*
defeat in 1940 behind their *unreal* victory in 1945, were
condemning themselves to the perpetuation of a costly

sham, whose ultimate product was the war in Indochina. Whatever his theory may have been worth, it aroused the indignation of the blindly chauvinistic French authorities, who had little use for handsome Friedrich's subtle paradoxes. They showed their wrath by harassing him in a thousand petty ways. Although Sieburg possessed intelligence, cultivation, and eloquence to an exceptional degree, there was one thing he did not know how to do, even when it was manifestly in his own best interest: keep quiet. His irrepressible enthusiasm for words nearly did him in. One night, I heard him holding forth in French to a group of people who may have seemed admiring when in fact they were only attentive: "When the truth about the Soviet camps is known, the Nazi camps will look like so many 'Embarkations for Cythera' by comparison." There were a few laughs, but the next day he was obliged to leave town.

The other great talker held an important position in the Social Democratic Party. Born in Perpignan to a French mother, Carlo Schmid was among other things the author of an excellent translation of Baudelaire's *Fleurs du mal*. At the time he was minister of justice in the government of Wurtemberg, a modest title that he himself mocked with half-feigned arrogance: "With me," he said, "Wurtemberg is living beyond its means." He had ambition enough to run for the presidency of Germany in July of 1959. But the Social Democrats' time had not yet come. A pity. Heinrich Lübke, the Christian Democrat who was elected instead, is remembered only for his blunders and bad grammar. Carlo Schmid would have brought to the post a luster of culture worthy of the founder of the German Federal Republic, Theodor Heuss.

I had gone to Germany with the intention of studying philosophy, and I fulfilled my ambition. I studied with

such eminent teachers as Eduard Spranger, Wilhelm Os-
terreich, Romano Guardini, Enno Litmann (the translator
of *A Thousand and One Nights* into German), and old Teo-
dor Häring, who claimed that one could not understand
Hegel without speaking the Swabian dialect, which I immediately set out to master. He was freezing to death in a
beautiful, book-filled house on the banks of the Neckar. I
shared my coal with him, and he gave me a handsome
edition of Schelling in return.

But in all honesty I must confess that horses occupied
me even more than philosophy. I had begun riding at a
very early age. While in boarding school at Alençon I had
endured the rigorous training of the First Cavalry's riding
school. In Tübingen I availed myself of both a little-used
stable (the German "peasants" were no more entitled to
ride in those days than were the serfs of the Middle Ages)
and the lovely Swabian countryside. What is more, King
Widmer and his major-domo Withechurch were both
horsemen. Though excluded from the royal court as a student (the authorities taking a rather dim view of suspect
intellectuals who maintained the most deplorable relations
with the occupied population), I made my entry as a
horseman. The splendors of the Court of King Widmer
were all the more impressive for the way they stood out in
a country ruined by war and defeat. Dressed up as a page,
I served in hunts, rallies, and races. One day the horses
were trucked off to Lake Konstanz. That night, after a
long ramble through the Baden countryside, we dined on
the illuminated bridge of a paddlewheel steamer as it
cruised along the Swiss and German shores of the Boden-
see. High living!

Among German contemporaries who became my
friends in this period, first mention belongs to Helmut

Waller, whose current position as chief prosecutor of West Germany both delights and terrifies me. He played an important role in the writing of *The Ogre* and later became its translator. But I must also mention little Thomas Harlan, who carved out an important place in my life for three years before disappearing as mysteriously and suddenly as he had appeared. His father, Veit Harlan, UFA's number-one director[14] and all too well known for such films as *The Gilded City* and *Jew Süss,* had been indicted as a war criminal and was at that time defending himself with all the ferocity of a cornered boar. When Thomas first came to Tübingen he was seventeen years old and resembled Rimbaud upon his arrival in Paris in August 1870. He was torn by three passions: love for his father, shame for what his father had done, and like nearly all young Germans in those days a frantic desire to flee a Germany in ruins and still stinking with the odor of the Nazis. Easier said than done. I worked unceasingly to get him a passport and visa to visit France, and when I finally returned to Paris in 1950 he was able to go with me.

He introduced me to his father. Harlan had divorced the famous actress Hilde Körber, Thomas's mother, in order to marry the Swedish actress Christina Söderbaum, to whom he gave a starring role in all his subsequent films. Immediately after the war he set up a touring company and directed its plays, with Christina naturally in the leading roles. Just before one of these tours was to begin, Thomas took me to Hamburg. "We'll bid them good-bye," he said, "and then have papa's apartment to ourselves." Apparently he still did not know his father very well, for the old man wouldn't hear of it. For us to stay in Hamburg was out of the question. We had to go on the road with the company, and of course there was always

room for two more. Thus we were given the opportunity
to enjoy the same play in city after city, and to my embar-
rassment I confess that I remember nothing about it except
that Christina struck me as a ravishing starlet without an
ounce of talent. Recently I saw her again in a television
screening of *The Gilded City,* in which I thought she made
up for her rather unpleasant looks with her considerable
talent. Who knows where the truth lies? Everywhere we
were received royally, whether by the American military
authorities or the barons of the Ruhr, and the ponderous,
gaudy luxury to which we were treated at every stop
seemed not so much to clash with the hideous misery of
the devastated cities as to be its normal and almost obligatory counterpart. I imagine that the India of the mahara-
jahs offers an even better version of this strangely harmonious diptych. The truth is that nothing goes better with
the most sordid destitution than the most ostentatious
luxury.

Veit Harlan radiated vital energy. Speaking volubly in a
German filled with juicy images that he seemed to mold
with his short, powerful fingers, and constantly playing
himself—outrageous, theatrical, naive, and childish—he
anticipated every doubt and forestalled every accusation.
The press feasted on his trial, part of a general program of
"de-Nazification." Former prisoners came and testified
that their guards had treated them more harshly after
seeing *Jew Süss.* Lifting his arms to heaven and invoking
God, the devil, and all the angels, Harlan claimed the immunity of the artist, to say nothing of the traditional privilege of the court jester. Evidently he had forgotten that
the jester's immunity was supposed to allow him to insult
his masters, not fawn on them. He told me a rather illuminating anecdote about Hitler. One day, while walking

with the Führer in the gardens of the new chancellery in Berlin, he noticed a building whose upper stories were being demolished because they overlooked the very garden in which they were walking. "I am afraid that someone might attempt an attack with a rifle and telescopic sight," Hitler explained. "I'd like to be able to walk in these gardens without fear that someone will shoot at me from that building." Harlan pointed out that he was not afraid to show himself in public, where surely the risk of an attack was just as great. "No," Hitler replied. "When I'm in the midst of a crowd, I'm on my guard. My whole being gives off an aura that protects me. When I relax in this garden, I am naked and vulnerable."

Thomas bore the full brunt of his father's powerful personality and was crushed, annihilated, and subjugated by the vehemence of Veit's convictions. The novelist Hans Habe based his novel *Christopher and His Father* on this pair, but to my way of thinking he made them if not implausible then totally uninteresting.[15] He cast Christopher as a cold, vindictive, judgmental son and his father as a pitiful wretch. The reality was far more profound and disturbing. In the presence of his terrifying father I watched Thomas revert to being a blind and affectionate little boy. Only much later did I learn that, traveling under a false identity, he had gone with Klaus Kinski (star of the film *Aguirre, the Wrath of God*) to work on a kibbutz, after which he had conducted an investigation in Poland and gathered evidence about a massacre committed by members of the SS who were still on the loose. The name Harlan was a difficult one to bear.

When I saw him for the last time, he was still possessed by the conviction, typical of adolescent psychology, that one's existence could be justified only by an impressive achievement or spectacular act. He vanished with a poet of his own age by the name of Marc Sabatier-Lévesque, of whose suicide I learned shortly thereafter.

We daily witnessed the liquidation of the old Germany, the Germany of the Third Reich and Kaiser Wilhelm II, and the birth of a new nation with limited but unthreatening objectives. As time went by, the American, British, and French Occupation Zones shed their colonial-type administrations and were merged into a republic. When I met, as I sometimes did, former Nazis still immured in their old faith, I had doubts about the sincerity of some German leaders, who assured the world that their only ambition was to "turn Germany into one big Switzerland." I was wrong. It must be admitted that West Germany is today the most democratic country in the world. It might be argued that, after the Third Reich, the Germans had no other choice. Of course not, but the fact remains that they did what they had to do.

The Germany of the "economic miracle" was born before my very eyes, literally overnight. On Saturday, June 19, 1948, Germany looked as devastated, desolate, and wretched as it had for the past several years. On Sunday, June 20, as if struck by a magic wand, the cities came to life, the markets filled with stalls, and the shop windows with merchandise. Ration cards were abolished, and with them went the black market that inevitably accompanies, and mitigates, any organized system of rationing. How did this miracle come to pass? Through recognition that the defeated Germany's economy was in a state of total collapse, leading to the complete withdrawal from circulation of the existing currency, the Reichsmark, and its replacement by the new Deutschmark. But this was no mere exchange of one set of bills for another, as had occurred in France three years earlier. No matter what quantity of Reichsmarks you submitted to the bank, you received in return no more than sixty Deutschmarks in two lump sums. This sudden transition from a subsidized, collectivist, centralized economy—a socialist system, in short—to an uncontrolled liberal economy governed solely by the law of the marketplace injured many people, as everyone now had to contend with a poverty shared by all. But the resulting spur to production yielded spectacular results, from which an indelible lesson was learned. I recall the stupefaction of a French engineer assigned to dismantle certain German factories and transport their contents to France by way of war reparations. "The Germans are incredible," he told me one day. "They write asking me to speed up my demolition work in such-and-such a factory, because the new machines have arrived and they don't know where to put them." I suggested that he leave the old machines in place and requisition the new ones, but he said that my proposal went beyond the established guidelines.

Nevertheless, my thorough exploration of the Germany of that time revealed some hidden realities. One of the most impressive was a Swabian peasant, almost too Swabian to believe, to whom I offered some cigarettes and soap in exchange for a few dozen eggs, a common enough exchange prior to the monetary miracle. Recognizing that I was French, he suddenly began speaking to me in an accent that smacked more of French farce than of the hills of Wurtemberg. He explained that he had been a French soldier captured and held in Germany as a prisoner of war, and that when peace came he had no desire to change his life yet again. So he had asked for and received naturalization as a German citizen. Perhaps he was telling the truth.

Or perhaps I was dealing with some obscure collaborationist or with a veteran of the French Volunteer Legions who fought the Russians and "Bolshevism" alongside the Wehrmacht, someone caught up in the maelstrom of defeat who had been issued false papers by the Nazis prior to their demise. This metamorphosis of fate fascinated me all the more because I myself felt so strongly drawn to Germany at the time. A few years later André Cayatte dealt with the subject in his film *Le Passage du Rhin* ("The Crossing of the Rhine"). A bakery worker, played by Charles Aznavour, married to the boss's daughter, is abused by his wife and in-laws. Taken prisoner along with two million other soldiers in 1940, he ends up working as a handyman on a beautiful farm in Bavaria. As Germany moves deeper into the war and closer to defeat, more and more men are sent to the front, even the children and the elderly, and in the absence of other men the prisoner's situation steadily improves. The handyman becomes the lover of the farmer's daughter, runs the farm, and issues ration cards at the town hall. For him, liberation is a catastrophe. He returns to his oven and is once again subjected to the abuse of his wife and in-laws. But not for long, because he has discovered another life—in Bavaria. The film ends with an image of the little baker heading back across the Rhine with a pack on his back, but this time in civilian garb.

This theme of the prisoner discovering his homeland in exile and his freedom in captivity touched me all the more because during the Occupation I was more than once haunted by thoughts of all those Frenchmen being held in a country that they had every reason to detest while I suffered the pangs of an enforced separation. In the converted, naturalized, and assimilated prisoner, moreover, I saw a beautifully trimphant and provocative image of *amor fati,* of that strength in a man that manages to turn a terrible blow into a blessing and the most disastrous of fates into happiness. So I knew very early that if ever I were to pour my experience, my disillusionments, and my enthusiasms into a novel about Germany, the principal character would be a Frenchman taken prisoner in 1940 and glad of it, crossing the Rhine with the certainty of never returning to France. But of course the literally autobiographical content of *The Ogre* is slim, because I was too young to have been called up in 1939 and was therefore never taken prisoner, nor had I ever set foot in East Prussia at the time I wrote the book.

I found myself confronted with two pieces, the prisoner and Nazi Germany, which somehow had to be fitted together, and shaped with that end in mind. It soon became clear that using the myth of the ogre as the central theme was the way to do it. In Germany at the height of Nazism's rise I had been a mere child, hence an object of the ogre's attention, for I had been keenly aware of how much the new German regime focused on me and others of my age. Fascism characteristically overesteems youth, which it holds up as a value, an end in itself, an incessant theme of propaganda. In Italy a common slogan insisted that fascism was a youth movement, of and for young people. It must be said, moreover, that there is something childish about fascist politics. With its constant parades, celebrations, fireworks, hikes, and youth groups, fascism manifests itself in ways accessible to the youngest of children. The new Wehrmacht, with its shiny new equipment, looked more like a toy army, an army of tin soldiers, than any other army in the world. The Nazis had cleverly exploited the youth groups known as *Wandervögel* ("migrant birds") that had flourished in Germany after the First

World War; members of these groups were drawn into the Nazis' own youth organization, the Hitlerjugend.[16] Adding racism to this "juvenophilia" introduced some maniacal aspects. For the Nazis were interested in children from birth, and not merely as soldiers but as the biological substance of the German people; hence juvenophilia turned to pedophilia. Specific physical characteristics were singled out for praise. To be good, the child had to be blond, blue-eyed, and dolichocephalic, hence the dark-haired, dark-eyed, and brachycephalic were perforce bad. In the end, of course, both the good and the bad physiques were destined for destruction by the system: the bad in massacres, slave labor, and extermination camps, and the good as cannon fodder in the service of the Thousand Year Reich.

As my research progressed, I gathered abundant proof of the Nazi regime's ogreish nature. One of the most striking was the solemn celebration held on April 19, when all the little boys and girls who had turned ten within the past year (a million children in all, in nice, round numbers) were inducted into the Jungvolk if they were male and the Jungmädelbund if they were female. Why April 19? Because April 20 was Hitler's birthday. The Führer thus assumed the aspect of the Great Ogre, the Minotaur to which an entire generation of children was sacrificed as a birthday offering.

In my investigation into the Third Reich, I was most efficiently assisted by Helmut Waller, whose post as Staatsanwalt or state prosecutor sometimes required him to investigate war criminals, making him a kind of expert on the subject even apart from his personal memories as a former member of the Hitlerjugend and soldier of the Wehrmacht. We communicated less often by letter than by magnetic tape, which made it possible to record in a very short time the equivalent of several letters' worth of material and which offered the additional charm of recreating the sonic environment of a household, with shouts of children returning home, ringing bells, purring cats, and the drone of passing aircraft. I wanted to know everything there was to know about the so-called *napolas* (National-politische Erziehungsanstalten), the SS's military training schools, where a hand-picked elite was raised to become the cream of the future Reich. In Munich I introduced myself to Baldur von Schirach, former head of the Hitler Youth, who had just completed the twenty years in Spandau Prison to which he had been sentenced by the Nuremberg tribunal. When I mentioned the word *napola,* he threw up his hands. They had not been his responsibility. The napolas were purely SS operations, closed to ordinary party members. The party had its own schools, which rivaled the napolas: the Adolf Hitler Schulen. Schirach's sons, who remained with him during our interview, confirmed that they had been educated in the latter and not in the napolas. Once again I discovered that the Nazi state, far from having the monolithic structure with which it has often been credited (particularly in Eugen Kogon's book *The SS State),* was composed of many factions at times in open conflict with one another.

At this point Helmut Waller's assistance proved invaluable. Not only did he put me in touch with a colleague of his who had been educated in a napola, he also informed me that by an almost incredible coincidence the former SS officer August Heissmeyer, at one time chief of all the napolas, lived in his own home town of Bebenhausen, a few miles from Tübingen, where since the end of the war he had managed the regional Coca-Cola distribution facility. While staying with Waller I went to see Heissmeyer several times, and he introduced me to one of his sons, who as was only fitting had been educated in a napola. The son lived in a handsome old wooden chalet with his wife, once a prominent pillar of Third Reich society. She showed me a copy of the *Völkischer Beobachter* (the official Nazi daily newspaper) in which she appeared on page one in the guise of Mater Germania, very beautiful, very blonde, very much in braids, and surrounded by a vast brood of children. Obviously Waller and Heissmeyer had neither the desire nor the occasion to meet, but one day the former SS man learned that I was living nearby in the home of his sworn enemy. He simply remarked that one of his grandsons and one of Waller's grandsons were the best of friends. Sancta simplicitas . . .

My investigations of Nazism also took me to Belgium. In Namur I had a terrifying encounter with a bizarre collector. Before the war Ray Petifrères had amassed an extraordinary collection of weapons from every time and place, from prehistoric stone axes to World War I trench mortars. When the Nazis came to power his collector's instincts found another outlet. He moved his original collection from his home to the fortress of Namur, where it acquired the name Namur Weapons Museum, with Petifrères as curator, and transformed his home into a Nazi museum. It takes a strong stomach to linger in the main room, which is filled with paraphernalia of the Third Reich, all carefully arranged by Petifrères. The walls are papered with Nazi flags, swastikas, propaganda posters, and parts of uniforms. In the windows, on the tables, and on the floor are piles of daggers, revolvers, clubs, rifles, machine guns, grenades, helmets, and belts adorned with the insignia of the SA, SS, HJ, NSDAP, and the like. A library contains a sampling of the major Nazi classics. And as if that were not enough, the rooms are filled with department store mannekins, poised as if ready to dance and with cajoling smiles on their faces yet dressed in the black uniforms of the SS, the brown of the SA, the green of the Landser, or the blue of the Kriegsmariner. There is even a little boy in the uniform of the HJ (Hitlerjugend), a little girl in that of the BDM (Bund Deutscher Maedel), and a young woman in mouse gray. Behind a curtain lies the sanctum sanctorum: a cake of soap made from Jewish flesh, a dish of ashes from one of the crematoria, and a parchment made of human skin, authenticated by the presence of a tattoo.

A most solicitous and attentive Petifrères placed all these wonders at my disposal and even offered, if my work dragged on, to have a cot set up for me among the mannekins. Then he left me to work on a monumental book he is writing, which will trace Hitler's movements *day by day* over the course of his entire career. Petifrères himself was conscientiously retracing the Führer's steps, attempting to eat at the same tables and sleep in the same beds where Hitler had eaten and slept.[17]

Like so many French prisoners, my hero was supposed to be sent deep into the heart of the Reich, to East Prussia. The choice of this particular province had more than one point in its favor. In the German mind it had always been enveloped in prestige and invested with poetry. Every country finds it useful to have some remote territory that can be used as a repository of myths and a place to send saints and miscreants. For England this role was long filled by India. In the United States it was the Wild West, which ultimately found its fulfillment in Hollywood and California. For a century France populated the Sahara with its missionaries, foreign legionnaires, and daughters of Atlas. To German eyes, East Prussia—the cradle of Prussia, whose first king was crowned at Königsberg—had the vague boundaries of a mythical land, with its Teutonic Knights, Porteglaives, and shifting dunes covered with swarms of migrant birds and a fantastic array of animals, including the auroch, or European bison, the wolf, and the black swan. Added to these claims to fame is now the misfortune of having been the first German territory to be invaded by the Red Army, an irretrievable calamity, since it led to the province's being divided between Poland and the Soviet Union, with Danzig becoming Gdansk and Königsberg, Kaliningrad. For obvious reasons I was not at all troubled by never having been there. Indeed, I would say that it was very nearly a blessing.

But imaginary does not mean imprecise. I was obliged to make up for my lack of intimate knowledge by providing a wealth of incontrovertible detail capable of withstanding the closest scrutiny. For years I snapped up all the maps, photographs, memoirs, historical studies, and tourist guides that I could find. My greatest discovery was the publishing house of Gräfe & Unzer, once headquartered in Königsberg. After decamping to Munich it kept memories of the old country alive among two million "repatriated" East Prussians by steadfastly turning out books of photographs, souvenirs, calendars, recipes, and humorous stories recounted in dialect. I also had the good fortune to stumble upon the memoirs of Walter Frevert, the last conservator of the Rominten game preserve, where Göring built the hunting lodge of his dreams, the Jägerhof, and carried on in grand style as the Third Reich's Master of the Hunt. This remarkable document had passed unnoticed even by discerning Germans, for it had been published by a house specializing in books on fishing, hunting, and farming. Thanks to this invaluable source, all the details of Göring's life at Rominten mentioned in *The Ogre* are accurate, to a degree that astonished the few survivors of that regal circle of hunters. Albert Speer, Hitler's architect and minister of war materiel, mentioned his surprise when we met: "How did you, so young and a Frenchman, manage to obtain an invitation to the Jägerhof?" I later learned that after the loss of Rominten, which became part of the Soviet Union, Walter Frevert had gone to West Germany, where he became the administrator of another game preserve—which obviously could not hold a candle to Rominten—near Kaltenbronn in Baden-Baden. I was struck by the similarity between the name of this locality and the imaginary fortress of Kaltenborn where I had placed the East Prussian napola in my novel. I attempted to arrange a meeting with him and had just established contact when I learned that he had killed himself by firing a rifle into his mouth.

By contrast, luck was with me when I called upon André Brébant, a carpenter in Chevreuse, to panel my attic ceiling. Since everything was out of plumb, every panel had to be cut individually and the pieces fitted together like a jigsaw puzzle. The work took three months. One day, while absorbed in studying a map of Masuria, I heard my French carpenter's voice: "That's where I was held prisoner. Four years. Liberated by the Russians. Came back to France via Odessa, the Black Sea, and the Mediterranean." I stared at him wide-eyed. He could not have been more dazzling in my eyes had he been wearing the luminous armor of the archangel Michael. So much for panels, nails, and jigsaws. We had work to do.

"But listen," he said cautiously, "I was no lion during the war, you know."

Precisely! It was not a lion's war that I wished to recount, but that of a poor giant, an ogre hungry for affection, myopic and visionary, continually making a cradle of his enormous hands to receive yet another small child.

The next day, my new collaborator brought with him a tiny notebook in which he had recorded, in a minuscule script, the details of his Masurian adventure, and with merciless insistence I forced him to relive that wretched period of his life and to share with me episodes and details that no one could have invented. It was from him, for instance, that I took the episode of the pigeon-fancying commando forced to eat his own pigeons, as well as the blind elk who knocked on doors in wintertime asking to be fed.

A cheap color print attached to the wall of the prison camp barracks was to change the life of the carpenter from Chevreuse. It was a picture of Senegal, symbolized by a white sand beach. Palm trees bowed gracefully toward the blue waves, and a proud woman advanced majestically, preceded by a bosom shaped like a ship's prow. In that interminable northern winter this vision of voluptuous warmth became the prisoner's obsession.

After returning home in May of 1945, our carpenter made a disastrous marriage, and several months after that he took off once again, this time for Senegal. For seven years he ran a carpentry shop in Dakar, returning in 1952 with enough money saved to buy a small house.

"Dakar after East Prussia! What an adventurous life for a quiet man!"

"Listen, I had to do it. The idea got stuck in my head while I was living in the cold."

"But the white beach, the leaning palms, the hot sand, the shapely women—don't you miss all that in a damp winter like this one?"

"Sure, a little. But mostly I miss Masuria. I'd really like

to go back there for a bit, just to see if it's still the way it was."

But Nazi Germany and its legendary East Prussia were only half the novel I had in mind. The other half was my hero, an auto mechanic employed in a Paris garage, a simple, realistic figure but at the same time a fantastic ogre, whose fate is secretly linked to the fate of the world. The technical problems raised by a character with two such different aspects were more easily solved than might at first appear possible. I never had any intention of writing fantasy. My aim was to achieve a realism that became fantastic only through an extreme of precision and rationalism: hyperrealism plus hyperrationalism.

This is perhaps the time to state my position on surrealism in literature and art. What separates me from the surrealist writers brings me close to the surrealist painters, namely, that to be a surrealist one must first be a realist. Surrealism, I think, is mastery of *technique*—in the academic sense—so perfect that it ends up being anti-academic. For me, that is the distinguishing characteristic of surrealist painting. Ernst, Picabia, Magritte, Delvaux, Dali, and Fini paint with such consummate skill as to produce meticulous, polished, finely brushed images that render reality with more precision than a photograph. They turned their backs on fauvism, cubism, and even impressionism and revived the meticulous style of such nineteenth-century traditionalists as Meissonier, Gros, Flandrin, and even Horace Vernet. Aiming to penetrate by stealth to the very heart of being, they trusted in the infallible firmness of draftsmanship rather than the shimmering haze of dreams. The more literally one copies reality, the more intimately one interferes with it. Such was the aim of the surrealist painters.

∨   The surrealist writers could have made the same choice. Leaping over late romanticism and symbolism they could have taken their inspiration from the naturalist tradition. They could have forgotten Mallarmé, Verlaine, and Rimbaud and taken up the tools of Théophile Gautier, Flaubert, and Maupassant, aiming to achieve an objectivity bordering on hallucination. Instead they chose the opposite course, relying instead on vagueness, fantasy, the unconscious, and the approximate, on automatic writing and free association.

It is with the painters that I feel at home. If I wish to provide a novel with nonliterary underpinnings, I call upon classical metaphysicians, not philosophical quacks. Given a choice between artistic vagueness and photographic precision, I have no hesitation whatsoever, particularly since the minute precision of the surrealist painters bears that discreet but inevitable hallmark of every truly great and profound work of art, namely, humor. By comparison, André Breton and his friends are like stolid schoolmasters, distastefully pale and solemn.

There is no better way to portray systematic, logical madness than to allow one's characters to speak for themselves. The reader is then confronted directly with a person's own explanations for his actions; he bears the full brunt of the character's convictions, while the self-effacing author remains hidden, a voyeur enjoying the confrontation. I know of no other way to give fancy free rein while at the same time respecting the fundamental choice of a realistic narrative. When Abel Tiffauges hopes that his school will burn down before he must face a disciplinary board, and that school does in fact burn down, then it is only natural for him not even to consider the possibility of a coincidence and to believe that fate has deliberately taken a hand. For him this is the only possible interpretation, and it is important that he explain it directly to the reader. Any authorial interference would only weaken the force of Tiffauges's vision. Similarly, when Robinson Crusoe spills his seed upon the earth and sees mandragoras grow on the very spot, he is convinced (in accordance with an ancient legend) that the plant has grown from his sperm, and that the fruit is his daughter and the island its mother. The author must neither corroborate nor contradict this conviction, which is one of the moving forces behind the novel's fantasy. Two things are certain. Mandragoras do exist; they do grow on the Juan Fernandez Islands (I've checked). And Robinson believes that he is their progenitor. I claim no more than this. It is in this sense, at once absolute and limited, that Abel Tiffauges, the hero of *The Ogre,* is indeed an ogre, which is to say a kind of fairy.

It is true that, in characterological terms, he is an ogre type. He is big and fat. All signs are that the digestive function is dominant. His enormous hands serve as intermediaries between the external world and his mouth; they are predatory, murderous hands, but at the same time obliging, supportive, and caressing. They combine all the characteristic features of what I call phoria. Like many mythological giants, his vision is poor. He is reminiscent of Orion, a giant but a blind hunter. And of the Cyclops in the *Odyssey,* who had but one eye, which was put out by Ulysses. And of Colin the Mallet Man, the giant warrior of Flanders, who fought with a mallet: deprived of his sight by a wound, he needed a squire to guide his blows. The ogre has a keen nose; he "smells blood," according to Charles Perrault.[18] And we know from biology that the sense of sight in animals is frequently inversely proportional to the sense of smell. Birds and monkeys with keen eyesight have a mediocre sense of smell. The hare, whose scent is fabulously keen, can barely see.

This digestive character is obsessed with fresh things—milk, salads, and raw vegetables—which he consumes in great quantities. Much preoccupied with digestion, he is terrified of constipation, a trait he shares with the aristocrats of the seventeenth century. At the court of Louis XIV—a court of ogres—the enema and the clyster were king. Jovial, the ogre is much given to telling scatological jokes but relatively reluctant to tell erotic ones. His personality is of the anal rather than the phallic type, as can be seen from his two greatest literary exemplars, Gargantua and Pantagruel. In his evaluation of the human body he chooses tails over heads. His focus is on the buttocks and anus. What is more, he is anxious about the small size of his penis (microgenitomorphism).

The ogre is a magus and predator. The magic of Perrault's ogre resides in his seven-league boots. Abel Tiffauges's magic resides in the coincidence that he believes to exist between his personal destiny and the course of history, or, more precisely, in the proofs of such coincidence offered by reality. Saint Christopher's School burns down so that he will not have to appear before a disciplinary board, and twenty years later war breaks out in order to spare him from appearing in court. The reason for the war is to free him from prison, or so he thinks. Once again the school has burned down. But life's greatest miracle is that ogreish Germany is given him as a gift, for after he is made a prisoner and catechumen it collapses before the onslaught of the Red Army and lies prostrate at his feet.

The ogre-magus finds a northern embodiment in the erlking, or king of the elves, made famous by Goethe's ballad *Der Erlkönig* ("The Erlking"), in which the erlking first attempts to win the child's favor and finally takes the boy from his father's arms and kills him. Made even more famous by Schubert's lied, Goethe's poem has always been *the* German poem par excellence for every French schoolchild embarking upon the study of German literature, a symbol of Germany herself. The odd thing is that the poem originated with an error of translation by Herder, who introduced the Germans to Danish folklore. He rendered the Danish *Eller,* or elves, as *Erlen,* meaning elms, because in the dialect spoken in Herder's native town of Mohrungen in East Prussia, the word for elm was *Eller.* It is unlikely that Goethe would have been interested in the banal legend of the king of the elves. But his imagination was inspired by the precise and original evocation of the elm, because the elm was considered to be a dark and evil tree that flourished beside stagnant ponds, just as the willow is a green and beneficial tree that flourishes beside fast-flowing streams. The marsh elm evokes the foggy plains and dunes of north Germany, and the Erlkönig is the ethereal, child-loving ogre who hovers over those mournful flatlands. The pedophile passion of the king of the elves is amorous and even carnal. Yet it is not quite pederastic, even though the victim in Goethe's poem is a young boy. (Perrault's ogre also had it in for boys, and if in the end he slit the throats of girls, they were his own daughters, and it was the result of a terrible mistake.) The most ambiguous line of the poem, and the most difficult to translate, is obviously the famous

Ich liebe dich. Mich reizt deine schöne Gestalt,

which has traditionally been weakened by translation as

I love you. Your handsome face pleases me,

whereas a more literal translation would be

I love you. Your beautiful body excites me,

for all the German-English dictionaries give *excite* as the primary equivalent of the German *reizen*. But to translate the line this way would surely be to go beyond Goethe's intentions. For that reason, in the translation that I published at the end of the novel, I proposed the following reading:

> I love you. Your handsome body tempts me.

This avid desire can be interpreted in a variety of ways, and no possible reading is foreclosed.[19]

Lazy, superficial, and tiresomely hostile critics have interpreted Abel Tiffauges as a pederast in a way that obviously conflicts with the whole shape of the novel. As a consistent ogre, Tiffauges is passionately in love with the following things, in order of intensity and also in an order corresponding to the three stages of his life story: first, freshness and that which embodies it (raw vegetables, dairy products, and clear voices); second, small animals; and third, children. At first he makes no distinction between girls and boys, but fate pushes him in the direction of the latter. In the first place, only the male "quarry" is worthy of the hunter. Killing a female animal has always been considered a relatively ignoble act (when the animal is butchered, there is always the question of the fetus), particularly in that most noble form of hunting, riding to hounds. No one hunts a doe on horseback. Second, the tradition of the male prey was continued and developed by the Nazis. The napolas were exclusively for males, for the simple reason that only male flesh is suitable for cannon fodder.

In any case, Tiffauges's relationship with his youthful prey is not sexual in nature. It is presexual, protosexual. Tiffauges is not an adult. He is characterized by a deep-seated and irremediable immaturity (symbolized by his tiny penis). The child's erotic instinct—that virginal, spontaneous force which society attempts to channel and shape for the purpose of perpetuating the species—remains, in Tiffauges's case, in its original undifferentiated state. From the outset he finds himself in the condition to which Robinson Crusoe is reduced by twenty years of solitude in my novel *Friday.* Crusoe has experienced a loss of those social institutions to which he owed, among other things, his sexual identity as a father and head of a family. His years of solitude alter him to the very core, leaving him free, unspoiled, and open to innovations of the most extravagant sort.

Less open, Tiffauges follows his own inner genius, which is that of an ogre. For a while he feels his way until the rites and forms of *phoria* have been established. He appears first as a mass of perversions, but perversions not yet fully developed, still malleable and inventive. Unfortunately, most deviations from what is exclusively regarded as "normal" sexuality become mired in forms and rituals even more limiting and oppressive than the "norm." Because, when all is said and done, the norm is a perversion shared by nearly everyone, it seems ultimately to offer a wider field to those who accept it than does the purely individual "norm" of perversion. There is no limit to the maniacal insistence of some perverts on the performance of certain precise rituals, without which they cannot experience pleasure. In one reported case, a man was unable to ejaculate unless a third party present in the room pronounced a rather lengthy sentence without omitting a single word—his orgasm required a magic formula, as it were. In another case, a person had to deposit his feces on the ground in a precise pattern. And so on. Thus, when Freud said that the child was "polymorphously perverse," he effected a no doubt unconscious union of contradictory terms, perversion being "unimorphous" by its very nature.

Not, however, in the case of Abel Tiffauges, who in the course of a phoric cycle that is not completed before the final page of the novel reveals a host of insidious perversions: vampirism (the episode of Pelsenaire's injured knee), cannibalism (his interpretation of the Eucharist), coprophilia (passim), fetishism (his penchant for shoes), pedophilia (passim), necrophilia (Arnim episode), bestiality (with his horse Bluebeard), and so on. The very plurality of his perversions ensures that he will possess a certain innocence, for the true pervert is punished by his self-imposed obligation to perform the exact same act over and over again.

A murk that hides a thousand and one perversions: an image not only of Abel Tiffauges's soul but also of that of his creator, indeed I believe of any novelist. To create a character and his world there is nothing like the polymorphous and exploratory adaptability of infantile sexuality. It would be a mistake, however, to succumb to the illusions of the dream world and to mistake what is merely projected in the imagination for something that exists in reality. Just as Balzac was not the millionaire businessman seemingly reflected in some of his novels, nor Stendhal the young and irresistible seducer who seems to have inspired his finest prose, polymorphous perversity in a writer ends with the initial inspiration, with the glow of inception. The jack-of-all-trades does not get very far, and pays for the diversity of his desires by the number of his unfinished projects, all of which resemble fiascos. I know one who tried his hand at virtually everything but always stopped in midcourse. An impotent necrophiliac, unsuccessful heterosexual, inept pederast, reticent zoophile, indigent fetishist, appetiteless coprophage, and impatient pedophile, he looks in his mirror and immediately his head nods in anxious self-indulgence. Fortunately, there remains the resource of literary or artistic creation, of fictional overcompensation. Nowhere does the possible proliferate as well as upon the ruins of the real. Drawing, painting, poetry, and fiction give new life to any number of abortive perversions, forcing each to yield a happy and adventurous life— but in an imaginary key.

Abel Tiffauges avails himself of a historical situation miraculously well attuned to his complex and nostalgic aspirations. The product of this harmony of the individual with his times is phoria, Tiffauges's specific perversion and the ogre's primary act. The word comes from the Greek *phoreō* (to carry), a root that can be found in such words as doryphorus (spear carrier), euphoric (literally, bearing well), and Christopher (bearer of Christ).[20] But before expounding the notion of phoria, which is the novel's only real subject, I want to preface my remarks with a word or two about an admirable—and phoric—deed of heroism.

The act in question was much in the news at about the time I was finishing *The Ogre*. The hero of the affair was a gym teacher by the name of Jean-Pierre Chopin. On January 15, 1970, he was teaching in a classroom from which it was possible to see the upper stories of the building across the street. He saw an eighth-floor window open and a child of about five climb up on the guard rail. It was obvious that the child was going to fall. Chopin ran down the stairs and into the street and placed himself directly below the child, who was by this point crawling around the building's gutter. The fall came. The tiny body plummeted earthward for the longest time, turning over and over as it fell. But Chopin managed to break its fall, stopping the hurtling child as though it were a rugby ball. The impact knocked him to the ground, and he broke both his wrists. But the child was unhurt. It was a little Moroccan boy, whose mother had locked him in their tiny apartment while she went out to work.

The reader can well imagine my enthusiasm when I learned of this feat of courage, strength, and skill, to say nothing of luck. I felt that if I had had the opportunity to perform a phoria as splendid as this one, I would not have needed to write *The Ogre,* and I would have been happy till the end of my days. But naturally it was too good a story for a work of literature. I could cite innumerable instances of this sort, in which reality confirms my ideas in a way that is too blatant to use. In any event, good phoria, phoria that is immaculate and salutary, is not always so triumphant and athletic. The exemplar of the good phoric hero, Saint Christopher, humbles himself by ferrying travelers across a river upon his back, as though he were a beast of burden. For there is abnegation in phoria, but of an equivocal sort, secretly possessed by the inversion of malign and benign, a mysterious operation which, without causing any apparent change in the nature of a person or thing, alters its *value,* putting less where there was more and more where there was less. Thus, the good giant who becomes a beast in order to save a small child is not so far from the predatory hunter who devours children. He who carries the child carries him away. He who serves him humbly embraces him criminally. In other words, the ghost of Saint Christopher, bearer and savior of children, is the erlking, abductor and murderer of children.

All the mystery and profundity of phoria lies in this ambiguity.[21] Serve and subjugate, love and kill. Such is the terrifying dialectic that governs the lives of so many couples: the kept woman, the pimp, the gigolo, the mother who abuses her stunted child all exemplify in one

way or another the phenomenon of phoria, which beyond
the extraordinary case of Abel Tiffauges affects all mankind.

The Ogre, one critic said, is a musical novel. He was allud-
ing, of course, to the Schubert lied that borrows its title
and theme from Goethe's *Erlkönig.* But the fact is that it
was not Schubert's music to which I listened over the four
years of writing, but Karlheinz Stockhausen's *Song of the
Jewish Children.* Stockhausen's "étude" was inspired by an
episode in the book of Daniel.

King Nebuchadnezzar had erected a golden statue sixty
cubits high and six cubits wide. Before it he summoned all
the satraps, prefects, governors, counselors, treasurers,
judges, and magistrates and all the officials of the provinces, who listened as a herald read out his orders: "You
are commanded, O peoples, nations, and languages, that
when you hear the sound of the horn, pipe, lyre, trigon,
harp, bagpipe, and every kind of music, you are to fall
down and worship the golden image that King Nebuchadnezzar has set up; and whoever does not fall down and
worship shall immediately be cast into a burning fiery furnace."

Three Jews appointed by the king to oversee his affairs
in the province of Babylon were accused of refusing to
serve Nebuchadnezzar's gods. Their names were Shadrach, Meshach, and Abednego. Nebuchadnezzar summoned all three. The horn, pipe, lyre, trigon, harp, and
bagpipe were sounded. The three men refused to prostrate
themselves. The king then hardened his heart toward
Shadrach, Meshach, and Abednego. He gave orders that
with naphtha, oakum, pitch, and vinestocks the furnace
be heated seven times hotter than usual. The three Jews

were bound together and thrown in. The fire was so hot that the guards who pushed them in were also incinerated. Yet the three Jews marched into the flames praising God and blessing the Lord as with one voice. An angel of the Lord had gone down into the furnace and made it as fresh and cool as the dawn breeze. Thunderstruck, Nebuchadnezzar suddenly rose up and addressed his counselors: "Did we not cast three bound men into the fire?" And they answered: "True, O king!" And the king said: "But I see four men loose, walking in the midst of the fire, and they are not hurt; and the appearance of the fourth is like a son of the gods." Then he approached the door of the furnace and said: "Shadrach, Meshach, and Abednego, servants of the Most High God, come forth, and come here." Whereupon Shadrach, Meshach, and Abednego came out of the fire.

I have retold this wonderful story primarily for the pleasure of the telling, but also because the ways in which it is commonly distorted bring me back to my subject. To take only the work of Stockhausen, notice first that the three Jewish officials of the Bible, presumably adults, have become adolescents (*Jünglinge*) according to the very title of Stockhausen's work. But this is only the first step. If you listen to the work, you will find that the only voices that can be heard are those of prepubescent boys. As if logic required those being burned alive to be small boys. The ogre is not far off. The joyful and triumphant end of the Bible story is of no interest to Stockhausen. He keeps only the sound of crystalline voices rising out of the torture of the flames. Bodies tortured in the fire are represented by voices tortured in a thousand ways by sophisticated electronic devices. Voices? In fact there is only one voice, for the recording is made with a single child's voice, electronically multiplied by repeated recording and superimposed upon itself; the child sings in chorus with himself. Children, torture from which there is no escape, a single voice superimposed upon itself—in all these ways Stockhausen's piece resembles *The Ogre*.

What about the overall design, the original ambition? In this I was aided by another piece of music, one of the richest, most rigorous, and most moving works ever composed by the mind of man or set down by human hand, an unsurpassable ideal that anyone who would create in any form ought to keep constantly before his eyes: Johann Sebastian Bach's *Art of the Fugue*.

The final work written by the cantor of Saint Thomas's Church, it was interrupted by the composer's death. With no hope that his genius would ever be recognized, Bach never imagined that the work would be performed, and he composed *in abstracto,* without instrumental markings. He continued to work on the prodigious composition up to the moment of his final breath, despite failing eyesight and eventual blindness. With the diligence of a good pupil who has been studying his lessons throughout his life, the old master set down the four measures of his subject, a short, wrenching melody whose gemlike simplicity mysteriously blossoms into a horn of plenty. With the greatest artistry Bach works his magic, as the piece proceeds through development, stretto, antiphon, inversion, counterpoint, coda, mirror writing, and other devices. In the eleventh fugue we are alerted to the impending conclusion of the work by the appearance of a theme whose notes (B-flat, A, C, B-natural) in the old German system of notation spell the name BACH. This is indeed the end of the work, which devoured its author; his supreme sacrifice cannot be outdone. The BACH theme is treated in counterpoint in the unfinished fifteenth fugue, the manuscript of which bears the following words in the hand of Carl

Philipp Emmanuel Bach: "The composer was found dead over this fugue, in which the name BACH figures as countersubject."

Starting with the theme of phoria—as simple as the act of placing a child on one's shoulder—I attempted to construct a novel whose architecture would be defined by purely technical developments, based on a series of figures governed by an underlying logic. Phoria takes root in the Adam of prehistory and is subsequently developed, inverted, disguised, refracted, and heightened in a variety of forms—phoria, antiphoria, superphoria, hyperphoria, and so on—with a light mantle of psychology and history laid over the work's bare bones. For the true springs of the novel are no more psychological and historical than the pistons and connecting rods of a child's electric train set are really the cause of the locomotive's motion. The book is driven forward by its own unique energy. Hence at the end of the novel one must not ask *who* has impaled the three children, Hajo, Haro, and Lothar, upon the ornamental swords in the castle fence. Who? Why naturally the whole novel, the irresistible force of a mountain of small facts and observations accumulated over the previous four hundred pages! It is Nestor, for example, when he declares that "alpha and omega must be joined by a single stroke." And it is Abel Tiffauges's three favorite carrier pigeons (corresponding to the three children of the napola), when they are broiled on a spit and eaten. It is above all the theory set forth by Major von Kaltenborn, according to which symbols, in this case the daggers formally given to the children, undergo a malign inversion, so that instead of men bearing arms, arms bear men, just as Christ, after carrying his cross, is carried by it.

Of course the danger in such a complex construction is one of formalism leading to coldness and indifference.

There is reason to mistrust the evolution of certain novelists, whose works contain more and more form and less
and less substance. But once again the *Art of the Fugue* offers encouragement and an incomparable model. For that
work is charged with human and cosmic substance all the
more abundant and moving for being subjected to the
most pitiless formal constraints. That monumental construction is heated to incandescence, one might say, by the
violence of the rules of counterpoint, just as an electric
current bursts forth in blinding light when forced to pass
through a diaphanous filament, itself enclosed in an empty
bulb. *The Ogre* will have been a success if its architecture,
apparently so close to the earth, to men, and to beasts, is
able to move, frighten, and amuse, all the more so since it
is in fact governed by its own secret virtues and subject to
an order that derives solely from itself.

For me, *The Ogre* had a belated and unexpected epilogue.
Having worked from 1965 to 1970 to create in my mind's
eye (and with the aid of documents) an image of East Prussia, I finally went there for the first time in 1975. When the
book appeared in German translation in 1971, I received a
letter from Count Hans von Lehndorff, a surgeon living
in Bad Godesberg. He thanked me for the pleasure the
book had given him. But, he said, East Prussia is not the
austere place you describe. In fact it is a lovely and hospit-
able part of Germany. In any case, he added, I have made
up my mind to revisit my former estates before I die, and
I invite you to come along.

The name Lehndorff was not unfamiliar. I knew that the
Lehndorffs had been one of the oldest and most important
of the East Prussian Junker families. A Lehndorff had been
in charge of the imperial stables at Trakehnen. Most im-

portant of all, Count Heinrich von Lehndorff, my correspondent's cousin, had been implicated in the attempt on
Hitler's life on July 20, 1944, and had been hanged in the
most grisly fashion. He left a wife and three children,
among them a little girl named Vera who was to become a
famous fashion model under the name Veruschka, notable
for her shaved head and elongated body.

I had more or less forgotten this letter when in July of
1975 I received a call from Bad Godesberg. It was Lehndorff. He told me that he would be leaving for East Prussia
on August 22 and that there was room for me in the car.
Naturally I accepted at once.

Lehndorff and his wife welcomed me to their home in
Bad Godesberg with all the cordiality that their natural
timidity and reserve allowed. He was as I would have
imagined him had I pursued my deductions further. I had
expected a tall, thin man. He was indeed very tall (6'3")
and as thin as a skeleton. He was also obviously quite ill
and alarmingly weak. I knew that he had chosen to become a surgeon solely in order to devote himself to the
service of others. I was told that he had donated the roy-
alties on his books (including his *East Prussia Diary,* of
which 390,000 copies were sold in Germany) to the ecu-
menical community of Taizé. I had imagined him as a
pious, selfless man. I found myself confronted with a lay
saint, a man who radiated spirituality. He had not taken an
active part in the July 20 assassination attempt, but his
cousin had kept him informed. That was enough to have
spelled his doom. Hour after hour he waited first for news
of the plot and then, after learning of its failure, for the SS
to come and arrest him at the Königsberg Hospital, of
which he was then director. Some months later, he shared
the fate of that city's population, Königsberg being the
first large German city to be occupied by the Red Army.

With admirable serenity he recounts the time of occupation, captivity, and exodus in his *Journal*.[22] "My parents
thought I was happy," he told me during the trip, "and I
would not have caused them pain for anything in the
world. But the truth is that I was oppressed by those vast
estates, castles, and servants and by all that wealth. I hated
being a privileged young aristocrat, and I count it one of
God's blessings that I lost everything. On that day a new
life truly began for me, my real life."

The third member of this expedition, in fact its orga-
nizer, was another giant but this time of the gastronomic
sort, combining weight, strength, and joviality with an
impressive waistline. Philip Janssen initially described
himself to me as the "Fauchon of Bonn," by which he
meant that he owned a gourmet food store that dispensed
caviar, salmon, and foie gras to West Germany's political
elite. Hence it went without saying that his huge Mercedes 350, white with cream upholstery, was chock full of
choice culinary items for his Polish friends.

I quickly understood that Janssen's devotion to and respect for Lehndorff were truly boundless, and that he
never tired of playing Sancho Panza to this sublime and
fragile Don Quixote. Throughout the journey he literally
carried Lehndorff in his arms, attending to his slightest desire and giving in, albeit not without occasional grum-
bling, to his most unreasonable whims.

He told me how milk had saved his life during the war.
He had studied to be an agricultural engineer and had spe-
cialized in cattle breeding. When the war came he was
among the first to be sent to the front, and, as he put it,
"my height and girth made me such a good target that I
really had no chance of coming out of it alive." But then
came the milky miracle. The Führer decided one day that
the quality of German milk production left something to

be desired. The Thousand Year Reich wanted large families of pink, blond children, and children required the best milk that Germany could produce. A search was conducted to find the savior of the Reich's milk supply and turned up Janssen, who was forthwith recalled from the front and invested with the title *Reichsmilchinspektor,* in charge of squeezing the udders and tasting the milk of all of Germany's cows. Later on, this vocation naturally developed into a passion for children. The gentle giant confessed to me that he could not travel, particularly in underdeveloped countries, without fighting down a desire to adopt every child he met so that he could feed it and shower it with affection. I was struck, for my part, that when I finally came to visit East Prussia, it was in the company of a giant who was fond of milk and children, just as I had imagined Abel Tiffauges.

I quickly came to think of my trip to Poland as a kind of movie, a movie about what once had been East Prussia and of which I was the only spectator. No doubt this was due in part to my having assumed a totally passive role from start to finish. Surrounded by food items in the back seat of the enormous automobile, and lending a somnolent ear to the conversation of the two giants seated in front of me, I let myself go without a worry as to our itinerary or stopping places, as inactive as a spectator in a movie theater. This no doubt contributed to the impression of unreality that surrounded everything I saw. Only action gives weight to reality. Dreams are perceived as dreams because they are endured passively, hence experienced as baseless images.

The first leg of our journey took us to Berlin. This was not my first visit to that pseudo-capital, an absurd and tragic symbol of the division of Germany because of the ideological war between East and West. Without great difficulty I had chosen it as the end point of the journey of initiation in *Gemini,* in which Paul thinks he has located his brother Jean and goes to Berlin, where he suffers ritual mutilation in preparation for his meteorological apotheosis. The novel thus provides the real reason for the construction of the notorious wall between the twin cities on August 13, 1961: it was in order to separate *my* twins, Paul and Jean, and to consummate the sacrifice of Paul that Walter Ulbricht ordered the wall built. An *apparently* historical novel, *Gemini* elevated the event to the plane of mythology, deducing history from fiction.

Whenever I walk down the Kurfürstendamm, my steps quite naturally lead me to the odd Gedächtniskirche, which so admirably illustrates the grandiose, tragic, and humorous fate of Berlin. Nothing could be more bizarre than this neo-Romanesque ruin (the church was built in 1895), filled with memories for old Berliners, maintained in the same dreadful state in which it was left by the war, and incongruously incorporated into a hideously "modern" glass and metal edifice consisting of an octagonal nave and a campanile a short distance away: the powder puff and the stick of rouge, as Berliners are fond of telling visitors. Together, the ruin and the new building make one think of the blackened stub of a decayed tooth between two false teeth, a metal molar and canine. But to my mind, at least, the church stands for all Berlin.

We found ourselves there once again on that August 22, this time to listen to a sermon in the purest Berlin style. As we slipped into a pew, a young pastor—the name Gerhard Kiefel was displayed on a sign at the door—performed a strange pantomime at the pulpit, sweeping the air first with his right hand, then with his left, as if he wished to slap the thin air. Indeed, it was a slap, for the theme of the young preacher's sermon was Jesus' advice in

Matthew 5:39: "But if anyone strikes you on the right cheek, turn to him the other also." The right cheek? Yes, it was the right cheek on which our young theologian dwelt, for as he explained with the aid of gestures, in order to strike the right cheek of one's "neighbor" one must use the left hand. Now, why in the world did the New Testament specify a left-handed cheek-slapper? How much simpler and clearer the text would have been had it said, "If anyone strikes you on the left cheek." But it says the right. Then came a digression on the significance of left and right in the Bible, with numerous illustrations of the primacy of right over left. If the good thief is crucified on Jesus' right and the bad thief on his left, is it not because wickedness belongs on the left, because it is left-handed, in short, perhaps leftist, and because slaps are administered preferably with the left hand? But Luther himself had pondered the paradox of the right cheek and proposed another explanation. It is possible that the slap was indeed administered with the right hand, but with the back of the hand, thereby striking the "neighbor's" right cheek. O wondrous subtlety! What a pleasure it was to expound endlessly on the different meanings of the two slaps, the one given with the palm of the hand, the other with the back! Compare the blunter, stronger, more resounding, physical, maternal, and childish *smack* with the symbolic, insulting, humiliating backhand *slap,* which might well mean a challenge to a duel and the spilling of blood. Thus there was born on that twenty-second of August, 1975, in the Gedächtniskirche on the Kudamm in Berlin the first glimmer of a new science, which I call *colaphology.*[23]

The next day we took the autobahn toward Pomerania and the Baltic coast. There were few formalities upon entering East Germany and still fewer to enter Poland. Thus our first discovery was that it is easier to enter the countries of the East than it is to leave them. We were to verify this axiom upon our return.

Gdansk, alias Danzig. Old memories returned, of the Danzig corridor and a resounding article by Marcel Déat[24] entitled "Die for Danzig?" And of Danzig Goldwasser, a kind of brandy with flecks of gold leaf floating in spirits. We were shown the city by a teacher who spoke French as well as German. Proud of his country's progress, he made this observation: "Just think! We have reached the point where we are thinking about importing immigrant workers." Pointing to some filth on the sidewalk, he added, "Yes, there is more and more work that Poles just will not do anymore."

Our journey was to end in Cracow. But the highpoint was Olsztyn, alias Allenstein, on the fringes of Masuria, where I had placed the imaginary fortress of Kaltenborn. This was to be our center, and from it we planned to travel out in search of the castles and subjects of the house of Lehndorff, or so we hoped. But our expeditions ended more often than not in astonishment before charred walls and violated graves rather than in floral gardens with graveled pathways. What most disoriented Lehndorff was the transformation of the gardens. After thirty-five years, some trees had fallen, others had grown, old paths had been covered over and new ones laid down. Living nature is constantly moving and changing, turning things upside down, and people who before fleeing had buried their silver at the base of a tree, as though in the benevolent shadow of an immovable object, returned years later in bewilderment, unable to find either the tree or the silver. One day we walked for hours through a forest in search of a manor. Three times we happened on living souls, as one says, but souls living in bodies so bizarre, twisted, and cackling that we were overcome by doubt and anxiety.

What black forest had we wandered into? Finally the buildings loomed ahead, apparently in good shape and well kept but strangely haunted: they had been turned into an insane asylum. Steinort Castle, where Heinrich von Lehndorff was arrested in 1944, was being restored, as was the castle of Preussich Holland, with such care that a painter was at work refurbishing the arms of the Dönhoff family to which it had once belonged. On the other hand, more illustrious residences had been reduced to ashes by the Russians before they turned the territory over to the Poles, including Finkelstein's castle, where Napoleon had lived in 1812, and the Teutonic fortress at Schönberg. In Rastenburg, Hitler's Wolfschanze, completely destroyed by bombs, presented the impressive spectacle of windowless bunkers leaning every which way, at once ruined and indestructible.

Lehndorff's meetings with his estates' game wardens, craftsmen, and peasants drained the last drop of his physical and spiritual strength. After an effusive exchange of greetings and lengthy evocation of the past, he was invariably obliged to accept the hospitality of everyone he visited and to spend the night with them, and Janssen and I returned to our very comfortable hotel in Allenstein, leaving Lehndorff to squeeze his long, pain-wracked carcass into a hastily prepared folding bed. The people he visited were German-born but had become naturalized citizens of Poland. The elderly confessed that they had never been able to learn the language of their new homeland. Those in their forties spoke both languages tolerably well. The children spoke only Polish. Their poverty was extreme, but neither better nor worse than before the war. To the well off, like us, it might seem that at this humble level of existence political regimes and economic systems can come and go without changing the daily routine one iota.

No doubt this impression is illusory, for if the price of potatoes or milk rises by even a few cents, the effect on these people's lives is dramatic.

A high point of the trip was a day spent at the Liski stables, nothing less than an entire village devoted to the breeding of Trakhenian horses. Six hundred horses were maintained on some six thousand acres of land, nearly two thousand of which were in pasture. In a hunting coach drawn by two mares and driven by a liveried coachman we toured this splendid farm in the traditional style, with its calves, cows, hogs, and flocks of geese, turkeys, and ducks. There were even storks living in enormous nests of branches perched precariously on chimney tops. This old-fashioned Polish farm—a hymn to the tranquil and pleasant life—was probably much like the French farm of fifty or a hundred years ago, and once again I had the sense that socialism has vindicated itself by the splendid way in which it conserves the treasures of the past.

It is quite true that in Poland the horse is king, and those traveling by car are frequently delayed on the narrow roads by smart teams driven by women with muscular forearms and brightly colored scarves. It is said that there are no fewer than 2.5 million horses in Poland, and no matter where you are you can hear the pleasant and familiar sound of horseshoes clacking against pavement. It would be unjust, however, to pretend that progress has not made itself felt even here: carts and wagons are now equipped with rubber tires.

As for the countryside itself, I would be lying if I were to claim that I found East Prussia as I described it in *The Ogre*: "This empty space, this silvery gray earth with its somber facing of heather and its single slender birch, these sands, these peat bogs, this great flight eastward which must lead as far as Siberia, and which drew him like a vortex of pale light." The description cannot be entirely false, for many East Prussians as well as French soldiers who were held prisoner there wrote to say that my novel had reopened the past for them. But a landscape is a state of mind, and my state of mind in that August of 1975 in the back seat of that white Mercedes 350 filled with delights from the Fauchon of Bonn was such that I saw only rich, lovely fields, gentle valleys, majestic trees, picturesque lakes filled with young people in canoes—rather like the French Limousin, in short, but dotted with lakes.

I mentioned the storks, whose familiar, angular silhouettes can be seen perched on the chimney tops, and which one can see cautiously padding about the marshy meadows. We also saw black swans, and from the shores of one lake we saw an island entirely taken over by cormorants. Clustered in black and white bunches on huge beech trees coated with droppings, they migrate south every autumn but come spring return to reclaim possession of this one island in this one lake, avoiding all the others nearby.

I mentioned earlier that Herder was inadvertently responsible for Goethe's ballad *Der Erlkönig* and hence indirectly for Schubert's lied and Tournier's novel. One of our excursions included Mohrungen (now Morag), a small town graced by a museum in honor of Herder, a big square house flanked by bronze cannon, relics of Napoleon's retreat from Russia. For it was in Mohrungen in 1744 that Johann-Gottfried Herder was born, the son of a man who served both as sacristan and schoolteacher.

Innumerable letters, manuscripts, prints, and maps in this little museum bear witness to a refusal to choose between science and poetry, mechanics and mysticism, typical of the early romantics. Herder, a pioneer of romanticism, was throughout his life as curious about the external world as were Diderot, Lessing, d'Alembert, and other

Encyclopedists and men of the Enlightenment. With romanticism, the object of curiosity changed but not the curiosity itself. Herder's first work was a collection of the works of that great and anonymous poet, the people, based upon research conducted in seamen's bawdy houses, dance halls, rural churches, and country inns. He then undertook a vast journey through France and northern Europe in search of material to finish off his great work, *The Origins of Language*. In 1770 in Strasbourg he met the young Goethe, five years his junior, and taught him to accept only two models: nature and Shakespeare.

Upon leaving the little museum with its abundant records of journeys and legends, we were accosted by a small boy who had obviously been waiting for us. His long blond hair, blue eyes, and madonna-like face with jutting cheekbones and sharp chin reminded me of Novalis, the angelic mechanic, who so admirably accommodated metaphysical reveries to his work as a mining engineer. The boy followed us, repeating a word that we had difficulty making out. He seemed to be repeating, "Mutter, mutter." Why was he speaking to us about his mother? We had reached the Mercedes, that white, powerful monster lying idle in the sun, when at last the mystery was dispelled. "Mutter," the Polish child repeated, pointing to the car's low chrome-plated snout capped by its three-pointed star. Motor! He wanted to see the motor!

The hood was raised, and the romantic angel half-disappeared as he plunged his golden curls into the machine's smoking, greasy entrails. With loving respect he stroked the still-warm rocker covers beneath which the engine's eight cylinders would soon unleash their awesome power.

I watched him with a pensive eye. Would he ever lift the sheet and bend down with such fervor over the body of a sleeping woman? No doubt the question would never have occurred to the pre-romantics, equally enamoured as they were of nature and mechanics.

The trip ended in Cracow, a royal residence, religious center, and living museum miraculously spared by the war. On Sunday morning the churches were filled with extraordinary crowds. We were told that for Poles the Church is the ancient and indestructible fatherland, an impregnable fortress strong enough to daunt even the government, which takes its orders from abroad. And we heard an anecdote that made the rounds some years earlier when Monsignor Feltin visited Warsaw. He had attended Sunday mass and like us had been impressed by the number of worshipers, who overflowed into the square in front of the church. "How do you entice all these people into church?" he rather naively asked the priest. "What do you mean?" the priest responded. "I just ring the bell."

The next day we headed west. Entering East Germany at Görlitz was an arduous affair, involving three hours of searches and interrogation by customs officers. The reason for all this was that we wanted to explore the country in its living reality rather than follow the safely disinfected route of the autobahn as we had done on the way out. For me the return trip was a revelation, because we passed through Thuringia, through the same villages and towns in which I had played as a small boy with other children of my age. In contrast to West Germany, where the prewar world has been swept away by progress and prosperity, in East Germany I found everything just as it had been forty years earlier, miraculously preserved. At every street corner something akin to Proust's madeleine awaited me in the look of the houses, the shop windows, the smell of the stores and kitchens—a mixture of red cabbage and furniture polish—and even the way people dressed. Will anyone believe me if I say that even people's anatomy remained the same? Children in the West nowadays are usually gangly giants, but such a type has yet to appear in the socialist zone, or so it seems. There the children are small and broad-shouldered, as we were at their age, and they dress as we dressed, the boys in lederhosen and the girls in dirndl aprons. Socialism apparently descended upon East Germany like a monstrous cold wave, freezing everything just as it was after the war (the war itself having been a conservative force) and turning the country into a vast "preserve," carefully protected from foreign contamination.

For a long time West Germans refused to refer to East Germany as anything other than "the Zone" (meaning the zone of Soviet occupation). But since then relations between the two Germanies have been "normalized," and the appellation Deutsche Demokratische Republik (German Democratic Republic) has entered the West German vocabulary. Has recognition made a nation of the G.D.R.? I have my doubts. Not as long as it takes the threat of the Red Army to keep the regime in power and mine fields and barbed wire to keep the people from fleeing to the West. A nation is first of all a consensus. As long as there is no consensus to hold the G.D.R. together, it will never by anything more than the punishment inflicted on Germany for the Third Reich.

West Germany has become an economic and military power of impressive proportions. After being stripped of half its territory, suffering the loss of five million of its citizens killed and seventeen million held captive in the

East, physically reduced to a pile of ruins and morally an outcast in the eyes of the world, the country, as I have said, came back to life before my very eyes, and with astonishing vigor. This miracle has been credited to American dollars. The argument is that the Americans, anxious to contain Soviet power, made sacrifices in order to create this new and powerful nation on the socialist East's western border. But this interpretation of events gives too much credit to American strategy and not enough to the basic laws of the capitalist market. The truth is that a Germany in ruins represented an ideal locale for foreign (that is, American) investment. Notwithstanding its own wishes or the wishes of its benefactors, it beckoned powerfully to foreign capital, much as a center of low pressure invariably draws the wind. For the free economy, unlike socialism, is not a theory that springs from the mind of man but the market itself, governed by laws of its own.

The miraculous postwar German revival illustrates a truth of the utmost importance: namely, that the wealth of a people lies not in its mineral resources or in the extent of its territory (Hitler's ridiculous *Lebensraum*) but in the quantity and quality of its citizens' gray matter. And the oxygen upon which that gray matter depends is freedom of information and expression. Any limitation of that freedom therefore diminishes the national wealth. Tyranny is the most ruinous of luxuries. This is true at every level, and in a country where poets are imprisoned or exiled, it is inevitable that housewives will be obliged to queue up at shop doors.

Germany's gray matter achieved an unprecedented apogee in that astonishing product of the vagaries of history: the German Jew. I shall leave to others the pleasant task of figuring out why those two elements combined to form such a happy marriage, yielding among other things the three pillars of modern Western civilization: Marx, Freud, and Einstein. I shall also leave them the sad task of analyzing what caused their terrible and brutal divorce. Consummated by a murderous wave of anti-Semitism, that divorce was the beginning of the end for Germany. So fertile in men of genius, the country was destroyed by the man with the bangs and the little mustache. For Germans the disaster was of incalculable proportions. I am one of the few Frenchmen to fully share their misfortune. Dream a little: had there been no Nazi madness, no war and no defeat, Germany and its outposts in Vienna, Zurich, and Prague would have formed an economic and cultural unit comparable in power and influence to France in the seventeenth or England in the nineteenth century. With the barbarians of East and West held at bay, the world would have continued to be European, and it would have been German. I remember a scene that took place in 1943. My father and I had been listening to the news from London. German cities were ablaze following American air raids. The Wehrmacht was retreating on the Russian front. With exclamations of glee I once again moved to the left the line that marked the front on a wall map of the Soviet Union. "Yes," my father said, "the news is good. But also very bad. You have to laugh with one eye and cry with the other. For the backbone of Europe is in the process of being broken." And it was broken, because its name was Hitler, and an American shook hands with a Russian over the smoking ruin.

Those who, like us, had chosen German culture might have felt cheated. Because the Americans had won the war, it was their language that one had to speak to become a hotel porter or an airline pilot. But we were not really cheated, for the twentieth century was still built upon a German foundation, or at any rate upon works written in the German language. I mentioned Marx, Freud, and Einstein. I should add Hegel at one end of a line that stretches all the way to Werner von Braun, with Engels, Jung, Kafka, Reich, Heidegger, Schönberg, Marcuse, and many others in between. There are few places where one can scratch the earth without coming upon the soil of old Germany. "Over there, on the horizon, beyond the floating bridge of sixty ships—do you know what lies there?" asked Gérard de Nerval. "Germany! The land of Goethe and Schiller, the country of Hoffman. Old Germany, mother of us all!"

3

THE MYTHIC DIMENSION

I am a lie that always tells the truth.
—Jean Cocteau

When I ask myself whose disciple I might have been, I draw a frustrating blank. My father was too discreet and modest ever to have thought of exerting any influence whatsoever on his sons. Within the family he maintained a rather corrosive atmosphere of mutual derision, bracing but frigid as the north wind. As I came to know myself better, I detected in my own personality the same penchant: the more I like a person, the harsher my mockery. My mother and I were father's favorite targets, and his hail of darts was seldom interrupted. Today, having inherited this flaw, I understand that he loved us best.

As for writers and philosophers, I can think of only two whom I might have wished to meet, Jean Giono and Jean-Paul Sartre. Presently I shall have more to say about Sartre, whom I missed by one year having as my philosophy teacher at the Lycée Pasteur in Neuilly. As for Giono, I began reading him when I was twelve and for years he was my god, but it never occurred to me to go see him. I exaggerated the difficulties. How does one visit a famous man? I imagined him surrounded by a court of admirers, all of whom I hated sight unseen. And then his books stood between us, infinitely magnifying the actual distance.

The only teacher I saw with any regularity was Gaston Bachelard.[1] Two of his books, *The Psychoanalysis of Fire* and *The Formation of the Scientific Spirit,* which I chanced to find in a Dijon bookshop at a time when books were so scarce that people indiscriminately bought whatever was published, persuaded me that I ought to take first my *licence* and then, in 1941, the *agrégation* in philosophy. From Bachelard I received the sudden revelation that philosophy was the great "Open, Sesame!"—the key to everything, a wonderful burglar's tool for entering all that the vulgar take to be hermetically sealed, irremediably obscure, arcane, and unapproachable. All at once literature and poetry and even science became vast pumpkins filled with the drollest, most delicate things, through which the great knife of dialectic could slice with a single blow. Those who did not know how to wield that wonderful implement had to content themselves with merely rubbing their fingers over the pumpkin's smooth and undulating surface. Bachelard taught me not only the versatility of dialectic but also that hallmark of all genuine philosophical investigation, laughter. The deep and I would almost say divine humor in Bachelard's work was made flesh when he lectured, as students at the Sorbonne discovered in 1942, but it would be a serious mistake to interpret the philosopher's clowning, pantomime, and grunting, or the crazy ideas that he loved to hurl at frightened students, as the mere ebullience of a jovial and gourmand Champenois nature or even as concessions designed to ensure his immense popularity with that youthful audience. No, the truth is simply that laughter is the sign of man's approach to the absolute.

Bachelard began as a student of science—primarily chemistry, which he taught himself while working as a postal clerk in Bar-sur-Aube—and seemed destined to take his place in a long line of great French epistemologists that includes Boutroux, Meyerson, and Brunschvicg. Although he did indeed fulfill that promise with a series of magisterial works in the philosophy of science, his most original contribution was to have invented the new discipline of demystifying science, a discipline that he then shaped with superb skill or, perhaps more accurately, that he allowed to shape him. In *The Formation of the Scientific Spirit,* for example, he observed that the scientific investigator is often blinded by certain very powerful, very seductive images, which, being devoid of scientific value, divert him from his goal or impede his progress. He shows, for instance, how the image of *digestion* wreaked havoc in chemical research because the reactions of compounds placed in stomach-like receptacles were likened to the digestive process in animals, an explanation that may have been reassuring to the scientist but that meant nothing and led nowhere. In the course of thundering against such monsters of the imagination as the sponge, the bridal chamber, and the idea of transmutation, however, Bachelard became enamored of these images and began to collect and nurture them. Perhaps his choice of chemistry as a subject rather than mathematics or physics was a harbinger of this turn in his career. For chemistry is the science of the sensory qualities of substances, of their visual, olfactory, and tactile properties. Moreover, chemical phenomena are distinguished from physical phenomena by their irreversibility, which makes them more like life. (An iron bar expands when heated: a reversible, physical phenomenon. But it rusts when moist: an irreversible, chemical phenomenon.) Now, the obvious way for Bachelard to add to his collection of teratological wonders, his catalog of monsters of the imagination, was by studying the works of alchemists, mystics, and poets. His books about the four elements, which offer a precise record of his evolution from the openly critical and defensive stance of *The Psychoanalysis of Fire* to the enchanted, enthusiastic embrace of *Water and Dreams,* revolutionized not philosophy, of which these works were to be sure merely a derivative application, but certainly literary criticism and, even more, the interpretation of poetry.

Nevertheless, Bachelard was not a philosopher in the strict sense of the word and to my mind was slightly intolerant of philosophy. A provocative thinker and midwife of many a vocation, he himself fell between the stools of science and philosophy. His sarcastic, antisystematic mind made him more akin to Socrates and Diogenes than to Plato and Aristotle.

Yet the truth, I think, is that I found my true masters principally among the members of my own generation. Our philosophy teachers at the Lycée Pasteur were named Daniel-Rops and Maurice de Gandillac.[2] Yet the most illustrious star in the firmament was to be found among the students. At that time Roger Nimier was a plump youth, slow-moving and facetious, whose slightly monstrous precocity, rare intelligence, and keen memory made relations with his fellow students difficult. He never stopped eating (and those were the days when cookies laced with vitamins were distributed in the schools), nor did he stop expounding subjects of which we understood not a word. It would be interesting to dig up the old class newspaper entitled *The Red Globule,* which he wrote and edited single-handedly. There is something of him in *The Ogre*'s Nestor. His terrifying maturity perhaps presaged the brevity of his career and his life: first novel published at eighteen, last book published at twenty-eight, dead at thirty-six, one is tempted to say of old age. Years later I was asked along with other artists, writers, and public figures to fill out the so-called Proust questionnaire for a well-known weekly magazine. The last question was: By what motto have you lived your life? I rummaged through memory for a phrase I knew was lying about somewhere: "One must live a life of devil-may-care panic, taking nothing seriously, everything tragically." I was congratulated on this epigram and asked to elaborate. All I knew was that the words were not my own, but where had I dug them up? I thought about it long and hard. Finally an angel whispered the answer in my ear: it was Nimier, indeed Nimier at his purest and most unadulterated.

Another classmate, Jean Marinier, introduced me to Gilles Deleuze,[3] who was in his next-to-last year at the Lycée Carnot. We differed in age by only one month, but since that difference capriciously fell between December and January, we were a year apart in school. My modest scholastic advance did not count for much, however, in the face of the newcomer's intellectual rigor and speculative reach. The arguments that my friends and I tossed back and forth among ourselves were like balls of cotton or rubber compared with the iron and steel cannonballs that he hurled at us. We soon came to fear his talent for seizing upon a single one of our words and using it to expose our banality, stupidity, or failure of intelligence. He also possessed extraordinary powers of translation and rearrangement: all the tired philosophy of the curriculum passed through him and emerged unrecognizable but rejuvenated, with a fresh, undigested, bitter taste of newness that we weaker, lazier minds found disconcerting and repulsive.

In the darkest days of the war, some of us, depressed by the oppressive restrictions, formed a small group united by a common idea of philosophy—a narrow, even fanatical idea that might well have gone hand in hand with tumbrils and the guillotine. I was foolishly about to write that Deleuze had been the "soul" of this group when suddenly I had a vivid image of the brickbats and howls with which that hated word would have been greeted by the adolescents we were then. Our one public manifestation came in the form of a single issue of a journal called *Espace* (Space), edited by Alain Clément,[4] which ceased publication immediately thereafter. Its one issue was devoted entirely to an attack on the notion of an inner life, and it opened with a photograph of a toilet bowl captioned "A landscape is a state of mind." In any case, Deleuze did set the tone of the group, and it was he who sustained our ardor. Anyone who has never known such a feverish need to delve deeply, to think systematically and use one's mind to the full, who has never experienced such a frenzied passion for the absolute, will I fear never know quite what thinking means.

One idea that we did not question was that an object or set of objects is real precisely to the extent that it is rationally consistent. The dream world is universally held to be unreal. We dismiss its claim to reality because it is so disjointed, chaotic, and incoherent. Suppose, instead, that our dreams were perfectly coherent and that each night they resumed precisely where they left off the previous morning. Then our lives would consist of two parallel, intertwined, interlarded strands, two equivalent worlds between which we would transit upon going to sleep at night and waking in the morning. Yet even the real world, for all its strict rationality, for all its infinitely greater solidity than the dream world, is consistent only in a relative sense. Science, or more precisely scientism, pretends that this relative is an absolute. In fact, the real world, rife with contradictions and bristling with absurdities, is a fabric full of holes. Hence it is possible—*and within the power of our brains alone*—to conceive of entities more consistent than "reality" and hence more real. Such entities exist, and are called philosophical systems. They can be counted on the fingers of two hands. Their dimensions vary (some being miniature systems, or models of systems). All are denser and more solid than reality, just as reality is more solid than the world of dreams, which looks foolish in comparison. Are philosophical systems the work of the great philosophers, as they might appear to the naive causalist? Obviously not. Since the more coherent is always the cause of the less coherent, a philosophical system with its matchless coherence is the cause of everything and the effect of nothing. The philosopher is nothing more than the detritus that the system drops into the empirical world as it is being created, much as the placenta falls upon the birthing bed when an infant is born.

Since philosophy was to be our calling, life for us held only two possibilities. Most of us would become guardians of those twelve citadels of granite named for their "placental" progenitors: Plato, Aristotle, Saint Thomas, Descartes, Malebranche, Spinoza, Leibniz, Berkeley, Kant, Fichte, Schelling, and Hegel. As professors of philosophy we would be responsible for initiating young people into the study of these historical monuments, grander and more majestic than anything else mankind has to offer. But by an improbable decree of fate any one of us might become the first ("placental") witness to the birth of a new system and by causalist aberration be named its author.

As one might imagine, such radical intransigence meant that hell as we imagined it was bursting at the seams. We roped science and religion together with humanism and the clammy "inner life" and pitched them all into the flames. For laughs we read the *Pensées* of Pascal and split our sides over ideas such as these: that painting is a frivolous activity because its object is to reproduce imperfectly objects already devoid of value in themselves; that translating from a foreign tongue is no problem because one has only to replace each foreign word with the corresponding French word; that the face of the world might have been different had Cleopatra's nose been shorter; that the truths of mathematics are less certain than the affirmations of faith since no one ever died for mathematics. And we read of wagers so foolish that Flaubert would never have dared to fob them off even on the likes of Homais or Bouvard and Pécuchet. To us, Pascal, the man who sewed bits of paper into the lining of his coat, was like the drunken helot. He was a bigot who moaned as he pursued his vain search, and we much preferred to think of the metaphysician as one who laughed at each new discovery. We held, moreover, that in good philosophy the solution always precedes the problem. The problem is nothing but the shadow cast by its solution, a fountain of clarity that spurts *motu proprio* into the empyrean of the intelligible. The existence of God, for instance, only became a problem on the day the ontological argument was invented. Like young Saint-Justs[5] of the intellect, we held our swords aloft and divided all the products of man's mind into just two categories: philosophical systems and comic strips. Anything that was not a system—or a study of a system—was a comic strip, and into that contemptible category we indiscriminately tossed Shakespeare and Ponson du Terrail, Balzac and Saint-John Perse.[6] We were intoxicated with the absolute and with the power of intelligence. Physicists had discovered that matter is made of energy, an idea to which we subscribed with the proviso that the energy of which matter is composed is *mental* in nature. In other words, we held that it was within the capacity of our brains to bring about whatever changes we wished in the world, to create and to destroy, provided we had the requisite brain power, just as with enough muscle power one could move any weight, be it feather or mountain.

One day in the fall of 1943 a meteor of a book fell onto our desks: Jean-Paul Sartre's *Being and Nothingness*. After a moment's stupor there was a long mulling over. Weighty and hairy, the book exuded irresistible power; it was full of exquisite subtleties, encyclopedic, proudly technical, with an intuition of diamondlike simplicity running through it from start to finish. Already the clamor of the antiphilosophical rabble could be heard rising in opposition in the press. There could be no doubt about it: a system had come forth into the world and been given unto us. We were exultant. Like Socrates' disciples in fourth-century Athens or Hegel's students at Jena in 1805, we had the extraordinary good fortune of seeing a philosophy born before our very eyes. We spent that dark and frigid wartime winter wrapped in blankets, our feet bound in rabbit skins but our heads on fire, reading aloud the 722 dense pages of our new bible. And the final sentence on the final page filled our heads with dreams: "We shall devote a future work," it said, to the questions left unanswered by this one.

On October 28, 1945, Sartre called us together. It was a mob scene. An enormous crowd pressed against the walls of the tiny hall. The exits were blocked by those who had not managed to gain entry to the sanctuary, and women who fainted had to be piled on a convenient grand piano. The wildly acclaimed lecturer was lifted bodily over the crowd and onto the podium. Such popularity should have alerted us. Already the suspect tag "existentialism" had been attached to the new system. Having tumbled into the darkened nightclubs of Paris, the new star attracted a grotesque fauna of singers, jazz musicians, soldiers of the Resistance, drunkards, and Stalinists. So what was existentialism? We were soon to find out. Sartre's message could be stated in six words: existentialism is a form of humanism. And to illustrate his point he told us a story about peas in a matchbox. We were floored. Our master had gone and fished up that worn-out old duffer Humanism, still stinking with sweat and "inner life," from the trash heap where we had left him, and now he trotted him out along with the absurd idea of existentialism as if he had invented both. And everyone applauded.

That night we gathered in a café to mourn our loss. One of us thought he had found the key to what went wrong in a novel that Sartre had published in 1938 called *Nausea*. In it is a ridiculous character, a failure whom the narrator calls the Autodidact because he is educating himself by reading, in alphabetical order, all the authors in the town library. This imbecile claims to be a humanist and, more comical still, confesses to his friends that it was in the warm and promiscuous familiarity of a World War I prisoner-of-war camp that he discovered the ineffable value of what is eternal in man. To top it all off, he joins the socialist party. Suddenly it was all too clear. Taken prisoner in 1940, Sartre had come back as the Autodidact. Around the table we were unanimous in our forecasts of disaster: "He will become a socialist. He will take up a collection for the children of China. He will become a Great Man [and for all of us the Great Man was something akin to the giant masks that people used to parade about in the carnival at Nice], the Gandhi of Gaullist France. He will write comic strips." And the future seemed to bear us out, as comic strip followed comic strip, novel, pamphlet, play, farce, newspaper article, political essay, and memoir. Of course it was all infinitely superior to everything else being done in those genres, for these parings were nevertheless scraps of the System, yet to us they seemed just good enough to make us mourn the death of the author of *Being and Nothingness*.

This reaction to Sartre should be taken for what it was: a liquidation of the father by overgrown adolescents afflicted with the awareness that they owed him everything. With hindsight I can see all the juvenile excess in our condemnation. Yet I cannot help thinking that it contained a grain of truth. Sartre seems always to have suffered from an excess of moral scruple. Acute fear of drifting into the camp of what he called the "SOB's" undeniably diminished his powers and his creative potential. I am convinced that one cannot live a full and healthy life without a minimum of indifference to the woes of others. Such indifference, which in most people takes the relatively untroubling form of pure and simple animal selfishness, necessarily acquires a tinge of cynicism in one more clearheaded and intelligent. Sartre's misfortune was that in this respect he never made up his mind where he stood. And perhaps it is also worth mentioning that he was a Marxist who was never able to give up the secret ambition of becoming a saint.

Then came the year of the *agrégation*, that bloated, hypertrophied, Ubu-esque[7] institution, the most dishonest and nefarious test in the whole educational system. Our little group was cut to pieces by the examiners. Only Gilles Deleuze and François Châtelet[8] came out of it relatively unscathed. The jury balked at stooping as low as it would have had to have done in order to have chalked them up among its victims. The rest of us had to renounce our one true calling and toss our metaphysical-clerical robes into the bushes; we had to convert to careers in journalism, radio, publishing, manufacturing, or, like Michel Butor[9] and myself, fiction writing.

So if a date is to be assigned to the birth of my literary vocation, one could do worse than to choose that July of 1949 when in the courtyard of the Sorbonne Jean Beaufret informed me that my name did not appear on the list of qualifiers. My response was all the more passionate because quite frankly I judged myself to be the best of my generation. But the truth was that my years of study in Germany, which furnished the grounds for my belief, had taken me so far away from the blind man's buff that it is the French examination system that I had no hope of success. I angrily dismissed the idea of accepting a teaching post with a lower-level qualification and of retaking the exam year after year. And in all frankness I must add that I also nursed an illusion. I imagined that one could do philosophical work alone, outside the academy, without benefit of colleagues and students. Having slammed the door of the university behind me, I believed that I would be able to pursue the same course I had been following for the past seven years, like a defrocked monk who thinks he can observe the rule of his former order while earning his living as a laborer or merchant.

I was living at the time with some amiable weirdos of my own ilk in the Hôtel de la Paix at 29 quai d'Anjou on

the Ile Saint-Louis. By April my view of the barges on the
Seine and of the Pont Marie was obstructed by an undulating curtain of poplars along the bank. Among my fellow residents were Yvan Audouard, Georges de Caunes,
Armand Gatti, Pierre Boulez, and Georges Arnaud, and,
on the distaff side, the photographer Ina Bandy and the
"comtesse de la Falaise," a tall and splendid Irish lass who
worked as a fashion model. I saw a great deal of the painter
Fred Deux and of Karl Flinker, Gilles Deleuze, and Claude
Lanzmann. Besides strolling in espadrilles along the banks
and quays of the Seine and among the bistros of the Ile
Saint-Louis and the Place des Vosges, I earned my living
by putting together radio broadcasts and knocking off
thousands of pages of translation for the Plon publishing
house. I had no idea that those two expedients for putting
food on the table were doing a very efficient job of preparing me for my profession as a writer.

Translation is a most profitable form of exercise for the
apprentice writer. To translate English into French is not a
problem of English, it is a problem of French. Knowledge
of English is naturally indispensable. But the knowledge
the translator needs is of a passive, receptive sort, incomparably easier to acquire than the active, creative knowledge necessary to write French. Therein lies the whole difference between reading and writing. It explains why the
only way to gauge a student's mastery of a foreign tongue
is to have him translate into it. Translation from the foreign language reveals only his knowledge of his own, and
the prizes invariably go to those who write their own language best.

The objective of translation being to formulate an alien
thought in a style that is as fluent, faithful, supple, and
familiar as possible, the translator is obliged to become a
past master of the cliché, the proverb, the maxim, the fa-

miliar turn of phrase, and of all the common idioms of the language in which he writes, the absence or scarcity of which is the hallmark of that abominable tongue known as "translatorese." I quickly saw the advantage of compiling a catalog of gallicisms, to which I referred so often that I soon committed it to memory. Rarity of the common phrases in this catalog gives away the fact that a text is a translation. In English, for example, there is no verb corresponding to the French *falloir* (to be necessary). So whenever the translator from English to French encounters "I must," he will write *il faut que je* in preference to *je dois,* for although the latter is briefer and just as clear it smacks of the "Anglo-Saxon."

This, as it happens, turns out to be excellent preparation for doing original work. By constantly manipulating those little snippets of language that people continually use unconsciously, the writer learns not only to make them work to advantage in his translations but also to disguise them in his own work, if not to eliminate them altogether. In fact, distortion of familiar phrases is a valuable stylistic resource in prose and still more in poetry. Poets often use language in much the same way that certain contemporary sculptors use sewing machines and automobile engines, transforming machinery into art by creative destruction.

To return to translation, every language has its own aura and allure. Therefore the prerequisite of good translation is to escape from that aura and allure and write freely in whatever language one adopts. The problem is similar to that of launching a satellite into orbit: the first thing is to overcome the earth's attraction. I hit upon a method that I recommend to all translators. I chose a French writer having some affinity, however remote, with the foreign author I had to translate and immersed myself in his writing before setting to work. I then attempted to translate my author not merely into French but into Flaubert, Maupassant, or Renan. Thus I translated two novels by Erich Maria Remarque "into Zola," whose influence is certainly perceptible to any reader of my translations.

Incidentally, those commissions gave me the opportunity to meet the author of *All Quiet on the Western Front*. A native of Osnabrück in Lower Saxony, famous the world over for his antimilitarist views, Remarque, with his straight back, severe, rectangular face, and ever-present monocle, looked for all the world like a Prussian officer of the old school. He invited me to lunch at the Relais Bisson where at his behest I sampled a dish I had never tried before: sea urchins. "This is the first time," he confessed, "that I have been able to converse in my own language with any of my translators. The others—the American, the Italian, the Russian—spoke German as though it were a dead language, like Latin or Greek." He congratulated me on my translations but encouraged me to think of them simply as preparatory exercises for my own future work. "Still, you must not mix translation with your own writing. I was surprised by two things in your otherwise excellent translation of my last novel. First, some pages of the original were missing." Worried, I asked him what the second surprise was. "That I found certain pages in the translation that were not in the original." I was twenty years old, I was a pretentious little fool, and my esteem for the prose of Erich Maria Remarque was not boundless. After a good deal of blushing and stammering I was insolent enough to answer, "Well, what matters, isn't it, is that the latter were better than the former?" He was generous enough to smile. I did not yet know that the translator is only half a writer—the humbler, more mechanical half. The apprentice writer who does translations not only acquires mastery of his own tongue but also learns patience and the virtue of conscientiously performing a thankless task for which he has no hope of receiving either money or glory. Thus translation is a school of literary virtue.

The lessons I learned from my work with the French National Broadcasting Network and later with Europe One were of a very different sort. When you are locked in a soundproof studio and the red light goes on to indicate that you are on the air and it is time to speak, the emotion you feel is of the same sacred order but more sudden and immediate than that which comes from seeing your name printed in a newspaper or on the cover of a book. I talked and people listened. What people? The question cannot be answered. My words were hurled into the void by a formidable network of transmitters to fall I know not where. In this mystery there was at first prodigious excitement as I sensed the obscure yet vital presence of that million-headed hydra, the "listening public." The experience was made even more overwhelming by my brief experience with the mail sent in by listeners, a vast, discordant concert of the most grotesque, frightening, and distressing letters, voices of every sort writing about everything and nothing, complaining about an illness, a husband, a tax collector, a mistress, a grandson, a stroke of bad luck, poverty, boredom, or solitude, and complaining to you, a total stranger who is nevertheless somehow there via the miracle of the airwaves and who can therefore do anything, who is, in a word, God. Anyone who reads listeners' mail knows all the wounds of that whining female monster, the crowd, and has a fairly accurate idea of what God and his saints must hear in the daily prayers lifted up to them by a multitude of voices. Thus as I strolled in my espadrilles along the banks of the Ile Saint-Louis and sharpened my pen through translation, I simultaneously became aware of a great din like an ocean wind in my ears, which as a student ensconced in my ivory tower I had haughtily ignored: the collective spirit of my contemporaries, what might be called public opinion, the voice of the masses, the vox populi.

With the advent of the privately owned radio station Europe One this discovery would take on its full significance, and I was at the same time destined to meet one of the most astonishing men I have ever known. Europe One was the brainchild of Charles Michelson. A Romanian-born Jew, Michelson, who mysteriously remained a man without a country, had gotten his start before the war with a trial run in Tangier of a radio station that would have been a master stroke had the war not intervened. Under the terms of an agreement with the international authorities in charge of the city since 1923, he was granted the exclusive right to build and run a private radio station on its territory, naturally in return for payment of a substantial share of all advertising revenues to the city's treasury. But events called a halt to the experiment before Michelson's Radio Tangier could begin broadcasting. The city was occupied first by the Spanish, then by the Americans, and in the end was returned to Morocco. Nevertheless, Michelson, brandishing his contract before the International Court at The Hague, obtained reparations for the damage sustained by his station while Tangier was under the control of three successive regimes.

This was a mere jaunt, however, compared with the major maneuvers conducted by Michelson in the Saar. An independent state until 1957, the Saar was in many ways similar to the former international zone in Tangier. Michelson signed an agreement with its government authorizing him to set up a transmitter in Saarlouis. Europe One was born, but not without difficulty, for the first broadcasts caused quite an uproar. The state monopoly on radio and television broadcasting in France had been established in 1945, primarily at the behest of the print media. Anyone observing the debates might have assumed that it was somehow the vocation of the press to exercise the most scrupulous vigil over the integrity and freedom of expression guaranteed by the Constitution. Such an observer might have been astonished to discover that the press so insistently called for an end to the free use of the airwaves—astonished, that is, until he remembered that not even the most sacred principles count for much against the power of money. The press, afraid that its advertising revenues might suffer, hastened to nip the potentially dangerous competitor in the bud. In other words, the press campaign against Europe One was a sordid conspiracy with purely selfish motives. This crime was to be punished a few years later, however, when the state-owned television networks began to accept commercial advertising.

During November and December of 1954 Europe One hired large numbers of people, with preference going to those who had worked in the past for the French state radio, to whom far greater salaries were offered than the state had ever paid. I found myself in the company of many others wriggling in Charles Michelson's net. In my first meeting with him I was fascinated as well as terrified. I knew his background and admired the fact that this lone wolf and man without a country somehow managed to negotiate with governments on an equal footing, holding his own and occasionally forcing them to the mat. The story of David and Goliath has no more impressive modern exemplar. Physically he breathed intelligence, strength, and tenacity. He was a dead ringer for Edward G. Robinson, another Romanian Jew made famous by his movie *Little Caesar*. Except that Robinson in his films never exuded sympathy and charm the way Michelson could. Money meant little to me, however, and in our first meeting he sensed my resistance. The station was a place of feverish activity, full of people whose imaginations had run away with them, and too many wore faces ardent with ambition and greed, which repelled me. I much preferred my ambles along the quays and bridges of the Ile Saint-Louis. Yet I lacked the courage to say no to this bull of a man, whose conviction was so powerful that it seemed to brook no opposition. To his great surprise I asked for three days to think it over. "We can do great things together," he said as he ushered me out. "Europe One Radio is just a springboard for Europe One Television. Think of the power in that, of the masses we will be able to reach. Use your imagination, and don't for a moment think that all we're interested in here is lining our pockets." Then, in all candor and with a disarming smile he added, "But naturally we're not ruling that out, either."

Three days later I had made up my mind: definitely no. Armed to the teeth, I was ready to repel the assaults of the tempter. Or so I thought, but if I had really been prepared to say no, why didn't I just send him a short, friendly note rejecting his offer? But no, I had to see him again, to justify my decision, and somehow I wanted to convince him that I was right to refuse. In fact, my dangerous need to confront him again was all his doing. I was unsettled by the welcome I received from his secretary, sweet Madame Thibault. The boss was out of town, but he had left instructions concerning me. For one fatal moment I wavered. A minute later I was in my own office for the first time in my life, with my own desk, my own telephone, my own secretary, and a guaranteed paycheck at the end of the month.

The odd thing was that I had nothing to do. The station was not yet in operation, for the transmitter building in

Saarlouis, extraordinarily bold in its design, had collapsed, destroying the transmitters. In any case, my first interview with Charles Michelson had left me with the impression that he had no more idea than I did what he wanted me to do when things finally returned to normal. In the meantime my relations with him were familiar but stormy. I started off by coming in at eight in the morning. He would greet me with outrage: "Lucky you to sleep in so late!" One morning I arrived at six. He shouted, "Look, do you think I come in this early to be disturbed by pests like you? Go home and go back to sleep." Another time he took me aside the minute I arrived and in a very quiet voice, as if telling me a secret, told me that he was already frantic and that I should disregard any insults that might come my way. Periodically we went out to the Saar. I acted as his interpreter, but he was impatient and used to interrupt me and speak directly to whomever he was dealing with in an astonishing pidgin compounded of German, Romanian, Yiddish, and English. We waded through the mud at the Saarlouis site. They had been putting up the antenna tower when the roof of prestressed concrete had cracked. We set up some programs for Telesaar, the local television station that Michelson had acquired at some point in his travels. Several times I made the trip in the company of colossal men with cauliflower ears, for those were the days when tag-team wrestling was all the rage on TV. Twenty years later, when I returned to Saarbrücken to give a literary lecture, I surprised my audience by revealing what had occasioned my last visit to their city.

Meanwhile, a battle raged around Europe One, whose audience grew steadily. Oddly enough, all the broadcasts originated in Paris studios and were sent out to the transmitter in the Saar via telephone lines. The French Post Office could simply have cut the lines and Europe One would have been finished. But the station's enemies were never powerful enough to make that happen. Pierre Sabbagh and Maurice Siegel's news broadcast had already attracted a large enough audience to prevent any such high-handed action against the station, so its enemies went after its creator instead. The minister of the interior signed an order compelling Charles Michelson to live in Corsica under police surveillance. He had the power to do so without stating his reasons and without possibility of appeal, since Michelson was a man without a country. French law tolerated this latter-day version of the *lettre de cachet*. The purpose of the maneuver was to force Michelson to sell the stock that gave him control of Europe One; it succeeded.

Management of the station passed to Louis Merlin, the man who had worked miracles in advertising at Radio Luxemburg and who came to us with one ardent passion in his heart: the circus. What would happen next remained to be seen. As a newcomer to the airwaves, Europe One (the name, intended to be a mark of prestige, was an invention of Merlin's) had to win a large audience quickly if it was to survive. This was accomplished through a series of bold strokes, the boldest of all being the work of Jacques Antoine and Pierre Bellemare, the creators of a program entitled "You're Really Something." The show, whose purpose was basically to sell the products of its sponsor, the drug and cosmetics firm Oréal-Monsavon, turned out to be a smash hit, and I really ought to say a word or two about its style, for it typified the new relation between "recipient" (consumer, moviegoer, spectator, listener, reader) and "giver" (producer, director, impresario, writer) in the media age.

Despite what is often said to the contrary, generally with little thought, forms of expression constitute a hierarchy: certain arts are preeminent, others "minor." Where to draw the line? It depends, I think, on the quantity and quality of co-creativity expected and demanded of the "recipient." I call minor any art that demands nothing more than passive receptivity and limp docility from those to whom it is addressed, any work in which practically everything is given and nothing remains to be constructed. Paul Valéry wrote that inspiration is not the state in which the poet finds himself while writing his verse but the state in which he hopes to place the person who reads it. Poetry, which demands more inspiration of its audience than any other form of expression, should therefore be considered the most eminent of the arts. At the other end of the scale, movies require nothing of their spectators except that they sit still in a dark room staring at a flickering screen in a semihypnotic state somewhere between daydreaming and sleep. The ideal moviegoer is the hero of Stanley Kubrick's *Clockwork Orange,* who is held immobile by a straitjacket, his eyes kept open and facing the screen by a mechanical device while a nurse drips distilled water into his eyes to compensate for the failure of his lids to blink. There you have a consumer whose passivity would be hard to beat— a poor spectator, actually, and worthy of a poor spectacle. So, whether the problem is to involve a reader in a poem's sonic construction, a listener in a symphony's abstract dance, an art lover in the deconstruction and reconstruction of his world view via line and color, or, at the most trivial level, to sell soap, the recipient's passive resistance must be overcome by provoking active complicity.

In the case of the radio listener, passive resistance is compounded by man's awesome ability to do something else while listening with half an ear to advertising jingles. If the audience is busily cooking food, making beds, or making love during the broadcast, how effective can radio be? This deplorable failing of the medium was quickly and effectively remedied by "You're Really Something." The dinnertime broadcast began with a solemn but vigorous rendition of an excerpt from Prokofiev's *Love for Three Oranges*. Thus prepared, the listener relaxed after a hard day's work while an announcer's voice narrated a true-life drama, taking great care to leave the ending in suspense. Then the listener was told that his help was needed to make sure that everything turned out all right. He must put his coat and shoes back on and go back out and do something to help. In other words, rather than lull the listener to sleep in a twilight of sweet dreams, "You're Really Something" took the opposite tack. It shook him awake and forced him to put his life on the line. The most astonishing thing was that he obeyed, and in consequence the advertiser's message penetrated him to the quick. The bull in his raging charge impaled himself on the picador's pike.

To illustrate the method I shall describe the programs of May 15 and October 30, 1956. On May 15 listeners heard a touchingly idyllic tale. The daughter of a railway crossing guard on the Paris-Charleville line was a paralytic, confined to her bed. One of the engineers had noticed her, however, and every time his locomotive passed her house, he greeted her with a blast of his whistle, a friendly and slightly mysterious note in an otherwise monotonous, bedridden life. Of course Andrée Jammet (the shut-in) and Robert Ferret (the engineer) had never exchanged a word.

"You're Really Something" set out to change all that with a stroke of its magic wand. On that Tuesday, May 15, 1956, thousands of listeners heeded the radio's imperious call and rushed, arms laden with gifts, to railway stations in Paris, Lagny, Meaux, Esbly, and La Ferté-Milon. A solitary locomotive driven by Robert Ferret picked up the presents and at long last halted in front of the Jammet home. The young invalid finally met her mysterious friend, who laid a thousand gifts at her feet.

At the end of October Hungary was crushed beneath

the boots of the Red Army. Throughout October 30 the radio broadcast the sounds of battle and the agony of the people of Budapest. That night, "You're Really Something" shook French households out of their torpor. A DC-4 capable of carrying four tons of cargo had been chartered and was waiting at Orly Airport. It would take off for Budapest the following morning, loaded with medicine. From every town and village in France at least one volunteer was needed to collect the medicine that people were urged to bring to their town halls for shipment to Hungary. The volunteer would load all the packages into his automobile and set out for Orly. People drove all night from cities as far away as Brest and Nice, only to arrive just as the plane was taking off. But what difference did it make? What mattered was simply the effort, the sacrifice, the vanquishing of passivity.

Certain of the program's activities just kept on growing until they had taken on enormous national, even international—and farcical—proportions. One of these episodes was triggered by the program broadcast on January 22, 1957. Its hero was an American industrialist by the name of Abraham Spanel, who, after making a fortune in the manufacture of rubber products, began buying full-page ads in American newspapers in praise of France and in defense of its policies. On the night in question, "You're Really Something" urged its listeners to send postcards from their towns and villages bearing the simple message, "Thank you, Mr. Spanel." A total of 1,361,000 cards were sent. Someone had to carry them. Who? A French mailman. Which French mailman? How about one named Lafrance? Unfortunately, the postmaster general reported that there was no mailman in all of France by that name. Well, then, how about a mailman from the village of Lafayette? Unfortunately, the village was too small to have a mailman of its own and was served by the post office of a nearby town. Something had to be done, and the time was short. The Post Office was persuaded to appoint a resident of Lafayette as its official mailman. Chosen was a citizen by the name of Abel Charbonnier. Now, Charbonnier means coal man, and this Charbonnier was too good a coal man to be true. He arrived in Paris for the first time in his life carrying a brand new leather mailbag. Then he flew across the Atlantic in a specially chartered Constellation, attended an embassy reception arranged by Abraham Spanel, and made a triumphal tour around the United States. Three weeks later, Abel and Abraham landed together at Orly. They were received at the Elysée by René Coty, at that time president of France. A special train was arranged to Chavaniac, and while en route the "minute-sculptor" Barteletty-Daillon carved a bust of Abraham Spanel in cathedral stone. When the train arrived the sculpture was unveiled in front of the town hall.

As a recently defrocked academic philosopher, still fresh from the pages of Spinoza's *Ethics* and Kant's *Critique of Pure Reason,* I felt that I was losing my virginity anew each day that I worked with the cynical—or simply insensitive—sharks of advertising, who dispatched me on countless adventures, the last of which took me to darkest Africa. What made the experience all the more overwhelming was that I was still leading the lonely life of the perennial student. Nothing drives a person more deeply into solitude than the warm din of a huge, anonymous crowd. The isolation of the rural villager of times past, cut off from the world but surrounded by neighbors, was nothing compared with the isolation of people today, obsessed with the mass media and informed about what is going on around the world by newspapers, radio, and television.

The mass media have replaced the neighbor with the mythical hero. Around each individual they create a void, which they then fill with allegorical figures of plaster labeled with the name of the pope or of some dictator or movie star or winner of the Nobel Prize in physics. Having read about the domestic squabbles of the shah of Iran in the morning paper, what is a married couple to argue about? Once I saw a man calmly eating in the company of wife, children, and friends when suddenly toward the end of the meal he lost his mind and ran totally amok: someone had awakened within, someone who had no idea what he was doing with all those strangers. In any event, somewhere between my modest translator's craft and the tempests of the world of advertising, which made me aware of the existence of a huge public, there was life, I knew, and there must also be a mythology, another, more fruitful, more profound mythology that would enable me both to express myself and to make contact with that public, a mythology that would make people better off by making them laugh, quiver, and cry, by changing the way they felt, saw, and thought, rather than by inducing them to buy soap and shampoo.

So literature was to be my life's work. But I vowed never to forget that I was an outsider in the world of letters and promised myself that I would always remain so. The study of metaphysics had equipped me with wonderful weapons, which I must never lay down. Naturally I intended to become an honest-to-goodness novelist, to write stories redolent with the smell of burning wood, autumn mushrooms, and wet fur, but those stories would secretly be set in motion by ontology and logic. I learned to write by studying Jules Renard, Colette, Henri Pourrat, Chateaubriand, Giono, and Maurice Genevoix—poets of concrete, savory, vibrant prose whose example explains why I feel so much at home as a member of the Académie Goncourt, which remains stubbornly faithful to its down-to-earth, naturalist roots. But underneath the leafy green canopy and brown furrows I wanted to make people feel the rock of the absolute shaken by the drumbeat of fate. My ambition was to take readers infatuated by tales of love and adventure and interest them in the literary equivalent of such sublime metaphysical inventions as Descartes's *cogito,* Spinoza's three types of knowledge, Leibniz's preestablished harmony, Kant's transcendental schema, and Husserl's phenomenological reduction. In other words, I found myself in the position of a factory manager at the end of a war during which his plant manufactured nothing but guns and tanks. Suddenly he must turn out refrigerators and stoves, if possible using the same machinery as before, because to tear down the factory and start over is out of the question. The problem was how to produce Ponson du Terrail with Hegel's typewriter. To borrow an analogy from Paul Valéry, I set out to play checkers with a set of chessmen. And by the way, it seems to me that a certain school of so-called modern writers is bent on doing just the opposite, playing chess with a set of checkers: using only implements inherited from the literary tradition, they want to break the bounds of literature in order to go if not farther then at least somewhere else.

My search was endless, and I was obsessed with the thought that it might all be pointless and vain, that what I was trying to do was absurd. I stubbornly insisted on stating the problem in *quantitative* terms, like a high jumper who knows that if he can just jump $7'4''$ he will be champion of the world. It was simply a question of genius or, to put it another way, of being intelligent enough, patient enough, and strong enough to sweep away all obstacles, break down all barriers, and create what I wanted to create. Youthful boasting aside (yes, I was a young Tarzan of metaphysics, pounding my pectorals), what did I know about the quantity of brain power at my disposal? For once the problem is simplified to the point where it can be stated in quantitative terms, the answer is also quantitative and irrevocable. Quality can be disputed. One can always muck about with subtleties. But quantity is unyielding. Some day every athlete and every metaphysician reaches a point beyond which he cannot go. And quantities are unforgiving toward one another. Spinoza said as much in an axiom in part four of the *Ethics* that one can mull over endlessly: any finite force can always be overcome by a still greater force. The strongest man in the world is a shrimp compared with a bull or an elephant. Even the champion highjumper must gawk in despair at the bar placed higher than he can jump, and as for myself, no matter what I write I am constantly aware, with tormenting clarity, of what might be done to make it better that I cannot do for lack of sufficient talent or genius.

This quantitative conception of the work is a burden I always carry with me. It is inseparable from my feelings about time, and especially about the very long time it took me to mature and develop as a writer. For writers are like runners: some are sprinters, others marathoners. Some can polish off a book in three weeks. It is said that Stendhal dictated *The Charterhouse of Parma* in fifty-two days. Others—the marathoners—need time, lots of time. I am one of them. It takes four or five years for a manuscript to ripen in my head and on my writing desk. It's something like a huge stew simmering on a very low flame, and every now and then I lift the cover from the casserole to add some new ingredient. Or like a house that I build around me: since I have no other place to live, I shiver at first in the bare frame, vulnerable to every wind. Gradually I arrange an increasingly habitable space for myself. The final year of work is both distressing and delightful. With the novel nearly complete, my mind is free to explore its rooms and outbuildings with naive pleasure, here and there making a minor improvement. Yet it is also tired of the whole oppressive and complex structure and eager to be rid of it and plunge into new and for the time being forbidden amusements. For nothing is more seductive than one's future works, of which one dreams while painfully bringing a long-running project to completion. Future works have all the unfettered and weightless novelty that is lacking in the work in progress, sullied by so much effort and doubt. Still, it hurts when the work is finally released into the world, and inevitably the moment is followed by a period of aimlessness and idleness.

Long maturation and quantitative vision are inseparable. The workman aware of his unfitness for the task at hand has no choice but to take his time and work carefully and patiently. Even the diminutive mason who can lift only one brick at a time will have moved tons of bricks by the end of the month. Suicide, too, sometimes takes a slow, roundabout course. A man who climbs the stairs of the Eiffel Tower with each additional step stores in his body a small amount of potential energy, and hundreds of such small amounts add up to a great deal. It is this very energy, which ultimately comes from his own legs, that will reduce him to a mess of porridge when he jumps into the void and crashes to earth. What it takes me four or five years to write will produce its impact on the reader in just a few hours. It would be a mistake for him to congratulate me on the force of the blast, which is simply a question of time and patience. If I deserve praise, it is simply for having known how to put together a tank or reservoir or storage battery in which energy could be stored for such a long time.

The author, moreover, is transcended by his work in two ways, one quantitative, as I have been saying right along, the other an example of the well-known transition from quantity to quality. To take the quantitative aspect first, the time that an author invests in a novel easily outstrips the duration embodied in his consciousness of self. When I say *I* or *at present* or *I am* I have in mind a certain duration, not limited to the present moment but rarely in excess of eighteen months. Beyond that limit there is the man I used to be and the man I shall become, and with those two gentlemen I identify only in a vague and abstract way. The writer who labors on a book for four years becomes that book and assimilates all its alien elements, which add up to a structure far more impressive, vast, complex, and learned than their author. Take Kurt Siodmak's celebrated novel *Donovan's Brain*.[10] A biologist grows a human brain in a beaker under such abnormally favorable conditions that it grows and proliferates until it becomes the seat of a superhuman mind, a genius that reduces the biologist to slavery, as a man might do to a dog. An author's relation to his book is somewhat similar. After a while my book is endowed with more parts, organs, gears, tanks, valves, and cranks than I could possibly imagine. I lose control, and it takes on a life of its own. I am then reduced to serving the work as gardener and handyman. Worse still, I become its byproduct: I am what the work gives off in its process of self-production. I wait upon a nascent, growing, proliferating monster, obedient to its most peremptory demands. When I wrote *Gemini,* for example, the manuscript kept issuing orders and asking questions like these: Go visit a trash incineration plant.

Go to Croix-Rousse and report on whatever you can find out about the old Jacquard looms. What is the place of the Holy Spirit in orthodox theology? What is life like in a home for the retarded? The work is all-consuming, a pious labor, a parasite. And when it has fed on me and sucked my blood, when it begins to make its own way in the world, I lie wan, drained, disgusted, exhausted, and obsessed with thoughts of death.

Further aggravating the imperious will of the proliferating work is a phenomenon common to all accumulation and expenditure, namely, the transition from quantity to quality. If water is cooled steadily, it will turn to ice when the temperature drops below zero centigrade. Water at $1°C$ is little different from water at $2°C$. But at $-1°C$ a qualitative change so profound takes place that the naive observer might wonder if he is still dealing with the same substance. If quantitative change is continuous, qualitative change introduces sudden, discontinuous mutations. Of course the suddenness and discontinuity of such a change are not incompatible with subtleness and harmony of structure, as can be seen if one examines a snowflake.

This dialectic of (continuous) quantity and (discontinuous) quality is an exciting subject for observation and contemplation. I attempted to make literal (and literary) application of it in a short story entitled "The Red Dwarf." The idea for the story came to me while I was reading Jean-Paul Sartre's autobiography, *Words*. In discussing his small stature, Sartre observes that he was still not small enough to be considered a midget. So I asked myself where the dividing line falls between the midget and the small man or woman. My story is about a tall midget. (Why do people always talk about tiny midgets?) In fact, he is so tall that if he wears elevator shoes he becomes a short man. He naturally obtains a pair of such shoes, but he remains quite unhappy. No one likes or respects or fears him. Everywhere he inspires laughter and scorn. One day, however, he ventures outdoors in his buskins. Wearing these thin-soled moccasins, he is astonished to discover that no one laughs at him. People look at him with awe and respect. The short man has become a midget, a sacred creature. On that day he seduces a woman for the first time, a woman who certainly would not have given herself to a short man but who found herself tempted and finally won by the prospect of experiencing love with a midget. By foregoing the extra inch afforded him by his customary elevator shoes, my hero crossed the threshold of abnormality and entered the realm of genius.

What is paradoxical and interesting about this fable is obviously the fact that a quantitative *minus* corresponds to a qualitative *plus*. This way of putting it is misleading, however. To say that there can be more or less of a given quality (a more or less intense color, say, or a more or less thirst-quenching drink or a more or less beautiful face) is perhaps to introduce an element of quantity into the realm of quality and is therefore impermissible. Bergson's philosophy is aimed largely at exposing this sleight-of-hand. Yet certain qualities do invariably make us think of quantities. Hercules' physique, a build designed for maximum efficiency even while asleep, inevitably suggests an abundant quantity of energy and evokes images of lifting and moving heavy weights.[11] Or to take a more familiar example, the obese man's belly, wads of fat, and slow, strenuous gait are qualitative equivalents of the numeral he reads on the face of the bathroom scale. These examples are relatively easy to grasp, however, because they illustrate the transition from quality (Hercules, obesity) to quantity (strength, weight).

The transition in the other direction, from quantity

(height) to quality (short man or midget), is more difficult to understand. For one can easily argue that quantity is but an aspect of quality, an abstraction, and that quantity can therefore be extracted from quality as one would extract the part from the whole. The inverse operation is shrouded in mystery. How, merely by cooling water vapor so many degrees, does one create something as unpredictable and original as an ice crystal or snowflake? A more familiar illustration of this inexplicable phenomenon can be found in the kitchen. What the cook does is purely quantitative: he or she adds a definite quantity of salt, water, or oil, performs some mechanical action more or less vigorously for a longer or shorter length of time, and so on. Yet the result is eminently qualitative: the flavor of the dish. The classic example is making mayonnaise: the mayonnaise has to "take," and that "taking" is nothing other than the transition from quantity to quality. A botched mayonnaise is one that remains in the quantitative state.

The plan and purpose of a novel are set at the beginning, hence it is highly unlikely that anything will deflect the course of the work. While working I concern myself almost exclusively with gathering my poetic energies, leaving them to make their own accommodation among themselves. So completely does this purely quantitative task absorb me, and so dwarfed do I feel by the magnitude of the project, that I am not really aware when it all "takes," when the work gels, when the quality without which it would be nothing but a shapeless mass first makes its appearance. Perhaps I trust in the cleverness of my design to crystallize the work, or in my reader's capacity to organize what he sees. Most likely I rely on both, the reader's vivifying gaze adding arabesques to my narrative's curve. But no matter how complex and subtle the calligraphy, no matter how finely tuned the book's harmony and structure (which ultimately even I come to recognize as I transform myself from writer into reader), I always wonder how much more beautiful it might have been, how much more delicate a shape it might have "taken" in the transition to quality, if only I had worked at it a little harder.

For me, the bridge from metaphysics to the novel was provided by myth. What is a myth? An immense question, to which I am tempted to give a series of answers, starting with the simplest: A myth is a fundamental story.

A myth is first of all a multistoried structure, each story being built according to an identical plan but at a different level of abstraction. Take, for example, Plato's myth of the cave. Plato asks us to imagine a cave in which a number of prisoners are bound in such a way that they can see only the cave's dark depths. Behind them is a large fire, and between the fire and the prisoners move people bearing various objects. The prisoners, however, see neither the people nor the objects but only shadows cast on the walls of the cave. They take these shadows to be the only reality and formulate conjectures about them that are inevitably either incomplete or erroneous. Told in this way, the myth is a mere child's story, a description of a puppet show and Chinese shadow play. At a higher level, however, it embodies a whole theory of knowledge; at a still higher level a theory of morality, metaphysics, and ontology. Yet it remains the same story.

The child's tale that is the myth's ground floor, as it were, is just as essential as its metaphysical summit. When I published my novel *Friday,* I was glad as well as proud to include in the paperback edition a rather technical afterword by Gilles Deleuze, while the very same novel was simultaneously being brought out in a children's version[12] and staged as a children's play by Antoine Vitez. For me, the proof of the novel's success is the response that it was able to elicit from two readers at opposite poles of sophistication: a child at one end of the scale, a metaphysician at the other.

A myth is a story that everybody already knows. While I was writing *Gemini* people sometimes asked about the subject of my new novel. I answered that it was the story of two twin brothers who looked exactly alike. Immediately the questioner's face would brighten. Twin brothers? Sure, the person would say, I know a couple of identical twins. One gets a cold in London, the other sneezes in Rome. How many times did I hear that story or one just like it? There was no point going into detail about my plans. Everyone already knew the details. *They* would tell *me.* I congratulated myself: here was proof that my subject was a mythical one. André Gide once said that he wrote not in order to be read but in order to be reread. By that he meant, of course, that he wanted people to read his works more than once. I, too, write in order to be reread but being less imperious than Gide ask only to be read once. My books should be recognized—reread—the first time through.

One way to get a better grip on the nature of myth is to compare a character in a novel with a mythical hero. Take, for instance, Julien Sorel and Vautrin. Both are prisoners of the novels in which they appear. Both have appeared from time to time on stage or on the screen, but only when the works in which they appear—Stendhal's *The Red and the Black* and Balzac's *Old Goriot*—were adapted in their entirety. And well known as both characters are, neither is as famous as Stendhal or Balzac.

A mythical figure like Don Juan is another matter entirely. Created in 1630 by Tirso de Molina, the author of *The Seducer of Seville,* he soon forgot and made everyone else forget about his origins. Has anyone ever heard of Tirso de Molina? Has anyone not heard of Don Juan? He crops up repeatedly in generation after generation, in comedies, novels, and operas. It almost seems as though every country and every period needs to invent its own version of the hero who embodies the revolt of sexuality against God and society, order and hierarchy. But perhaps there is a hidden and vital reason for the seducer's wandering from work to work. Surely Don Juan has so often been a spur to the imagination because he has his place in real life. If we encounter him in so many works, it is because we also encounter him in life. There are Don Juans in all of us, and there is a little Don Juan in each of us. He is one of the models through whom we give shape, form, and feature to our aspirations and moods. People crowd movie theaters and museums, go to plays, listen to music. What are they looking for, if not the same thing the hen is looking for when she eats bits of lime in order to make shells for her eggs? The *scrupulous*[13] hen, in need of an envelope for the white and the yellow of her egg—nothing could be softer, runnier, or gooier—invented a shape of impeccable purity, a supreme masterpiece of design: the eggshell. Similarly, the crowd experiences timorous feelings of desire. It dreams of encounters it would not dare to avow openly and emits inarticulate cries. It suffers from a malformation of the heart. Amorphous matter cries out for a sharply delineated form, a strict outline, a shapely body, an angelic face, a happy adventure. The crowd—*scrupulously*—reads novels, goes to the movies, hums songs.

That is not enough. One has to go beyond sociology to biology. Man rises above animality only by grace of mythology. Man is nothing but a mythical animal. He becomes man—he acquires a human being's sexuality and heart and imagination—only by virtue of the murmur of stories and kaleidoscope of images that surround him in the cradle and accompany him all the way to the grave. La Rochefoucauld[14] wondered how many people would have fallen in love if they had never heard the word. To be quite radical about it, the answer is, not one. For the person who has never heard of love is the victim of a total castration: he has been deprived not only of his genitals but of his emotions, his brain, everything. Denis de Rougemont touches on the same idea when he says that an illiterate shepherd who says "I love you" to his shepherdess would not mean the same thing by those words if Plato had not written the *Symposium*. The human soul is shaped by myths that are in the air. Even animals experience something similar in a process that might be called *animation* (*anima* = soul, animal, etc.), which in its own way reproduces the phenomenon I am describing. To understand what I mean by animation, remember that many animals, from insects all the way up to mammals, enter into relations with one another—and sexual relations in particular—only by means of odor. In other words, their souls are literally *in the air*. Deprive these animals of their sense of smell and you deprive them of their erotic and even their social life. Similarly, a child protected from all sexual and emotional "education" by a device that somehow filtered everything he saw and heard would probably be reduced to a sexual life consisting of nothing but dreamless nocturnal emissions.

That being the case, it becomes easy to describe the social—one might even say biological—function of the creative artist. The artist's ambition is to add to or at any rate modify the "murmur" of myth that surrounds the child, the pool of images in which his contemporaries move—in short, the oxygen of the soul. In general the artist affects this fund of myth in only barely perceptible ways, much as a great fashion designer may find in a cheap, ready-to-wear dress a touch or two taken from one of his unique, bold, absurd, and priceless designs of the year before. Occasionally, however, a writer will strike such a powerful blow that he succeeds in transforming the soul of man forever. Jean-Jacques Rousseau, for instance, *invented* the beauty of mountains, which for centuries had been regarded as prefigurations of hell. Before him everyone agreed that mountains were horrifying. After him, their beauty was obvious to all. He achieved the ultimate success, which is to say, he was overshadowed by his own discovery. (In this instance, in fact, his genius was to take the notion of the *sublime,* hitherto restricted to the sphere of morality, and introduce it into nature, where previously only beauty had been allowed. Following in his wake, Bernardin de Saint-Pierre and Chateaubriand extended Rousseau's sublime from the mountains into the oceans and deserts. Kant in his *Critique of Judgment* gave an aesthetic analysis of the distinction between sublimity and beauty: the former is open, imperfect, and infinite, the latter closed, balanced, and finite.) Or, for another example, take Goethe, who in creating Werther in 1774 also created romantic love and triggered a wave of suicides. It is indeed true that no one would love as he does today if Goethe had not written *The Sorrows of Young Werther.*

Literary and artistic creation are important because myths, like all living things, must be irrigated and replenished or die. A dead myth is called an allegory. The writer's function is to prevent myths from becoming allegories. Societies in which writers are not free to fulfill their natural function are hobbled by allegories, which are like so many plaster casts. At the same time the writer—domesticated, emasculated, inhibited by a comforting aca-

demicism, and celebrated as a "great man"—himself becomes a plaster cast who takes the place of his own
insignificant work. By contrast, the living, growing work
of art becomes a myth that pierces the heart of everyman
and there does its work, relegating its author to anonymity
and oblivion.

For fifteen years I filled my drawers with unfinished manuscripts. I had been unable to bring off the transition from
metaphysics to fiction, the fictional transmutation of metaphysics. In 1958 I tried to write a first version of *The Ogre*.
The enormous manuscript left off with the declaration of
war in 1939, the war itself being reduced to little more than
an epilogue. I then realized that only a third of the novel
was written, for I still had to tell the story of my hero's
activities during the "phony war" of 1939–40 and of
his captivity in Germany and monstrous flowering in
the climate of East Prussia under the Third Reich. I
doubted that I had the strength. More than once I gave up.
By then it was 1962. I began writing *Friday,* a novel into
which I hoped to pour the essence of what I had learned
while employed at the Musée de l'Homme, especially
under the tutelage of Claude Lévi-Strauss.[15] For the first
time I produced a manuscript, finished in December of
1966, that I deemed worthy of submitting to a publisher.
The book was published in March 1967. I became a naturalized citizen of the republic of letters. I would continue
to write novels, starting of course with the unfinished
Ogre. But when I attempted to finish it, I saw that the
whole manuscript would have to be tossed out and begun
anew. Somehow that first version was twisted in such a
way that it was absolutely impossible to go beyond September 2, 1939.

Naturally I could not imagine anything but a traditional

novel. Like any recently naturalized citizen, I scrupulously observed the customs of my new homeland. I set out to write like Paul Bourget, René Bazin, or Delly.[16] Whenever I sat down to write a new novel, it was always with the idea of rewriting Victor Cherbuliez's *Le Comte Kostia,* which had enchanted me as a child.[17] That reminds me of an anecdote that made the rounds in London a few years ago, at a time when Indians, Sinhalese, Afrikaaners, and Pakistanis were flocking to England, hoping to be admitted to the Commonwealth's "mother country" before the gates were permanently closed. One of them ordered a typically British suit from the finest tailor in the city. While admiring himself in the mirror, he suddenly collapsed in a chair and burst into tears: "The suit is splendid, but we've lost the Empire." I was that foreigner in the heart of the mother country, my complexion still rather dark from my long years under the metaphysical sun. But no sooner had I donned my handsome academician's suit than I realized that "we" had long since renounced our claim to the traditional elements of the novel: character, psychology, plot, adultery, crime, setting, and dénouement. So I stood up and said no, just as my naturalized Pakistani would have said no to Oxford students born and bred in England had he chanced to see them jeering the queen or the prime minister. In my case it was no to writers to the manor born who had availed themselves of their privilege only to burn the manor down. I needed that manor! My intention was to avoid formal innovation, to use only the most traditional, conservative, and reassuring of forms, but to fill them with a content having none of those qualities. Therefore some would say that I was bent on parody. So be it. But there is parody and parody. There is pastiche, which merely reproduces an author's tics and habits. But there is also Maurice Ravel. The bulk of Ravel's work—*Bolero, La Valse, Le Tombeau de Couperin, La Pavane pour une Infante morte*—is parody. *La Valse* may well be more of a Viennese waltz than anything ever written by the three Strausses, Johann Sr., Johann Jr., and Oscar. Parody may descend to pastiche, but it can also rise to quintessence. To my mind there are two traits—one positive, the other negative—that no work of literature can do without: humor and celebration.

According to Henri Bergson, organization, structure, and order are natural byproducts of society; they add to its stability but invariably threaten to impede its further development. We encounter this impediment at its most obvious when we respond mechanically to a situation seemingly like others we have encountered before but in fact different. In other words, our behavior is maladapted when we act like programmed robots rather than living creatures in a perpetual state of creative improvisation.

Laughter is the cure for such rigidity of response. Laughter hurts. It is a punishment that any observer is entitled to inflict when he catches someone else in the act of behaving like a robot. It is a call to order or, rather, to the disorder that is life, a perpetual challenge to yesterday's order. Those who are most deeply mired in changeless structures—bureaucrats, policemen, soldiers, doctors, aristocrats—and who are therefore more likely to behave in ways that clash with the rest of the world, like machines rather than people, are particularly comic figures, as playwrights and satirists have traditionally recognized.

This is Bergson's analysis of humor, and it is surely the best that has yet been said on the subject. It is hard to think of any major correction that needs to be made to Bergson's theory, though it should probably be broadened beyond the rather narrow sociological outlook so typical of his time, when the influence of Auguste Comte and Emile Durkheim was at its height. Bergson's humor is a social humor best exemplified in comedies of manners and circus performances. Although Bergson is aware of the bitterness in this kind of laughter, his humor is still quite rosy compared to black humor, which thumbs its nose even at death.

Yet even black humor is fundamentally social. It makes funereal comedy of undertakers, hearses, corpses, and mourners. Take this classic example of the genre: "At the gates of a cemetery a priest has been waiting for more than half an hour for a funeral to begin. He turns to the gravedigger, also waiting, and asks, 'By the way, when is the procession supposed to arrive?' The gravedigger looks at his watch and says, 'Well, Father, if they didn't stop for a good time along the way, it won't be long now.'"

The macabre circumstances plainly reinforce the comic effect by adding a tinge of cynicism and even blasphemy (these are things that ought not to be laughed about, it's bad luck, and so on), yet they do not alter its fundamentally social nature.

There is, I think, a third kind of humor, which to continue the color metaphor I shall call *white humor*. White humor has a dimension that black and rosy humor lack, a cosmic, metaphysical dimension.

Cosmic and comic. The two words seem to be made to go together, but in reality they are usually pushed apart. For the comic in its usual guise is a social phenomenon, a game whose playing field is normally the salon—as broad, flat, and superficial an arena as one could wish for. Comic success is actually measured in terms of horizontal propagation. There are jokes that are repeated all over Paris, all over France, all over Europe, even around the world. Such comedy is the antithesis of the cosmic, of the vertical intuition that dives straight down to the world's foundations and rises as high as the stars. To take some classic examples, Voltaire and Talleyrand were comic spirits, Rousseau and Chateaubriand cosmic ones. The two are as different as water and fire.

But there is also a cosmic comic, namely, the laughter—God's laughter—that invariably accompanies any appearance of the absolute in the tissue of relativity that we call our world. Life is a painted veil that we throw over the void, yet through that veil nothingness sometimes protrudes, much as a reef pushes up through the surface of the sea. Man suffers not only from animal fear of the dangers that beset him but also from anguish over the absolute, which lurks everywhere, sapping his words and deeds of meaning and heaping derision upon everything that exists. No effort is spared to prevent white humor from rearing its head. The grandiloquent abjection of a Napoleon or a Hitler—a tumult of proclamations, trumpet blasts, cannon fire, and collapse—neither adds to nor subtracts from the tragedy of the human condition, that brief passage between two voids. White humor derides the fact that everything human is transient, relative, and doomed to disappear. Had the Preacher of Ecclesiastes known how to laugh, he would have laughed white; but he didn't know. Bossuet[18] wrote: "When the wise man laughs, he trembles." What is astonishing about this remark is that our image of the Eagle of Meaux is of a man who neither laughed nor trembled.

The man who laughs white has glimpsed the abyss between the gaps in reality's fabric. He is suddenly aware that nothing is of any importance. Though in the grip of anxiety—indeed, *because* he is in the grip of anxiety—he feels delivered from all fear. Many have lived and died without ever experiencing such laughter. They know vaguely that nothingness waits at both ends of life, but in the meantime they hoist full sail, and for a few years, at least, the earth will not fall away beneath their feet. They are willing dupes of the consistency, solidity, and coherence with which society embellishes the real. Often they are men of science, religion, or politics, fields in which white laughter has no place. In fact, nearly all men are like this. Mankind walks a narrow bridge across a bottomless void, and when the loose slats underfoot begin to drop away, most men see nothing, but a few see Nothing. The latter stare at their feet without trembling, gaily singing that the emperor has no clothes. White laughter is their rallying cry.

The writers who join the comic and the cosmic can be counted on the fingers of one hand. At the head of the list is Nietzsche, in whose work laughter laps steadily at the roots of being, undermining the entire edifice. Although Nietzsche's humor resides primarily in his inimitable tone, it is possible to cite from his work any number of passages in which the cosmic source mingles intimately with the comic vein: "One must have a chaos within oneself to give birth to a dancing star." There you have a sentence with profound overtones, whose words make a joyful clatter. Paul Valéry—similar to Nietzsche in so many ways—drew from his own ironic metaphysics a thousand barbed shafts: "God made everything out of nothing, but the nothing shows through." "An angel is a demon in whose mind a certain thought has not yet taken shape." "A solitary man is always in bad company." Whole poems like *Le Cimetière marin* or *Ebauche d'un serpent* combine laughter with the absolute. Léon Bloy, prophet of the absolute, ungrateful beggar, and pilgrim of the Apocalypse, was not like Pascal a man who moaned as he searched but a trustee of truths

proclaimed amid bellowing laughter.[19] Not that his laughter ever brought much light to his fixed and mournful
mask, with its naive, round, protruding eyes, like those of
a sick, hallucinating child. It was inseparable, however,
from his thundering voice and vengeful outcry. In 1912 he
claimed responsibility for the shipwreck of the *Titanic,*
that ultramodern ocean liner making its maiden voyage
with a cargo of billionaires who reveled in a ballroom
filled with elegant women in scanty dress. "I am an ocean
of contempt," he cried, "and it is I who launched the ice-
berg that staved in the hull of the *Titanic.*" At the time he
would have been enraged, no doubt, to hear that this tirade
contained an element of humor, but only because he
would have mistaken the true nature of that humor, of that
often frightening, divinely inspired hilarity. Every page of
Bloy's work illustrates the truth that laughter and the absolute are inseparable. Concerning a contemporary writer
he wrote: "He wants to be a man of letters so badly that
he could not say hello simply even if nine choirs of angels
begged him on their knees." At the height of the Boer War,
at a time when French outrage against the English was at
its peak, Bloy wrote: "The more Englishmen they kill, the
more resplendent are the Seraphim." Funny it was, and
what is funny is heard in heaven.

Wherever the absolute is attained there is intense jubilation, an attenuated form of which can be found in certain
popular jokes. "Some sailors land on a desert island, where
they come upon an elderly man. 'What are you doing
here?' asks one of the sailors. 'I gave up everything in order
to forget.' 'To forget what?' 'I forget.'"

"A white man and an Indian are crossing the Rocky
Mountains. It is very cold. The white man is wrapped in
fur. The Indian is naked. 'But how do you do it?' asked

the white man. 'Aren't you cold?' 'You not cold in face?' replied the Indian. 'No,' said the white man. 'Me face all over,' answered the Indian."

A glance from the absolute is enough to send a whole scaffolding of convention tumbling down, thus liberating the comic in a way that is perhaps best exemplified in Jewish humor: "When anti-Semitism was at its worst, two Jews met in Paris. 'Somebody told me about a city where we can live in peace,' says one. 'What city?' asks the other. 'Kabul,' replies the first. 'Where's that?' 'In Afghanistan.' 'Afghanistan! That's a long way.' To which the first replies: 'A long way from what?'"

It hardly needs emphasizing that Jewish humor has nothing in common with anti-Semitic "Jewish jokes." The former is cosmic humor, the latter, with its tired themes of money and greed, mere social satire.

Thomas Mann was a writer more given to black humor than to white, despite his many characters with diabolical overtones, such as Adrien Leverkühn in *Doctor Faustus*. What could be more comically macabre than this passage from *The Magic Mountain,* a novel set in a tuberculosis sanatorium. Young Hans Castorp has fallen in love with a patient, Claudia Chauchat. She leaves the sanatorium but gives him a photo of herself, which he carries with him at all times and regularly smothers with kisses. It is no ordinary photo, however, but an "inner portrait," in other words, an X-ray of the young woman's lungs, ravaged by Koch's bacillus. Cruel comedy of this sort abounds in this admirable and powerful novel, but the humor in my judgment seldom rises above the trivial psychological level. Yet another passage in the same novel illustrates to perfection the notion of white humor that I am trying to define. It is the description of a patient who nearly dies of "pleural shock" after air is introduced into his chest cavity to collapse his lung as a therapeutic measure (cited here after the translation of H. T. Lowe-Porter):

> Then I hear the Hofrat say: "Very good"; and then he begins, with a blunt instrument—it must be blunt, not to pierce through too soon—to go over the pleura and find the place where he can make an incision and let the gas in; and when he begins moving about over my pleura with his instrument—oh, Lord, oh, Lord! I felt like—I felt it was all up with me—it was something perfectly indescribable. The pleura, my friends, is not anything that should be touched; it does not want to be touched and it ought not to be. It is taboo. It is covered up with flesh and put away once and for all; nobody and nothing ought to be allowed to come near it. And now he uncovers it and feels all over it. My God, I was sick to my stomach. Horrible, awful; never in my life have I imagined there could be such a sickening feeling, outside hell and its torments. I fainted; I had three fainting-fits one after the other, a green, a brown, and a violet. And there was a stink—the shock went to my sense of smell and I got an awful stench of hydrogen sulphide, the way it must smell in the bad place; with all that I heard myself laughing as I went off—not the way a human being laughs—it was the most indecent, ghastly kind of laughing I ever heard. Because when they go over your pleura like that, I tell you what it is: it is as though you were being tickled—horribly, disgustingly tickled—that is just what the infernal torment of the pleura-shock is like, and may God keep you from it!

This passage is white humor in the guise of fiction. Simply replace the individual patient by mankind in general and his pleura by the absolute and you will hear the cackle of white laughter. Being rests on a small number of props. Draw near one of them and you cannot help smiling; touch one and you cannot help bursting into laughter—white laughter.

Consider the following two anecdotes. Though the two are quite similar, the first is white humor and nothing more, indeed in its very simplicity offers a definition of what I mean by white humor, while the second introduces elements of lyricism and celebration. The first concerns the Parisian socialite Antoine Bibesco. A blasé, jaded skeptic, Bibesco was invited to visit a friend's new home. Now, this friend happens to have been a wealthy art collector, and his home was a paragon of refined beauty and tasteful luxury. At the end of his visit, Bibesco plopped down in an armchair and said, "Yes, all right, but why not nothing instead?"

The second story concerns a laconic remark of Jean Cocteau's.[20] Cocteau had been showing a journalist his apartment, filled with various mementoes and awards, and afterwards the visitor asked the usual question: "If the house burned down and you could choose only one thing to take with you, what would you choose?" To which Cocteau replied, "The fire!"

That single word *fire* threatens annihilation every bit as much as Bibesco's lengthier remark, but because Cocteau was also a poet of genius he instinctively added a dimension of eulogy and exaltation. White laughter signals literature's subversiveness and destructiveness, but writing also has another, wholly positive function, which I call celebration.

The writer magnifies everything he touches. If he is mediocre, he embellishes, bestowing upon things and creatures borrowed qualities, which, being alien to the object's essence, stick to it like so many useless ornaments. But the good writer truly adds nothing. He illuminates the object from within, bringing out the subtle and elegant structures normally hidden by the opacity of matter. This brings me back to the theme of *recognition*. In a good writer the reader should discover nothing new. Rather, he should recognize truths and realities that at the very least he always suspected. Can a writer deliberately create such an illusion? Perhaps. Perhaps the highest art is to create something new that nevertheless retains a reassuring air of familiarity, which somehow links what is written with the reader's distant past. Whenever I create a character, I also endow him with an invented past in order to make him more believable. Perhaps this process ought to be generalized in such a way that every image, every idea, every analysis or description is made retroactive and therefore capable of causing the reader to exclaim, "But I knew that already, I could have written it myself." This is no doubt one of the keys to what I earlier called the indispensable complicity between giver and recipient. It fulfills the dream of all creation, which is to become contagious.

There exist three forms of celebration: philosophy, fiction, and poetry. It would be an arduous and lengthy task to explain the function and inner workings of these three genres and to explore their similarities and differences. Note, however, how the relative importance of words and ideas changes. In a poem words take precedence over ideas, which follow along as best they can. The music of the rhyme is primary, the logic of meaning secondary. By contrast, in philosophy ideas take absolute precedence over words. The language of a philosophical work is never adequately docile to its ideas, so that the philosopher is continually obliged to create new words to express his thought more adequately.

This is the source of the philosophical jargon so often deplored by those too foolish to see its value. Other disciplines such as medicine, biology, physics, and mathematics have their own technical vocabularies, and there is no reason why philosophy should be any different. A technical term, moreover, is generally a guarantee that once its meaning has been understood and assimilated, its definition will not change. The word can therefore be relied upon as a key for unlocking the meaning of the text. Admittedly there are some philosophers who write in everyday language. They are the vaguest and most barren to read—in a word the most difficult. Take Descartes, for example—a philosopher of this sort—and compare him with Kant, whose terminological arsenal often frightens the novice. When Kant speaks of the *transcendental schema,* he is using a neologism of his own making, whose definition was from the beginning cast in bronze. In his work there are some twenty such neologisms, no more, and once the student has mastered this brief lexicon, as he obviously must do, he has half of Kant's philosophy under his belt. By contrast, when Descartes speaks of "clear and distinct ideas," he yokes together three words whose definitions are nowhere to be found in his work and probably vary from page to page. At best these common words give the lazy reader the illusion that he has grasped the meaning at once and can safely move on. A scrupulous reading of Descartes reveals the thorniest difficulties, however, and any interpretation, no matter how brilliant, is inevitably open to challenge.

It is a mistake—an act of terrorism—to impose limits on literary creation. It nevertheless seems to me that to marry poetry with prose fiction is unnatural and unlikely to produce fair offspring. Prose narrative has a forward thrust, a dynamism, that is the opposite of poetic contemplation. Standing midway between philosophy and poetry, prose fiction borrows the propulsive force of philosophy's arguments and intentions and uses it to power a vehicle freighted with plot and description. Philosophical concepts, being frictionless, dissipate no energy, whereas in a novel with characters and settings words become swollen with substance. Yet they must not be allowed to become so fat that the plot is slowed or prevented from reaching its climax. The energy of a philosophical system is virtually pure and moves in a closed circuit. By contrast, a novel's energy is a motor that must drive a vehicle forward, not expend itself as poetry does in static heat and light. The language of philosophy is as transparent as a concept, that of poetry as opaque as a substance, but the language of the novel must remain translucent, combining intelligence in equal proportions with color and fragrance. Incidentally, the level of linguistic concreteness determines the difficulty of translation into a foreign language. Insurmountable difficulties are rarely encountered in the translation of philosophy, while the translation of poetry is quite simply impossible. When a poem passes from one language to another, it becomes two poems drawing upon the same source of inspiration. The translation of a novel falls somewhere between comparatively easy and impossible.

The contrast between poetry and the novel is roughly equivalent to that between the still photograph and the film. Like the novel, the film is dramatic, propelled from start to finish by the power of a plot, each episode of which arouses both desire for and fear of the next. An image that is too beautiful—whose beauty is too static (but is not all beauty in some sense static?)—has no place in the unfolding of a plot, which it can only impede. Like the poetic novel, the photographer's film suffers from the crippling defects of an ill-advised hybrid. Photography wants to *retain:* that is its vocation, its reason for being. Just as a poem naturally wants to be learned by heart and recited again and again, the photograph, whether set on a mantelpiece or slipped into a wallet, wants to be looked at not once or twice but continuously and unremittingly. A humble, despised object, its demands are boundless, like those of paupers who, being utterly without hope, nurse limitless dreams. Whereas in theory there is no reason to look twice at a novel or film.

Again in contrast to the novel and the film, poetry and photography have two things in common: they rarely bring fame and never bring fortune.

Philosophy, fiction, and poetry are all by vocation apologetic, whereas the vocation of science is *reductive*. The sole purpose of scientific thought is efficacy. Science wants to accomplish things and make itself useful. It always proceeds from the complex to the simple, systematically reducing the profusion of the concrete to a dry formula simple enough to be used as a tool. To the physicist or chemist, Irish rain, the Red Sea, Lake Titicaca, and the morning dew in my garden are all H_2O. This formula tells us analytically what atoms will be produced if we break a molecule of water into its constituent parts, and synthetically what atoms we must introduce if we wish to make one molecule of water. The physicist asks no more. Philosophy, fiction, and poetry follow the opposite course, always proceeding from the simple to the complex, restoring dazzling freshness to the clichés on everyone's lips and celebrating the inexhaustible richness of the real and the irreplaceable uniqueness of creatures and things while at the same time creating that richness for our amazement.

For the past century two pseudosciences with similarly reductive claims have dared to venture into territory where true science cannot go. Both Marxism and Freudianism "reduce" the subtlest and most complex creations to a small number of distressingly threadbare patterns. Give them the works of Proust, Kafka, or Faulkner and they will tell you that they are products on the one hand of petty-bourgeois fear in the face of the rising power of the proletariat and on the other hand of a more or less successful resolution of the Oedipus complex. By contrast, a philosophical study of these works would reveal structures, architectures, and depths that escaped the notice of prior readers because they did not yet exist.

True criticism must be creative, must "see" riches in the work that are indisputably there though the author did not put them in. This proposition will seem paradoxical to anyone who clings to the traditional idea that the author "creates" his work, pulls it out of himself as one might take a smaller Russian doll from inside a larger one. But it makes good sense if you accept a suggestion that I have repeated more than once, namely, that the work produces itself and the author is only its byproduct.

4

FRIDAY

There is always another island.
—Jean Guéhenno

On January 31, 1709, a dinghy carrying six men in arms and an officer set out from H.M.S. *Duke,* an English warship of thirty guns, headed for the beach of Mas-a-Tierra, the largest island in the Juan Fernandez archipelago, situated in the Pacific Ocean 400 miles west of Santiago, Chile. The men were soon surprised to see waving at them from the shore a hirsute figure clad in goatskin. One of them asked this stranger where the best spot for a landing might be, whereupon the man, having pointed out a place, leapt down the rocks to greet them.

The man's name was Alexander Selcraig, but his sea name was Selkirk, the custom in those days being that a man changed his last name when he signed on as a seaman. In the spring of 1703 he had left his native village of Largo, a tiny port on the Scottish coast, and gone to London, where he joined the crew of the *Five Ports,* a ship of ninety tons with sixteen guns and a complement of sixty-three men, scheduled to sail to the Pacific with the *Saint George* in pursuit of Spanish galleons laden with silver and gold. At age twenty-seven Selkirk was no novice. Taken prisoner by pirates, he had been sold to a French buccaneer in Santo Domingo. There, for three years, he had hunted, killed, and butchered wild bulls and cows, whose smoked flesh brought handsome profits. His surname, which means "stone head," told a great deal about his character.

His difficulties with the *Five Ports'* captain, Lieutenant Thomas Stradling, began at the start of the journey and grew steadily worse, compounded by the fact that the voyage proved disappointing. When the two ships put in at Mas-a-Tierra in February, Selkirk therefore explored the island and surveyed its resources with a very specific purpose in mind. It should be mentioned that he was a sturdy, simple man who believed in omens, and in a dream he had glimpsed the most lamentable fate that lay in store for the *Five Ports* and its men. Still, there is something moving about Robinson Crusoe's first contact with his island. Though deserted, it was perfectly habitable. And indeed, it had had one previous resident: a Mosquito Indian had been left behind by a ship in 1680 and picked up only three years, two months, and eleven days later, in excellent health. In other words, Friday had preceded Robinson by more than twenty years, thus missing a memorable encounter. It would take the genius of Daniel Defoe to repair that error of fate.

In September the trouble between Selkirk and Stradling came to a head. The *Five Ports* once again put in at Mas-a-

Tierra but this time departed without the Scotsman. He was left on the beach with his sea chest, a rifle, some ammunition, and a Bible. At the last minute he suddenly appreciated the folly of his decision, and as the ship's launch pulled away from its stem-post's imprint in the sand he succumbed to panic. He begged Stradling to take him back aboard. The captain agreed but stipulated that Selkirk was to be put in irons as a mutineer and turned over to the English authorities at the first port of call. The terms were unacceptable. Selkirk was forced to resign himself to his fate. And a good thing he did, for as the omen had predicted the *Five Ports* shortly thereafter fell into the hands of the Spaniards, and its decimated crew was sold into slavery. Selkirk did not learn of this until much later, however.

For it turned out that although Mas-a-Tierra was on the whole an excellent place with a temperate climate, its few visitors were a most scurvy lot. The ships that came to replenish their supplies of water, palm cabbage, and meat flew either the Spanish flag or, worse yet, the pirate's skull and crossbones. More than once Selkirk escaped with his life only because his legs were good and he knew the island's interior like the back of his hand. It was four years and four months before an English ship arrived.

After a lengthy call at Mas-a-Tierra the *Duke* and her companion the *Duchess* resumed the hunt for Spanish and French ships. Heading the expedition was Captain Woodes Rogers, who in his memoirs would later tell of his encounter with Robinson Crusoe. Selkirk proved to be a fine sailor, and what is more his long abstinence had made him indifferent to alcohol and tobacco. Occasionally a captured ship would join the small convoy, and captain and crew would have to be found to man the additional vessel. In this way Selkirk came to be entrusted with the command of a ship rebaptized the *Increase*. In that capacity he performed brilliantly in the sack of the Spanish town Guayaquil in Ecuador. Not until October 14, 1711, did he set foot on the soil of the country he had left eight years, one month, and three days before.

His return created quite a sensation. Curiously enough, there was no dearth of tales of other, similar adventures. Long before Selkirk any number of shipwrecked sailors had returned after long, lonely years on some forsaken island, among them the Mosquito Indian I mentioned earlier. But none caused as much of a stir as Selkirk. The point bears emphasizing: for the first time the ground was ready to receive the seed of a new myth. I shall have more to say about it in a moment. Meanwhile, Selkirk became a figure of note; people flocked to see him, and some asked questions. The most perceptive searched for the traces that such a terrible trial of solitude must inevitably have left. Sir Richard Steele wrote in his review *The Englishman:*

> The person I speak of is Alexander Selkirk, whose name is familiar to men of curiosity, from the fame of his having lived four years and four months alone in the Island of Juan Fernandez. I had the pleasure frequently to converse with the man soon after his arrival in England in the year 1711. . . . When I first saw him, I thought, if I had not been let into his character and story, I could have discerned that he had been much separated from company, from his aspect and gesture; there was a strong but cheerful seriousness in his look and a certain disregard to the ordinary things about him, as if he had been sunk in thought. When the ship which brought him off the island came in, he received them with the greatest indifference, with relation to the prospect of going off with them, but with great satisfaction in an opportunity to refresh and help them. The man frequently bewailed his return to the world, which could not, he said, with all its enjoyments, restore him to the tranquillity of solitude.[1]

One might wish that Selkirk after his return had experienced an uncommon fate, that his life had been marked forever by the extraordinary adventure of his youth and been directed by some imperious vocation born on the bare cliffs of Mas-a-Tierra, a vocation of a literary, philosophical, religious, or perhaps simply perverse kind. For Defoe it was enough that he should be afflicted with wanderlust and unable to remain in one place. Another novel remains to be written about the great hermit of the Pacific and his impossible readjustment to society.[2] But the plain truth of Selkirk's life is that it ended as banally as it began. He married, sailed again, and in 1723 died on board H.M.S. *Weymouth*.

Did Daniel Defoe ever meet Alexander Selkirk? There is no evidence that he did, but there is a reason—admittedly inconclusive—for believing that he did not. Selkirk returned to England in 1711. Defoe's novel did not appear until 1719. If the writer had known his model personally, surely less time would have elapsed between the real adventure and its transcription in fiction. Would not this strange meeting, this irreplaceable eyewitness account, have stimulated the writer in his work? Of course this is nothing but conjecture. But note the many discrepancies between the true story and the literary work. For one thing, the locale is different. Robinson lands not on Mas-a-Tierra in the Pacific but on an island near the mouth of the Orinoco, hence in the Atlantic. Why this change? No doubt because the author, hoping for a popular success, preferred to set his story in a part of the world that was already well known and, unlike the Juan Fernandez Islands, the scene of innumerable existing tales and legends. Defoe also increased the length of the hero's stay from four years and four months to twenty-eight years. Art has certain imperatives. Selkirk had been abandoned

on Mas-a-Tierra for mutiny, or at any rate for incompatibility with his ship's captain. Crusoe is the sole survivor of
a shipwreck. That way the story is more edifying: fate's
blow is struck by none other than the finger of God. Yet
to my mind Defoe's most ingenious embellishment of historical fact was the invention of Friday. I shall come back
to it in a moment.

The book's success was astonishing in both senses of the
word. Poor Daniel Defoe, whose previous serious and
meritorious works had earned him nothing but misery and
persecution, suddenly found himself rich and famous, so
much so that he hastened to provide a sequel—sequels,
actually—to the adventures of Robinson Crusoe. The
reader who comes to a complete edition of the novel
for the first time may be somewhat surprised to discover
that the story of Crusoe's life on the desert island occupies
only the first third of the book, the rest of which ranges
over the entire world until Friday, after an ill-fated return
to the famous island, is killed by Indians who may well be
his brothers.

The success of Defoe's novel, great as it was, would have
been much like that of any number of other literary masterpieces had it not inspired innumerable imitations and
new versions throughout the world. Whether in English
or translated into other tongues, copies spread like seeds
in the wind, sprouting new works wherever they fell—
offshoots deeply influenced by the mental climate of the
host country. Among the best known of these are *Crusoe
in New York* by Edward Everett Hale, *The Arctic Crusoe* by
Percy B. St. John, and of course Wyss's *Swiss Family Robinson,* in which a father is interested primarily in availing
himself of the island's pedagogical resources for the benefit
of his children. More recent examples of the genre include
Saint-John Perse's admirable *Images à Crusoé* and Jean Gi-

raudoux's *Suzanne et le Pacifique,* in which a young woman from Bellac takes the place of Defoe's bearded Puritan. Each new generation, apparently, has felt a need to tell its story through that of Robinson Crusoe and by so doing to discover its own identity. Crusoe soon ceased to be a character in a novel and became a mythical hero.

Jules Verne's *Mysterious Island* (1874) is an instructive case in point. There is no doubt that Verne, in publishing his version of the Crusoe tale, intended to throw down a challenge to Defoe's hero, born some 150 years earlier. In his struggle for survival the original Crusoe had held two important trumps: civilization had given him a valuable going-away present in the form of his wrecked ship, and he had been stranded on a lush island with abundant vegetation and no animals more threatening than his famous goats.

Verne's five survivors, on the other hand, are confronted with nothing more than a rocky islet battered by heavy seas. They have been traveling by balloon, moreover, and arrive clinging to the rigging, having been forced to jettison the basket in order to avoid going down at sea. As they writhe like wet dogs in the island's dirt, we inevitably think of five magicians who roll up their sleeves, spread their fingers, and invite the audience to observe that there is nothing in either hands or pockets. What follows is a dazzling display of inventiveness, discovery, and ingenuity. The men light a fire, bake bricks, mine ore, and forge steel. But the best is yet to come. They go on to prepare nitroglycerin, manufacture chemical fertilizer, and then, with a single seed found in the lining of a coat, make wheat grow where once there was only stone. They blow glass, build a hydraulic elevator, and soon cap the whole fantastic adventure by producing electricity and a telegraph. Crusoe and his penned goats are outclassed, outdone, and ridiculed.

The point of the story is that among the five victims is that quintessential Jules Vernian hero, Cyrus Smith, an *engineer*—a wonderful word, compounded of engine and ingenuity—who embodies the triumph of applied science and technology. It would of course be easy to be ironic at the expense of these five survivors, who are never once visited by doubt, despair, or hatred. Crusoe may not have made electricity, but his religious crisis and thoughts of suicide give him a different, more human presence. To which Verne would no doubt respond that work is happiness and that there is no time for tears when one must manufacture sulfuric acid and glass out of thin air.

Yet Verne might also respond in another way. His heroes may have had little in the way of inner life, but his island did, and its name was Nemo. For the captain of the *Nautilus,* that somber metaphysician of the deep, lay hidden in his magic toy off the rocky coast. Smith was the hero of the nineteenth century dreaming of the twentieth. Yet for all his ingenious engineering Smith is but a small boy compared with Nemo, the grandiose solitary who plays Bach chorales on the organ of his submarine as an earthquake swallows both it and the mysterious island.

In this fracturing of the gem that was *Robinson Crusoe* we recognize two essential aspects of the mythical hero. He escaped from the work in which he first appeared in order to bring life to many others, and his popularity surpassed and eclipsed that of his author. The property of all mankind, Crusoe is one of the basic constituents of the Western soul.

No matter what aspect we choose, he is a living presence in each of us. His myth is surely one of the most topical and vital that we possess. Perhaps it would be more accurate to say that it possesses us. It is worth pausing a moment to consider a few of the ways in which the Crusoe myth shapes our fictions, a few of the ways in which it serves as a mold into which we pour our modern sensibilities and aspirations.

Crusoe is first of all a hero of solitude. Stranded on a desert island, an orphan deprived not just of parents but of the whole human race, he struggles for years against despair, madness, and suicide. Now, to my mind, of all the wounds from which contemporary Western man suffers, solitude is the most pernicious. It afflicts us all the more because we enjoy so much in the way of freedom and wealth. Freedom, wealth, and solitude are the three faces of the modern condition. Less than a century ago Europeans were bound together by family and religion, by living together in the same village or neighborhood, and by their fathers' professions. These bonds weighed heavily, preventing radical change and limiting freedom of choice. A man was barely free to choose his own wife, and once the choice was made he had little prospect of changing one woman for another. And besides these obligations he had to contend with the constraints of economics in an avaricious and impoverished society. Yet such servitude sustained and comforted even as it oppressed. Much the same situation can be seen today in the so-called underdeveloped countries. Are they truly underdeveloped? Surely not from the standpoint of human relations. Rarely does a stranger's smile go unanswered. It is returned at once, just as the dove sent out from Noah's ark returned bearing an olive branch. Unbidden, a child will come up to you in the street and invite you to tea with his family. A baby sitting on the sidewalk will tap the stone with his hand to invite you to sit down. Anyone who goes from a place like this to the airport at Marseilles or Orly is immediately struck by the wooden expressions on people's faces and the hostility that fairly quivers in the air.

We live locked in glass cages of reserve, coldness, and self-containment. From early childhood we are taught never to speak to strangers and to go about wrapped in a mantle of suspicion, making as little contact with others as possible. On top of this antihuman training is laid that obsessive distrust of the flesh which with us takes the place of morality. Puritanism conspires with its wayward daughters Prostitution and Pornography to perfect our isolation. If, while riding the subway, I venture to glance at my neighbor's newspaper, he will give me a dirty look and angrily stuff the paper into his pocket. The newspaper is his, you see, bought and paid for with his hard-earned cash. He was simply exercising his most inalienable right to read it in peace when I came along and allowed myself to be caught red-handed in the act of filching his property. You'd think he had caught me eating from his plate or rummaging through his pockets. I have no right.

This little anecdote calls to mind the opening scene of a wonderfully bitter and bracing book.[3] The setting is a railway dining car in which some sixty passengers are seated at tables of four. No one is looking at or talking to anyone else. When the dinner is over, the narrator's neighbor, a sturdy, open-faced Swede with well-chiseled features, orders a kirsch. He drops a cube of sugar into his glass and smiles at the narrator. "I smiled back," the author recounts. "He then dropped a second sugar cube into his kirsch and over the next few seconds slowly stretched out his arm toward me. Most likely he wanted me to taste the liquor-soaked treat he had prepared. But between us, between our bodies, there was a wall, an insuperable wall. The gesture was abruptly cut short."

As riches piled up, social bonds fell away one by one, and the emancipated individual found himself standing naked, expectant, and alone, with no one to whom he could turn for help in the nameless, faceless crowd. A tenement on the outskirts of Naples is something of a vertical village, where everyone knows everyone else. Of course that means that everyone is watched constantly, but in exchange people are surrounded and supported by their neighbors. They live with their doors open and eat in one another's apartments. By contrast, the inhabitants of a luxury apartment building in a fashionable neighborhood of Paris hide behind walls of discretion. Propriety forbids undue curiosity about even the names of one's closest neighbors. In travel you see the same indifference to other people. The driver's life—to say nothing of road safety— would be markedly improved if a way could be found to end the motorist's solitary confinement in his sheet metal cell. Every driver is obsessed, threatened, and oppressed by *other* drivers. And to those others he can say nothing. Even when he hurls insults at them, two windshields ensure that his angry words will never reach their ears. Technically it would be feasible to equip every automobile with a small two-way radio capable of communicating over distances of a few hundred feet. At first this would probably mean only that insults would attain their mark more surely and more quickly, but soon a kind of society would be instituted with its own rules of proper behavior, and driving attitudes would improve noticeably.

Unfortunately, it is more difficult to dispel the three scourges that threatened Robinson on his island than it is to calm the wrath of motorists. Madness, addiction, and suicide: these are the consequences of solitude, itself engendered by wealth and freedom. With growing prosperity and freedom of choice, more and more victims fall by the wayside, for some people are just too weak to bear the loneliness that is the dark side of progress.

The glass cage must be broken. And in order to break it we must first discover for ourselves that it exists and convince ourselves that it is neither inevitable nor good. Points of contact do exist, moreover. Temporary communities can be created, communities in which people understand one another even before they meet. The community of the highways has yet to be founded, but a community of motorcyclists already exists. Leather-clad knights exchange familiar greetings, lend one another a helping· hand, and hold huge rallies. There are also religious communities, Taizé being a fine and noble example. Such groups puncture the carapace of loneliness, and a society concerned about the common good should encourage and even organize them rather than greet them with suspicion or, worse yet, foolishly combat them in the name of some nefarious notion of law and order. I am thinking in particular of pop music festivals, or of those celebrations of the erotic known to take place in, say, the Bois de Boulogne by night—a most charming place, with all its mysterious confusion, furtive signals, silent commotions, and lascivious shadows suddenly illuminated by a burst of laughter or flash of light. I see, or at any rate I should like to see, the Bois by night as an image of wealth and freedom reconciled with pleasure, gaiety, and community.

Robinson Crusoe is not only the victim of his solitude but also its hero. In a curious reversal of values, the solitude that kills us and drives us crazy can also take on an aura of prestige, like those deadly fish that when first tasted seem to possess an indescribably pleasant smell and taste and produce an extremely agreeable sensation. Who has not dreamed of running away to a desert island? For many people the pleasant thought of vacation is inseparable from the idea of white beaches, palm trees, and crashing azure waves. Robinson had all of that. His sunny paradise required nothing in the way of work beyond a little gardening, a little building, and a little fishing, activities usually referred to as "do-it-yourself." And Crusoe is indeed the patron saint of the outdoor do-it-yourselfer.

It should be obvious, then, why Crusoe commands such respect: he was so marvelously adept at coping with the solitude that afflicts us all, even—perhaps especially—in the midst of a faceless and oppressive multitude, and he was moreover capable of erecting that solitude into a way of life. That, at any rate, is the way most people think of Defoe's hero, and it is an idea that tells us a great deal about how myth works. The mythical hero not only strikes his roots into the heart of every individual, even the most modest and prosaic, but also scales humanity's grandest heights. Paradoxically he is at once everyman's double and a superhuman hero to be set alongside the immortal Olympians. Hence every mythical hero—not only Crusoe but also Tristan and Don Juan and Faust—involves us in what I like to call *autohagiography*. How tall I am, how strong, how melancholy! cries the reader, as he lifts his eyes from his book to his mirror. He truly had no idea he was so beautiful.

Nevertheless, Crusoe's years of solitude—the only thing his adventure has in common with Alexander Selkirk's—are overshadowed by the novel's other great theme, for which in the end they merely lay the necessary groundwork, namely, the appearance of Friday. No doubt it was inevitable that at first only Crusoe would achieve the dimension of myth, for it was not until recently that the science of anthropology was developed and the great colonial empires were simultaneously dismantled. What was Friday to Daniel Defoe? Nothing: an animal, at best a creature waiting to receive his humanity from Robinson Crusoe, who as a European was in sole possession of all knowledge and wisdom. Once properly broken in by his master Crusoe, Friday could never aspire to anything

more than to be a good servant. The idea that Crusoe
might have been able to learn something from Friday
would never have occurred to anyone before the age of
anthropology.[4] The story's properly mythical quality is
most plainly evident here, for over the past few decades
the encounter between Robinson and Friday has taken on
a significance that Daniel Defoe was a thousand leagues
from even suspecting.

As I reread his novel, I could not forget my years of
study at the Musée de l'Homme, Paris's museum of anthropology, where I learned that there are no "savages,"
only men living in civilizations different from our own
and most rewarding for us to study. Crusoe's attitude toward Friday was of the most ingenuously racist sort and
heedless of his own self-interest. If you must live on an
island in the Pacific, hadn't you better learn from a native
well versed in methods adapted to local conditions rather
than attempt to impose an English way of life on an alien
environment? Am I advocating a revival of Rousseau's
myth of the noble savage? Not as much as it might seem.
For Rousseau, who lived in an age of exploration, cared
not a whit for all that was being discovered around him.
His noble savage was merely an abstraction that he used to
indict his own society, exactly like Montesquieu's Persian.[5]
All the virtues he imputed to the "savage" were merely
mirror images of the vices of which he accused the "civilized." And when he praised Defoe's *Robinson Crusoe* as the
only book he would choose for Emile's edification and
amusement, he explicitly excluded Friday, a character in
whom he saw nothing but the germs of society and domestic slavery: "Let us make haste to establish Emile on
this island while his felicity can still be assured within its
bounds, for the day will soon come when, if he wishes to
go on living there, he will not want to live alone, and

when Friday, who for the time being touches him but little, will cease to suffice." Rousseau is interested only in Robinson, the industrious hero, sober and ingenious, capable of supplying all his needs without society's assistance. What Rousseau does not see, apparently, is that Crusoe is destroying his desert island by reconstituting a civilization in embryo, just as he is perverting Friday by reducing him to the role of servant. Worse yet, he deprives Crusoe of all inventiveness and creativity, granting him only those paltry skills he brought with him from his native England.

Nevertheless, my novel *Friday* is not really an anthropological novel. The genuine anthropological novel remains to be written. Its true subject—and an exciting and rewarding subject it is—would be the confrontation and fusion of two civilizations personified by two representative narrators, and it would take place as if under laboratory conditions on a desert island. Robinson is an Englishman of a certain social class of the early eighteenth century. Friday is an Araucanian, a Chilean Indian, of the same period. Both civilizations would have to be described in full detail: economy, legal system, literature, art, religion, and so forth. The writer would then observe the encounter between the two, their struggle and fusion, and the emergence of a new civilization combining elements of both. Defoe never broached this subject, because for him Crusoe alone was in possession of the *only* civilization that existed, and he simply overwhelms Friday with it. In any case, my novel, conceived more as a philosophical venture, aimed at a very different goal. I was interested not in the marriage of two civilizations at a particular stage of evolution but in the elimination of every last vestige of civilization in a man subjected to the corrosive effects of inhuman solitude: the very roots of his life and being are laid bare, and he must then create from nothing a new world, groping in the dark, feeling his way toward discovery, clarity, and ecstasy. Friday—still more virginal, more bereft of civilization than Robinson even after his bath of solitude—serves the new man as both guide and midwife. Thus my novel was intended to be both inventive and forward-looking, whereas Defoe's was purely retrospective, confined to describing the restoration of a lost civilization with the means at hand.

This three-way drama (Robinson, Friday, and the island) provided a perfect springboard for the jump from philosophy to the novel. Some day I must repay the immense debt I owe to Paul Valéry, and then, like a truly thankless and rebellious child, I shall avail myself of the opportunity to publish the indictment I have been patiently preparing against him. It was Valéry who defined the kind of novel I was trying to write and who, with *Monsieur Teste,* provided me with a model. In reality he was himself following a model at once venerable and paradoxical: Descartes's *Discourse on Method.* The origin of *Monsieur Teste* is evident from its Latin epigraph: *Vita Cartesii res simplicissima.* In a letter to André Gide dated August 25, 1894, Valéry wrote: "I reread the *Discourse on Method* this afternoon, and it is indeed the modern novel as it might be written. It is remarkable that the autobiographical element has since been banished from philosophy. That is the point that needs reexamination, and therefore what has to be written is the life of a theory, too much having been written already about the life of a passion (sexual). The difficulty, though, is that, Puritan that I am, I insist that the theory be more than a fake as in *Louis Lambert.*" It was probably the beginning of the first paragraph of part two of the *Discourse* that roused Valéry to such a pitch of enthusiasm and illumination: "I was at that time in Germany, whither I had been called by wars still in progress, and while returning to the army from the coronation of the emperor the onset of winter compelled me to stop at a place where, finding no conversation to divert me and happily being untroubled by either care or passion, I remained closeted all day by myself in a room with a stove, where I had ample leisure to ruminate upon my thoughts."

In this there is indeed reason to rejoice. We are dealing with a mercenary. After serving in Holland with the prince of Nassau's army, he leaves to enlist under the colors of the elector of Bavaria. The winter of 1619 being harsh, he finds a billet on the upper Danube, closets himself in a room, and while the cannon of the Thirty Years' War roar and Ferdinand, king of Bohemia and Hungary, is crowned Holy Roman Emperor at Frankfurt, he invents the *cogito* and the ontological argument. In comparison with such a *romance,* it is not hard to imagine how pale later stories of made-up sexual adventures must have seemed to Valéry.

The problem, in short, was to relate a series of purely cerebral activities and discoveries without removing them from their historical and autobiographical matrix, to combine essay with novel in such a way that the more abstractly metaphysical the essay and the more adventurously picaresque the novel, the more brilliant the marriage.

Paul Valéry completed only one work answering this description. In *Monsieur Teste* he endowed an imaginary character with an extraordinary mind, turned him loose in nature, and observed what happened. As with Descartes, the monstrous nature of the man's mind created an insuperable distance between himself and events, thus affording the observer an ideal vantage point. Descartes, lost in thought, vaguely heard the blare of trumpets and the roar of cannon from the depths of his heated room and somehow these dimly perceived sounds entered into his meditations upon the fate of man. (One is also reminded of Hegel finishing the *Phenomenology of the Spirit* at Jena in 1806, while the flash and roar of cannon on the horizon attested to the rout of the Prussians under Prince von Hohenlohe by Napoleon's army.)

The fact that the story of Robinson Crusoe lent itself to a treatment of this kind, in which the cerebral adventure would be submerged in a classic novelistic context, did not go unnoticed by Paul Valéry. His *Histoires brisées* contains a brief outline: "Robinson reconstructs his intellectual life without the aid of books or notes. All the music he has ever heard comes back to him. . . . His memory expands to meet the needs of solitude and emptiness. He peers within. Books he has read come back to him, and he makes notes on what he remembers. These notes are very odd. First he *continues,* and then he creates." The name Friday crops up only once in these notes, but the problem of others, of their absence or ghostly presence, obviously must have occurred to Valéry, who provided this caption for the color frontispiece included in the first edition of *Histoires brisées:* "Although his island was deserted, he put a feather in his cap. By so doing it seemed to him that he was creating someone who was looking at the feather."

That is the miracle of the story. Crusoe's life on the island can be divided into two perfectly complementary parts, before Friday and with Friday. The drama of solitude issues in an appeal to a companion, an appeal suddenly cut short by the actual arrival of one. The companion who arrives, however, is of a surprising, totally unexpected, and bitterly disappointing sort, a Negro, yet he holds out the promise of a prodigious renewal of adventure and invention. It is clear, moreover, that a companion of the sort Crusoe was hoping for—another Englishman, another Robinson Crusoe—would have made the story fall flat.

In my novel *Friday* these two parts are preceded by a third, what I call "the swine's wallow," which gives the tale a dialectical structure. It was in the logic of the story that Crusoe, after hoping in vain that he would be found and trying to signal to passing ships and to build a boat, should experience a period of hopelessness and dejection. He discovers a mudhole to which a pack of peccaries comes to wallow during the hottest hours of the day. Imitating the animals, he wallows in the mud like a pig, allowing only his nose and mouth to protrude from the muck, and is reduced to a brutish stupor, is indeed nearly killed, by the noxious gases emanating from the marsh.

This episode is the low point of Crusoe's life on the island, after which he begins to reassert control over his destiny. He climbs back up the hill, sets rules for himself, and organizes and farms the island as though it were an English colony. I call this the "age of administration." The story takes place at a time when the English Puritans, Bibles in hand, were invading and colonizing the virgin territory of the New World, inspired by a morality of accumulation codified by Ben Franklin in *Poor Richard's Almanac,* which bridged the gap between Calvinism and free-enterprise capitalism. Imbued with this Puritan ethic, the Crusoe of the "age of administration" believes that productive labor is the only hope of salvation. Because he works in solitude, however, his labor is futile, and his output—grains, dried meats, fish, fruits—seems more like the folly of a madman than the soul of wisdom.

Friday at first seems to offer a justification for Crusoe's maniacal attempt to organize the island. He is to be the kingdom's sole "subject," General Crusoe's only soldier and Governor Crusoe's only taxpayer. To all these demands he good-naturedly accedes, or so it seems. But his mere presence is enough to shake the island's organizational structure, for it is clear that he understands none of it, and Crusoe, who at last sees himself with Friday's eyes, is forced to take the measure of his own madness. Friday sows the seeds of doubt in the heart of a system that had stood only by the strength of blind conviction. When Friday half-inadvertently causes the destruction of all Crusoe's accumulated provisions and of all the treasures saved from his wrecked ship, Crusoe's reaction is therefore quite mild, as if he had all along been expecting and almost hoping for such a disaster.

From here on out Friday calls the tune. He becomes the inventor and forces Crusoe to invent in ways that he had previously explored only with the greatest timidity, the administered island being nothing more than a scrupulous reproduction of the civilization Crusoe has left behind. Friday is an aerial, aeolian spirit, an Ariel. His attributes are the arrow, the kite, and the aeolian harp. His very virtues actually conspire to bring about his downfall, for he cannot resist the attraction of the first-class English sailing vessel that anchors off the island's coast. Crusoe at first belongs to the kingdom of the earth. He is like a peasant, slow and uncouth. He lives his terrestrial vocation to the full, loving his island as a child loves its mother (the cave episode) and, later, as a husband loves his wife (the mandragora episode). Then, however, he undergoes a slow metamorphosis, which begins with his turning toward the sun and is completed under Friday's influence. The formula of the novel can be expressed in the form of two equations:

$$Earth + Air = Sun$$
$$Terrestrial\ Crusoe + Friday = Solar\ Crusoe$$

It has been noted that the three stages of Crusoe's evolution are related to the three types of knowledge described by Spinoza in the *Ethics*. Knowledge of the first type comes from the senses and emotions and is characterized by subjectivity, contingency, and immediacy. Knowledge of the second type is embodied in science and technology. It is rational but superficial, mediated, and for the most part utilitarian. Only knowledge of the third type yields an intuition of the essence of the absolute. The swine's wallow, the administered island, and the solar ecstasy do indeed reproduce the three successive stages of knowledge described in the *Ethics*. There is even the same affinity between stages one and three, both of which are immediate and disinterested, as opposed to stage two (rational science and the rationally administered island).

Of course this parallelism was not deliberate. But apart from the fact that for me the *Ethics* is, after the Gospels, the most important book there is, its lesson deeply etched in my mind, I must point out that these three stages reflect a classical pattern that can be found in more than one religious and philosophical system. Even at the most trivial level—that of ordinary life—one can point to a rough equivalent of the same pattern. Three ways of living are open to every man and woman: a life of purely passive and degrading pleasures such as alcohol, drugs, and the like; a life of work and social ambition; or a life of pure artistic and religious contemplation. Crusoe's three lives thus bridge the gap between our everyday existence and the metaphysics of Spinoza.

A reader once rather pointedly asked me why I had not dedicated my book to the memory of the man who inspired it, Daniel Defoe. Was that not the least I could do to pay my respects to Crusoe's creator? I will admit that the thought never even occurred to me, for it seemed obvious that every page of the book paid tribute to its English model. The fact is that I had thought of another dedication, which I turned over in my mind for quite a long time before finally rejecting it. I had no way of asking permission to offer my foolish tribute, and the proposed recipient seemed too great, too worthy of respect, and too remote. For I had wanted to dedicate my book to all of France's immigrant workers, to those silent masses of Fridays shipped to Europe from the third world—some three million Algerians, Moroccans, Tunisians, Senegalese, and Portuguese on whom our society depends and whom we never see or hear, who have no right to vote, no trade union, and no spokesperson. It would seem only reasonable and just that a considerable part of what is published and broadcast in France not only be devoted to them but belong to them. Our affluent society relies on these people; it has set its fat white buttocks down on their brown bodies and reduced them to absolute silence. They sweep our streets, pick our strawberries, mow our lawns, carry our burdens, and beg at our doors, yet we behave as though they had nothing to say, nothing to say to us at any rate, nothing to teach us, and yet everything to learn by attending our schools, learning to speak the civilized tongue of Descartes, Corneille, and Pasteur, acquiring our civilized manners, and most of all by making us forget— stupid, blind Crusoes that we all are—who they are and where they come from. They are a muzzled but vital population, a barely tolerated yet totally indispensable part of our society, and the only genuine proletariat that exists in France. Beware lest these mute masses erupt one day with the sound of thunder.

5

THE METEORS, OR GEMINI

Thunder is a meteor, as is the dew.
—Joseph de Maistre

The Ogre was a novel about a solitary man in the grip of the subtle and irresistible machinery of fate. *Les Météores* (translated as *Gemini*) is the story of a couple so closely united that each member finds his fate in the other. Having repeated the lovely word *fate* twice in two sentences, I owe the reader a word of explanation.

Fate, says the dictionary, is a necessary but unknown sequence of events. To these three ingredients one must add a fourth, namely, an ego, a human being more or less implicated in this sequence of events, which eludes both his will (being *necessary*) and his understanding (being *unknown*). We would never use the word *fate* in speaking of a physical phenomenon or chemical reaction on an uninhabited planet. But we do speak of fate when events—events that make and unmake our lives—take place in such a way as to offer us a glimpse of some higher logic, some intelligible necessity. In both *The Ogre* and *Gemini* the lives of the heroes become more and more intelligible as events—primarily historical in the first novel, geographical in the second—give substance to and illuminate them. This gradual elucidation elicits ever more intimate assent to a story which as time goes by is revealed to be both strictly personal and closely intertwined with the cosmic order. Recognition turns *fatum* into *amor fati*. The true subject of both novels is the gradual transformation of fate into destiny, or, to put it another way, the transformation of an obscure, coercive mechanism into enthusiastic and wholehearted embrace of the future.

The twin theme had dogged my steps for a long time. It crops up in *Friday,* when Crusoe imagines that he is Friday's twin brother—not in the usual horizontal sense of kinship but in the vertical sense, a celestial twin, as it were. Even then there was a connection between *twins* and *meteors,* the idea being that twin brothers have a natural, intimate, and unique relation to the heavens.

In that initial brush with the theme I indicated that because twins have but one soul for two bodies, their flesh must be denser, richer, and somehow more intensely *carnal* than that of non-twins. This judgment was not without a basis in reality. Anyone who has observed twins is aware of the fascination exerted by their bodies, whose physicality is in some gross way emphasized by duplication. Such super-flesh inevitably attracted the attention of that connoisseur of young flesh, Abel Tiffauges. He first discovers the charms of twinship in a pair of pigeons that he requisitions for his unit (which uses carrier pigeons for its battlefield communications) and which he later eats, with mixed emotions. Still later, in East Prussia, he comes upon a pair of identical twins, Haro and Hajo. With fierce joy he takes them into custody, and later they are impaled on either side of their friend Lothar in a kind of child's Golgotha.

There is no question that *Gemini* was inspired by a fascination with the super-flesh of twins, but the twin theme quickly proved to be an enormously fertile one. In the first place, there is no better way to distinguish between the effects of heredity and the effects of environment on living things than through the study of twins. Identical twins carry identical genetic baggage, and if they are placed in different environments heredity is all they have in common and ecology is all that tells them apart.

Heredity and environment: few dichotomies are as rife with consequences as this. The controversy is first a question of biology. A living thing is nothing but a set of genes subjected to the stresses and caresses of various environments. Gregor Mendel and Ivan Pavlov provided two different ways of looking at life, one genetic, the other ecological.

But the debate over heredity versus environment rages well beyond the laboratory, affecting every sphere of life, including politics. It is often said, for instance, that the ideas of "right" and "left" in politics have lost all meaning and ought to be discarded as relics of ancient polemics, particularly since in recent years they have come to be associated with certain implicit value judgments—positive for the left, negative for the right—in consequence of which everyone claims to belong to the left and no one to the right. And in fact a tradition inherited from the nineteenth century does pit the wretched mass of the proletariat against a right-wing coalition of privilege and wealth

wedded to the status quo. Left is to right as progress toward justice is to preservation of an oppressive order.

But now that revolutions in a number of countries have
driven out the former rulers and landlords and replaced
them with socialist governments that have turned out to
be nothing but bureaucratic oligarchies, this picture has
naturally had to be retouched. The moment the left comes
to power it wants to stay there, and it is prepared to use
force to prevent not only further revolution but change of
any kind, which is automatically denounced as counter-
revolutionary. In other words, the left becomes conservative, and experience has shown that socialist conservatism,
with its harsh and reactionary opposition to every challenge to the established order, is no less adept at preserving
the status quo than the divine-right monarchies of the
past. Does it follow that there is such a thing as a reactionary left and a specifically left-wing tyranny, or should we
say instead that all power is by nature right-wing?

It is here that the distinction between heredity and environment becomes useful. As long as these two extremes
of biological thought continue to attract believers, there
will be a right-wing biology, which ascribes everything to
heredity, and a left-wing biology, which holds that the environment alone is decisive. And by extension there will
also be a right and a left.

The Old Regime based social privilege on a person's
ancestors and "quarters of nobility" and permitted titles,
offices, and wealth to be transmitted from father to son,
including the very highest office, that of king. Centuries
before any science worthy of the name biology existed,
and long before the principles of genetics were established,
heredity thus undergirded an entire social structure. Of
course it was heredity understood in the broad sense, because new branches could be grafted onto the family tree

by adoption and endowed with all the rights of authentic offspring. Racism was still a long way off.

Later, when the bourgeoisie seized power and supplanted the aristocracy, the biological basis of the hereditary claim to social privilege was bolstered even more. Certain people were said to be *physically* destined to cultivate the earth, work in factories, or perform servile chores. Such people could know happiness but only of a particular sort: they were fated to eat, drink, and sleep in a cruder, simpler style than that to which their bourgeois employers had become accustomed. A family of laborers had no more need of a bathroom than a horse of a bed. Indeed, to give them a bathroom would be harmful to their own interests "properly understood." Dickens tells us of a remarkable idea in which many people in Victorian England firmly believed, that it was an unforgivable, criminal act to offer meat to the children of the poor, for meat was by nature intended for their betters and giving it to the poor would only corrupt them, turning them into delinquents or rebels. Therein lay the true cause of strikes and riots.[1] This ideology proved particularly well suited to the colonies that the industrial nations were then in the process of acquiring.

The most radical form of hereditarian ideology was yet to come, however: the racism of the Nazis. According to the theorists of the Third Reich, there is good blood and bad blood, and in any particular individual the proportion of each is determined by fate. Bad blood—that of Jews, Gypsies, and Levantines—cannot be improved and must therefore be destroyed. In this overestimation of the importance of heredity there was, conscious or not, an uncompromising pessimism quite typical of right-wing ideology, in this case carried to an extreme that led logically to the extermination camps and crematories.

Left-wing ideology springs from the opposite premise: that all men are created equal at birth, not only in law but also in fact. All carry the same moral, intellectual, and emotional baggage. From the first hours after birth, however, the work of the environment begins—benefiting some, destroying others, and giving rise to an inequality that is but another name for injustice. Some must spend childhood and adolescence in families devastated by the effects of poverty and alcoholism. Others, even before they open their eyes, snooze surrounded by the rustle of culture and sophistication. Later on, the poor child's development will be systematically blocked, but by then the damage done in the first few years, during which the child's mind is shaped by a host of external impressions, will in any case have irrevocably limited his future growth.

If the assumption that heredity is decisive led to the worst crimes, the axiom that environment is all when pushed to the limit is no less insane. In the 1950s Soviet biology and agriculture were led down the primrose path to ruin by the followers of Lysenko and Michurin, who dismissed everything that had been learned about genetics as "bourgeois science" and who among other things claimed to be able to grow oats, rye, and barley from specially treated seeds of durum wheat. In reality they did nothing more than apply to botany a cherished principle of left-wing ideology: that with a proper education any child can be made at will into a mathematician, statesman, or stevedore.

The look of a tyrannical regime depends on whether it is based on an ideology of heredity or an ideology of environment. A hereditary tyranny, most recently exemplified by Nazi Germany, creates an apparently normal society in which a person can live without getting into trouble provided he refrains from attacking the government and its officials and does not belong to any of the groups slated for destruction by the regime. Thus the Nazi government was able to strike bargains with both the Catholic and Protestant churches. Death struck the condemned from above, like a bolt out of the blue. They were simply taken into custody and murdered, a perfect example being the famous "Night of the Long Knives," June 30, 1934.

Left-wing tyranny rarely acts in so direct a fashion. It begins by casting a broad net that captures the entire population in its toils and alters daily life down to the smallest detail. This is called bureaucracy, the primary form of what might be called environmental oppression. Oppression subsequently takes a form that is no less environmental, only now the environment is filled with booby traps and poisoned stakes, and the victim is pushed into it much as a hunted animal might be chased into a marsh. An example is the rigged political trial, the result of which is a term in the Gulag archipelago. It may seem surprising that a government so powerful would trouble itself with these formalities and stage great mock trials that fool no one and simply provoke international outrage. But by its very nature the government is committed to the principle that the environment is everything, and it is therefore obliged to attack its enemies indirectly, from the flank, whereas the right-wing murderer strikes directly at the heart.

Where is the truth? Certainly not in ideological bias. What ought to worry the left is that with the advent of genetics heredity is now an object of scientific study, and progress in the area has been rapid and steady. By contrast, the environment is a rather vague concept. Pavlov and his conditioned reflexes add up to very little compared with the impressive progress made in genetics and microbiology in recent years. No doubt the wisest thing to do would be to defuse the polemic by granting that man is determined 100 percent by heredity and 100 percent by environment. Man surpasses man, Pascal once said. Perhaps this 200-percent determinism is another way of saying the same thing, the evident paradox being the measure of man's freedom.

One thing is clear, at any rate, and that is that the child obtains both his heredity and his environment for the first few years of life from his parents, whose influence on him is thus doubled, for better or for worse. Anxious parents not only transmit to their children an anxious nature but also raise them in an atmosphere of anxiety. Thus the parental burden on the child is doubled, with disastrous consequences in a family of alcoholics but beneficial consequences in a family of talented musicians. But for every family of musicians, how many families of alcoholics are there?

Still, man's dependence on his environment is far less oppressive than the tyranny of heredity. One can change one's environment or choose another, but who can change a hereditary bent, the plan inscribed in the very heart of the living cell? Furthermore, observation of life and nature teaches one very clear lesson. The sexual creature bears its charge of heredity like a burden to be shaken off. Sexual reproduction shakes up the cocktail of chromosomes so as to produce an enormous diversity of individual types, whereas the agamic, parthenogenic, or fissiparous forms of reproduction practiced by "inferior" species transmit the hereditary charge unchanged and intact. With each new generation life attempts to erase all vestiges of the previous one, and whatever "information" is transmitted despite this cleansing of the slate is riddled with errors. When the adolescent asserts his identity in opposition to his parents, when he rejects their traditions and advice and insists upon starting from square one, he is unwittingly ratifying nature's view that every man ought to be the first in Creation. If respect for heredity and faith in the past are characteristics of the right, then nature is firmly on the left. The nontransmissibility of acquired characters is as good as a manifesto.

The dilemma of heredity versus environment has left its mark on literature, including even fiction. To take two examples of some consequence, it has been said that Balzac was a man of the right and Victor Hugo a man of the left. This assessment is confirmed by an application of our principle to those two illustrious escaped convicts, Balzac's Vautrin and Hugo's Jean Valjean. [2]

In characteristic fashion Hugo fills us in on the details of Valjean's background. He gives us nothing less than the genealogy of a criminal. Valjean begins his career in crime by stealing a loaf of bread to feed his widowed sister's seven children. For that he is sent to prison, where suffering, humiliation, and injustice are heaped upon his head. When he gets out he is as black as soot, and the rest of the novel traces his gradual rehabilitation, his reacceptance into a society from which he was excluded by a cruel trick of fate. Initially he was a perfectly normal, commonplace man—virgin wax. All the rest was a product of circumstances. [3]

The case of Vautrin is totally different. Balzac does not trouble himself to tell us about his background. We must take him as he is, a wild man with all his strength, joviality, and sleepy yawns. He is heredity to the core, massive, inevitable, and single-minded. He would be evil incarnate if there were not in him something of the innocence of a force of nature. In order to make his fate even more visceral, Balzac makes him a homosexual. What this means is that he will not only fall in love with Rubempré but will also hate women—in Balzac's eyes a doubly fatal flaw, for woman in his mythology stood on the one hand for morality and mysticism (Séraphita) and on the other hand for society (social success being granted by women, who hold the keys to fortune in their salons). Henriette de Mortsauf in *Le Lys dans la vallée* fills both roles at once. An angel of purity, she also guides Félix de Vandenesse's first steps in Parisian society.

Vautrin rejects all of this. He is part of the underside of society, which he seeks to dominate by his will to power. He, too, hopes to draw strength from love, but by using Rubempré as the docile instrument of his machinations. Unfortunately, Rubempré is weak and inconsistent, a young heterosexual in thrall to the social system, to its values and its women. In love with a woman and wild with social ambition, he denies Vautrin, who has been passing himself off as Rubempré's father, and then, like Judas, hangs himself in despair.

There is no question that Vautrin is a more three-dimensional character than Valjean, who looks quite insipid and superficial by comparison. Is this merely because Balzac is a greater novelist than Hugo? Is it because characters defined and guided by the environment—heroes of the left—are less impressive than those whose lives are shaped through and through by an inborn passion? The same question arises from a comparison of Corneille with Racine. Corneille's heroes are quiet family men propelled into tragedy by external and fortuitous circumstances—think of the slap that Don Gormas administers to Don Diègue—whereas Racine's heroes carry tragedy within themselves, like a secret of the heart. The controversy has raged on over the centuries, and at many levels. My philosophical predecessors stand in the wings, prompting me with an answer. If the drama of the right-wing hero is greater and more gallant than that of the left-wing hero, the reason is that the former's relation to the drama is one of essence, the latter's one of contingency. Now, whatever else can be said, essence is always superior to accident.

The motor of *Gemini* is fueled by this great controversy. The twins while still quite young are like a cell that lives solely on its hoard of heredity, but soon that cell must submit to the assaults of the external world. The twins react in opposite ways. Paul sees himself as the curator of their intimacy, the protector of their "gemel" games, while Jean shakes off his brother's tutelage and succumbs to the strange and bitter charms of the "single" world. Compared with the gemel society composed of Jean and Paul, single society might seem lame, impure, and vulnerable to the vicissitudes of time and age. Nevertheless, it yields satisfactions, meager and rare, perhaps, yet to Jean's taste incomparable in their flavor, tart and musky like certain desert berries. In other words, if one had to situate the two brothers politically, Paul would be on the right, Jean on the left.

I did not invent gemel happiness but discovered it in my conversations with twins and in numerous studies of twinship. It has negative as well as positive aspects. Statistics show that the proportion of unmarried twins is higher than that of unmarried non-twins. Why are twins less likely to marry? Obviously because they are given lifetime partners at birth. Lifetime? Not always. It is easy to imagine a twin, exasperated at being forced to share his life with another, leaving to savor the charms of solitude to the end of his days. An American researcher has analyzed lists of graduates of leading universities, names in *Who's Who,* and other presumed indicators of success. He found that twins were *fifteen times* less likely to succeed than their numbers in the general population would suggest. Twinship is obviously no advantage when it comes to success.

But if twins are less likely to succeed in life, is it not perhaps because their lives are already more successful than those of non-twins? In so many cases social and financial success is merely compensation for a deeper and less visible failure.

Gemel unhappiness—a tale such as that told in *Gemini,* in which one brother "betrays" the other—also follows a predictable pattern. An unmarried young woman whose twin sister had married gave me in an interview the following interpretation of their common history: "I was the one the fellow was courting. I turned him down out of loyalty to my sister. I wanted to preserve our happiness. So he turned to her, which was easy because of our resemblance. And that bitch ran off with him!" I do not necessarily accept this interpretation at face value. Very likely the sister or her husband would have told a different story. Whether true or not, however, this interpretation is typical of the twin's fate. Few twins live apart by mutual consent. The terrible words that I have Paul say after Jean's departure I actually took from a study of twinship: "After the intimacy of twinship, any other kind of intimacy can only be experienced as disgusting promiscuity."[4]

Is there a form of sexuality peculiar to twins? No doubt there is, but we must be careful not to interpret it in "single" terms. It is commonly acknowledged that the vast majority of children discover sex through masturbation. When twin brothers or twin sisters are brought up in conditions of complete physical intimacy, they will obviously discover masturbation *together* and thus experience from the first what the single know only as a second and often quite late form of sexuality, the couple.[5] The difference is important, and it gives twins a distinctiveness that is the principal subject of *Gemini.* Furthermore, the misunderstandings, conflicts, and disagreements to which the differences between two distinct physiologies normally give rise are largely smoothed out in relations between twin brothers or twin sisters. Each has an innate, prophetic, infallible knowledge of the other's body and nervous system. The two partners are immediately and congenitally attuned to each other. Thus to a twin, mating with a non-twin partner seems like a risky and rather scandalous adventure.

Is it correct to describe such relations as homosexual or incestuous? Certainly not, for even taken together those two words are far too feeble to describe the intensity of relations between twins—too feeble because homosexuality and incest as practiced by non-twins are but crude, imperfect approximations to *gemellarity*. The counterfeit does not account for the original, the original accounts for the counterfeit. If a business executive from the city spends his two-week vacation in the mountains, you might say that for those two weeks he lives like a mountain man. But you wouldn't say that a mountain man lives all year round like a businessman on vacation. From the standpoint of incest and homosexuality, gemellarity looks like an inaccessible absolute. It is an indubitably authentic original, compared with which incest and homosexuality are mere clumsy copies. Concerning the sexual happiness of twins and the couple's slow "emergence" from its cell on its way to "mixed" sexuality via maternal incest and "singular" homosexuality, let me cite from an (anonymous) letter that I received from a pair of twins after the publication of *Gemini:*

> Dear Mr. Tournier,
>
> We are identical twin brothers, so you can imagine what a personal interest we took in your long book *Gemini*. Now that we are grown up, our twinship has evaporated and we lead separate lives. Nevertheless, there remain between us a friendship and affection that will live, I believe, as long

as we do. Our psychological separation was accomplished without trauma when we were about twenty. In childhood and adolescence we were in every sense ONE. Physically we were dead ringers, both the same height, with the same brown hair cut the same way, the same face, even the same clothes. At school and summer camp no one ever referred to us by our first names; we were always "the twins." My brother was my best friend and I his. We were inseparable, quite literally identical. Being fairly good looking, we were attractive to classmates and teachers (and even teachers' pets), but we were jealous of each other and both rejected the advances of older children and adults, which occurred at camp. When one of us had a treat, he immediately looked to share it with his alter ego. Both of us remember one episode from our childhood as a particularly *emotional* experience: we met on the school playground, each with half a piece of pastry in his hand, worried that the other was nowhere to be found and that we would not be able to share our prize. Our relations were not only emotional but also physical. We masturbated together in the "boarding-school style," that is, mutually, ending with kisses on the mouth. Then, when we were about thirteen, we discovered fellatio. We swallowed each other's sperm just as in ordinary friendships two boys will mingle their blood. When we were fifteen or sixteen, we attempted a more intimate union and actually copulated, taking active and passive roles in turn. Our heterosexual desires were focused on our mother. Both of us had sexual relations with our mother from puberty to late adolescence. Instead of making us jealous, this little family secret oddly drew us together in a kind of conspiracy. Until we were eighteen, the only form of physical pleasure we knew was incestuous and "endogamous": between brother and brother and between mother and son. No one to my knowledge suspected the unusual nature of our family habits, although our parents were divorced and my mother had no regular lover. Perfect twinship is surely an aphrodisiac and a spur to incest. To love yourself mirrored in your partner's face is no doubt the secret attraction of incest, which is so powerful and so powerfully repressed. One has to experience the special flavor of incestuous love, which is ultimately narcissistic and which makes normal love seem pale by comparison. As adolescents our twinship elicited countless propositions to pose in the nude for painters and photographers. Amateur pornographers offered us large sums for striking incestuous homosexual poses. Even our own father, womanizer that he was, was not insensible to the ambiguous charms of his twin boys. He had a way of touching us that went beyond the usual fatherly affection and familiarity. One night at his house things actually went pretty far. (It is true that we were all pretty well drunk after celebrating our seventeenth birthday in a strip-tease joint.) The next day relations between us seemed strained, and the subject was never mentioned again. Yet another family secret! Sometimes alcohol brings out the dual sexuality that I think is in all of us, hetero as well as homo. After age eighteen, we sampled exogamy, what you call "single" loves— sampled it, but at first *together*. We had a mistress in common, an older woman, old enough to be our grandmother but quite a pervert and greatly stimulated by our being twins. We were also kept as a "couplet" by a wealthy widower in his sixties, obsessed with incest and twinship. In both of these triangular affairs, one with a woman, the other with a man, we were encouraged to make love to each other while they looked on. Yet at the age of twenty, by some mystery of nature, we embarked more or less painlessly on independent sexual lives. We were both able to sleep with girls and boys without the stimulus of a "twin" in the same bed. The purification of carnal desire through brotherly love strengthened the emotional and intellectual bonds between us, however, and heightened our need to exchange ideas on a daily basis. Sexually we are both still bisexual, though predominantly hetero.

Your book captivated us in spite of its length and the rather heavy-handed portrayal of certain characters such as Uncle Alexander, though neither of us is prudish or squeamish and both have been practicing homosexuals since childhood. We prefer the admirable *Ogre*.

With sincere regards,
Two Twin Readers

For these twins it is clear that incest and homosexuality were not part of their natural gemel state but first concessions to the singular world and stages along the way to mixed sexuality, that is, exogamy combined with heterosexuality.

That is why the two homosexuals in *Gemini,* Uncle Alexander and his friend Father Thomas Koussek, are secondary characters, despite Alexander's flamboyant and brilliant personality. There is a risk of misinterpretation here, and more than one reader has read the book as Alexander's story and been disappointed by his death, which, taking place as it does two-thirds of the way through, leaves an immense, incomprehensible coda. I concede that while writing I was overwhelmed by this somewhat too conspicuous and obtrusive character. My response was relatively mild. I might have cut him out altogether, but it seemed to me that with Alexander the novel gained not only in strength but also in subtlety. Chronologically the first two chapters should have been reversed. The story would have gotten off to a quicker start. But the imbalance in favor of Alexander would have been even worse, and this objection proved decisive. I console myself for the unforeseen excrescence of this character with the thought of two illustrious precedents. Surely neither Balzac nor Proust foresaw the extravagant importance that would be taken on by Vautrin in *The Human Comedy* and Charlus in *Remembrance of Things Past,* multivolume works with innumerable characters that no single figure was supposed to dominate. Every novelist should know that if he turns a flamboyant homosexual genius loose in one of his books, there is no hope of confining him within reasonable bounds. Patrick Modiano learned the same lesson in his subtle and delightful novel, *Villa Triste.*

Although Alexander is a secondary character, he is

nevertheless essential to the structure of the book. A number of mixed couples—Edouard and Maria-Barbara, Ralph and Déborah, Olivier and Selma, Urs and Kumiko—revolve around the pair of twins as satellites around a major planet. These heterosexual couples, immersed in the vagaries of time and history—of which their lives and the lives of their children form the very substance—are fascinated by the twin cell, by its very nature changeless, eternal, and sterile. And the heroes to whom they cling in order to alleviate the anxiety they feel as ephemeral creatures subject to death and decay are simply twins disguised as mixed couples but possessing the twin's privilege of eternal youth: Tristan and Isolde, Romeo and Juliet—couples that never grow old but for whom procreation is impossible.

Alexander establishes a bridge between the twin planet and its mixed satellites. He is a hybrid, a bastard, and as such a much more interesting character for fiction than the lawful and orderly. I say that Alexander is a hybrid because he partakes of both gemellarity and singularity. He was born a single individual, without a twin brother, but he refuses to accept his condition and claims the privileges of a twin. Instead of marrying and having children as a good "single" should, he longs for a twin brother who does not exist. Paul compares him to Molière's "bourgeois gentleman," condemned by his low birth to sell dry goods and marry off his daughters but who refuses this modest destiny and usurps a higher station in life by daring to practice fencing, dancing, and philosophy, privileges of the aristocrat.[6]

Being pseudo-twins, Alexander and Koussek hit upon certain pseudo-truths of twinship which despite their imperfection are not without interest. Koussek gives the novel a religious dimension. Religion was supposed to have been a major theme of the book, justifying my projected title *Le Vent Paraclet* ("The Paraclet Wind"), announced when *The Ogre* was published. Originally my plan was to restore the sacred character of celestial phenomena by combining theology with meteorology, the former embracing the spirit, the sacred, and the divine, the latter the very concrete poetry of rain, snow, and sun. The sky or heaven is both the air and the abode of God and the saints, and my intention was to eliminate the difference between these two meanings and continue the exploration of the solar cult begun at the end of *Friday*. By identifying the Holy Spirit with the wind and each wind with a different spirit I hoped to construct an aeolian theology. The twins would have occupied the central role as intercessors between heaven and earth. In a number of mythologies studied by Frazer in *The Golden Bough,* twins do indeed control the clouds and the rain. There is a perfectly logical reason for this, by the way, for a twin birth indicates a mother of exceptional fertility, and rains make the earth fertile. Thus there is a deep affinity between twins and rain, which is reflected among several tropical tribes by the custom of carrying twin babies in procession through fields made sterile by drought, much as Catholics carry the Blessed Sacrament in procession on Rogation Day.

In fact, however, the novel developed along much more profane lines. The sacred made only sporadic appearances. My research on Joachim of Floris, millenarianism, and the place of the Holy Spirit in orthodox theology, carried out with the assistance of Olivier Clément, professor of orthodox theology at the Institut Saint-Serge, proved exciting and enriching but did not find the place in the novel that I had hoped. I had expected that the Paraclete wind (the Holy Spirit returned to meteorology) would undergo a double metamorphosis, becoming both word and flesh. The third person of the Trinity is in fact responsible for impregnating the Virgin Mary as well as for bestowing the gift of tongues upon the apostles, actions commemorated respectively by the Annunciation and Pentecost. Thomas Koussek, Christ's twin, might have taken on major importance as prophet of the Holy Spirit. But the work, proliferating independently, developed along lines of its own, lines of space and time made concrete by Paul's great journey of initiation. Koussek, like Alexander, remains a mere sidelight, illuminating the overall structure of the edifice from a particular angle. He resolves, for example, the problem of broken symmetry created when one twin survives another (which is the subject of the last third of the book) by stating that the apostle Thomas Didymus (Thomas the Twin) is an absolute or divine twin, whose only twin brother is God himself in the person of Christ. He divides the world into three spheres: heaven under the jurisdiction of the Father; earth under the jurisdiction of the Son; and finally, under the jurisdiction of the Holy Spirit, an active and turbulent—in a word, meteorological—intermediate zone filled with humors and vortices and enveloping the earth like a muff. All of this is not unrelated to the final apotheosis of Paul, who lies in bed a helpless cripple yet by way of his amputated left limbs actually merges with the heavens. (The amputated limbs grow to tremendous size, as is known to happen with "phantom limbs.") Similarly, his direct, unmediated comprehension of the voices of plants and stars was anticipated by Koussek with his dreams of a profound language, a weighty tongue whose words are germs of things themselves rather than, like human words, their partial and misleading reflection.[7]

Alexander's strength lies elsewhere. In the first place he

is the twins' scandalous uncle, their father's brother. I believe in the importance of such a figure in children's eyes. The father stands for order, honor, and wisdom. The uncle belongs to the same generation yet is stripped of authority and responsibility. How attractive that makes him! I myself had a scandalous uncle. This is not the place to recount his sad, violent, and exemplary tale. And I hope that by now I have become the scandalous uncle of my own nephews and nieces.

Alexander had several models. The most important of these was a woman, Louise Falque, whom I met during her retirement at Barbizon; an authentic episode from her life appears in the novel. Now more than eighty, Louise Falque was raised by her father, a garbage-picker who lived off the dumps at Miramas. At age fourteen her father offered her a pipe to smoke for the first time, and she has never worn female clothing since. Seldom do I travel to the south of France without stopping at Barbizon for a visit. She is a tiny gnome of a woman with close-cropped gray hair. Propped up by two canes, she speaks in a gruff, bantering voice with her pipe clenched between her teeth. She has grown old in the company of her lifelong friend, the painter Germaine Hennes, and it is a distressing sight to see those two lonely women clinging to each other as they fall ever more tightly into the grip of madness and disease. Each one takes me aside to say, "My poor friend is very ill, but if she dies first I'll kill myself." During my last visit Louise told me that a pair of bandits had moved into the attic of the house (which has no attic), and that they were plotting to kill her. She heard them making plans at night. The older one spoke with authority to the younger, who was in fact so young that his voice was still changing. Louise had called the police, who had inspected the premises and done nothing but confiscate the hunting rifle that she had taken to keeping by her side at all times. "They thought I was senile!" she shouted indignantly. She was the person from whom I heard about the shipment of dead dogs, the first load of garbage sent from Paris after the exodus of June 1940 to the dump at Saint-Escobille, where she found herself all alone. Together with a horrified Lucien Clerge I visited the dump at Miramas (which serves the city of Marseilles) to check her memory. I know no one tougher than that diminutive little lady, whose spirit animates Alexander's combative, unyielding carcass.

I see Alexander as a person rather like Barbey d'Aurevilly or Maurice Barrès,[8] thin, stooped, insolent, old-fashioned, provocative, standoffish, and witty. Creating him was a two-stage process, as with my other somewhat monstrous characters: the twins, the Red Dwarf, and Tiffauges. After surveying him objectively from outside, I adopted his point of view and described the world and its inhabitants as seen through his spectacles. Just as the twin Paul revealed the "singular" world and the Red Dwarf taught me that the world is full of men who totter like stilt birds on long, fragile legs, Alexander served as my vantage point on heterosexual society. Therein lay the novelty of the character, which no doubt accounts for the indignation with which he was greeted by certain critics. Homosexual characters have long been a part of the novel, and if homosexuals are not yet first-class citizens in real life they are in fiction. But Alexander was not content simply to exist; he insisted on bestowing existence on heterosexuals as well. He talks about them endlessly, names them, marks them, paints them with rouge. Shocking! For heterosexuals have always pretended to be one with nature, the family, morality, and society and therefore believed they could simply melt away into the background, much as a brown-feathered partridge cannot be seen against the plowed earth. True, in recent years they have attracted plenty of attention with all the talk of birth control pills, abortions, divorce, and the demographic diarrhea of the third world. How could they think they would be able to go on passing themselves off as nature and morality incarnate? Alexander merely tore off the heterosexual's mask and splashed his astonished face with red paint. A hundred years ago it was a bold stroke to call homosexuality by its name in a novel. The bold stroke in *Gemini* was to call heterosexuality by its name.

As for the garbage dump, there you have the novel's degree zero. Previously, in *Friday,* Crusoe had wallowed with the pigs when the world became too much for him. In *The Ogre* Tiffauges had commented with subtlety and passion on his own waste. (Let me note in passing that the howls provoked by this passage of the novel reveal a certain ignorance of French literature, in which there is a veritable tradition of the man inspecting his own chamber pot. Without even doing any research I can recall scenes of this sort in Rabelais, Molière, and Huysmans.) As stated previously, my novels are all attempts to render certain metaphysical ideas in the form of images and stories. Well, it's a simple fact that ontology when tossed into the crucible of fiction undergoes a partial metamorphosis into scatology. The quagmire is not all negative, moreover. You can't simply avert your eyes and forget about it. It is subtly structured and full of meaning. Amid the noxious vapors of the wallow Robinson reeling from despair and lack of oxygen sees faces from his past. For Tiffauges human waste is the subject of a prolix and preposterous science, coprology, in which Göring is an expert. And Alexander sees in the heaps of garbage a vast accumulation of brainpower in the form of wrappings, envelopes, discarded paper, and so on—form without substance (or form whose substance is used up, such as an empty toothpaste tube), covered with signs, a loquacious literature without a subject, comprising instruction manuals, newspapers, advertising leaflets, declarations of love, poison pen letters, and who knows what else. It seems, moreover, that some people are capable of being revolted by the idea that garbage is not undifferentiated matter but possesses a thousand forms and a thousand voices.

In June 1972 I toured Iceland with Christiane Baroche. There we met Selma and Olivier, Selma acting as guide and Olivier her faithful and melancholy companion.

In April 1974 I went to Japan with Edouard Boubat. The 747 was three-quarters empty, and apart from Boubat, the wife of the French ambassador to Japan, and myself, all the passengers were Japanese. We were flying over the Arctic Circle when the captain came back to inform us that Georges Pompidou had died. I was reminded that I had been in southern Morocco when I learned three days after the fact of the death of Charles de Gaulle. Apparently my trips are not good for the health of French presidents. We spent two weeks in Japan, an absurdly short time for anyone who would write anything objective about the country. I circumvented the difficulty by casting the Japanese chapter of *Gemini* in the form of a journal kept by a French traveler—Paul—who is visiting the country for the first time and who stays two weeks. There being total coincidence between my hero and myself, I was in no danger of making a mistake. I should add that I had a splendid and expert guide in the eminent specialist in Japanese affairs, Bernard Frank, at that time director of the Maison Franco-

Japonaise. Acting as our guide and interpreter was a tiny, elderly woman with the amusing name Mitsu Kikuchi, who proved to be of inestimable service. One of my most vivid impressions was of a restaurant whose glass walls were licked by spray from the highly agitated ocean nearby. We left our shoes in a sort of cloakroom, put on slippers chosen from an enormous and rather filthy pile, and looked for a place among the crowd of revelers spread out over three stories. Whole families in their Sunday best sat or knelt around large, low tables. Some were celebrating weddings, and at those tables the women wore kimonos, the men suits, and the children school uniforms. People sang and clapped their hands. Pots of miso soup simmered on gas-fired hot plates. The most popular dish looked like a doughnut of fish and fried batter, and another consisted of a heap of raw shellfish, fish, and ice cubes, all topped by a live but tailless lobster, antennae still quivering. In this gastronomic caravansary I thought of Flaubert: it was an odd combination of the barbarian feast from *Salammbô* and the wedding banquet from *Madame Bovary*.

I also crisscrossed Canada, again in the company of Edouard Boubat, from the Magdalen Islands in the mouth of the Saint Lawrence to Vancouver, which we reached by taking the Canadian Pacific Railway over the Rocky Mountains. But the most vivid and rewarding experience of all was surely the trip to Tunisia.

Ralph and Déborah in their garden at Djerba belong to the world of fiction, as does Hamida, the girl Paul meets in Venice's Piazza San Marco. But they owe a great deal to another, very real couple whose bailiwick was not Djerba but Hammamet: Violett and John Henson.[9] Hammamet is the lushest North African beach I know, and the one with the most beautiful gardens. In 1927 John and Violett—he American, she English—bought a large piece of land on the gulf and set about building a house and farm. Not a day went by when they did not in some way add to the beauty of the place, and their life there was an unforgettable memory for anyone fortunate enough to visit. (Georges Pérec describes the couple in his novel *Les Choses.*) Violett died first, followed on July 2, 1974, by John. Their graves lie side by side in a grove of eucalyptus. To anyone who knew the public face of their life together—the conversations, receptions, and endless parade of prestigious dinner guests—and who after their death suddenly discovered the secret, intimate, private side, this house, with its silence, its fragrance, its cabinets and drawers filled with letters, private diaries, bills, press clippings, photographs, telegrams, estimates, and manuscripts, the sensation is like that of being thrown abruptly into another world, into a country of fantastic but disturbing beauty. The Henson house, lost in its tropical garden, is always open to me thanks to Leila Menchari, who has become its loyal and attentive caretaker. I hesitate to avail myself of this privilege, however, for the atmosphere is one of such oppressively populous solitude that I can sometimes scarcely breathe, especially when the nights are hot and I wander naked through the portrait galleries and across the damp patio and of course the bedrooms, which have their stories to tell.

One thing that makes the memory of this couple so dear to me is my long-standing regret at having failed to make what might have been a crucial decision in my life. When I returned to France in 1950 after four years in Germany and found my hopes of an academic career abruptly dashed by my failure to pass the *agrégation,* I should have gone to live in an Arab country. There I would have assimilated a new civilization, learned a new language, absorbed a new religion. My ferocious mental appetite was ready for such exotic nourishment.

(Is it too late? You're only as old as you want to be, and it's never too late until you decide that it is. Besides, for one who was anything but an early bloomer and who has made up his mind to live to be a hundred, there is always time to start anew. The big problem is wealth, modest though it may be: no stouter chain exists than the gentle pleasures of house and garden. Sometimes I tell myself that fifteen years is long enough. It's time to sell, go somewhere else, and start over. But the thought of selling is like the thought of cutting off an arm or a leg. The truth is that as you grow old you grow fat, not just in girth but in the amount of space you take up in the world, in the happiness that you create instinctively without thinking about it as the years go by and that closes around you like a trap.)

Which brings me to the very serious problem of the nomadic life versus the sedentary life. Who has not dreamed of living two lives at once, one a life of perpetual wandering, a cosmopolitan quest for flesh, images, landscapes, the other a quiet, stay-at-home existence behind a wall of books, devoted to fermentation of the gray matter and harvest of its precious distillates? Alas, we have but one life to live, and if we spend it on the road we accomplish nothing for want of opportunity to reflect and meditate. But if we stay at home, habit and laziness soon throw a gray pall over people and things and we cease to feel, see, or think. I travel a lot—far too much, grumbles the sedentary grump who lives somewhere within me—and it does me a lot of good. But I hate to leave home, and the whole time I am away I can never overcome the remorse and anxiety I feel at having left house, garden, and friends behind. People sometimes think that it is easier for a bachelor to travel than for a man with a large family. In fact, the opposite is true. For the man who travels with his wife and children brings the essential part of his life with him, its human core. Whereas the core of the bachelor's life is dispersed. It consists of friends, relatives, familiar faces that cannot be taken along. When the bachelor travels, he loses everything. He goes into exile and dooms himself to a frightful solitude.

Heredity versus environment, the nomadic versus the sedentary life: we thus come back to the final third of *Gemini,* to the break between Jean and Paul after the death of Uncle Alexander and to Paul's search for Jean. From a technical standpoint the death of Alexander was a danger-ous move. The untimely removal of such a powerful and colorful character sapped the novel of its tension, and more than one reader has told me that he lost interest at this point and put the book down. The hurdle was a diffi-cult one for me, too, and with Alexander killed off I went into a kind of stupor, a dreadful state of depression in which I remained for more than a month, incapable of proceeding with the book. That was in January 1973. But it was really a question of remedying a misconception. Al-exander had done all that it was in his power to do when he discovered the formula "ubiquity = twinship un-twinned."

This formula is suggested by a game of hide-and-seek, in which the twins turn up minutes apart at widely sepa-rated points in the city, so that if there were only one per-son involved, as Alexander initially believes, he would have to have been blessed with the gift of ubiquity. At the end of the novel Paul discovers the reverse of this formula, which crowns the book much as the formula $E = mc^2$ crowns Einstein's physics: "twinship untwinned = ubiq-uity." True, Paul arrives at this equation not by reasoning but through painful experience and after a lengthy journey of initiation. It sums up the meaning of the twins' great voyage.

Movement is a synthesis of time and space. Paul and

Jean's journey can be analyzed as the combination of twinned time with twinned space.

Languages derived from Latin such as Italian, Spanish, and French have only one word to denote what English calls *time* and *weather* and German *Zeit* and *Wetter*. But the Latins are not entirely wrong to conflate these two notions. They intersect in a number of ways. The seasons, for example, are defined by calendar dates and start and end at a precise *time,* yet each is associated with a definite kind of *weather*. The underlying subject of *Gemini* is nothing other than the lost coincidence of the two meanings of *temps* (time, weather) followed by the restoration of identity—a great theme, but not an entirely original one, for it is also the subject of Jules Verne's *Around the World in Eighty Days*.

Passepartout's first meeting with Phileas Fogg is a masterpiece of comedy. Passepartout is a tired nomad. He has tried every occupation including that of acrobat and traveled in twenty countries. He is looking for a haven, a place of rest, and an employer with nothing up his sleeve. Thus he is delighted to meet Phileas Fogg, for the Englishman comes on from the first as a stickler for promptness and regularity. A greater homebody cannot be imagined. He dismissed his previous servant for bringing shaving water at a temperature of eighty-four degrees rather than eighty-six. The two men are made for each other. As Passepartout says to himself, "I swear I've known gentlemen as lively as my new master at Madame Tussaud's!" He then inspects the premises and in the room assigned to him finds an electric clock that strikes "to the second" precisely the same time as the clock in Fogg's room. Indeed, the new master is a walking clock. Passepartout is ecstatic: "That suits me just fine! A veritable mechanic!"

A few hours later, Phileas Fogg returns unexpectedly.

Dumbfounded, Passepartout learns that they are to leave on a round-the-world tour in ten minutes.

Sedentary and finicky as he is, Phileas Fogg knows all the world's almanacs and schedules by heart. He is in his own way a traveler, an armchair traveler. He has an abstract, bookish understanding of travel, and he has deduced a priori that it should be possible to travel around the world in eighty days. The confrontation between this a priori knowledge and harsh reality is the heart of the novel, surely the most profoundly philosophical ever written. True, Cervantes' *Don Quixote* has a similar theme: the confrontation between the bookish notions of chivalry with which Quixote has gorged himself and the mediocrity of modern reality. But Cervantes does not even come close to the almost mathematical rigor of *Around the World in Eighty Days.*

A walking timepiece sets out to cross oceans and continents. The obstacles he must overcome are essentially meteorological in nature. The journey must be made *against wind and tide.* Passepartout with his blunders and tantrums embodies those obstacles, because for him, as a Frenchman, Time and Weather are one and the same, and he finds it normal that the hours counted out by the clock should be splattered with rain and illuminated by sunshine. While Fogg is identified with his chronometer, Passepartout is the man of the changing heavens, always in the grip of some unpredictable humor.

The implacable chronometer at first triumphs over the likeable acrobat. In the running battle with his servant Fogg scores a point with the forgotten gaslight, which continues to burn in Passepartout's bedroom. It is like an hourglass, a Foggian chronometer in Passepartout's private sanctum, which minute by minute is driving him further into ruin: he calculates that 1,920 hours' worth of gas will be deducted from his wages upon his return.

Yet this minor defeat will soon be eclipsed by brilliant victories. Initially the servant's blunders diminish Fogg's chances of success, but in the end the journey is triumphant thanks solely to Passepartout's efforts, and Fogg wins only by accepting his servant's confusion of Time and Weather. It is Passepartout who informs Fogg that by traveling from west to east, that is, ahead of the sun, he has gained twenty-four hours and is therefore returning to London after eighty days and not eighty-one as measured on his chronometer. Hence he has won his bet. It takes Passepartout's empirical, concrete, solar perception of time to recognize this simple fact. One is reminded of the passage in which Kant proves that the perception of space cannot be reduced to a mere concept of the understanding because of the existence of right and left. Even if there were but one hand in the world, it would have to be either a right hand or a left hand, a fact that the understanding for all its concepts will never comprehend.

Boldly taking the place of a dead rajah on his funeral pyre, Passepartout saves a pretty Hindu widow from the flames and takes her back to London. It soon becomes apparent that the impassive Fogg is not insensible to the young woman's exotic charms. Thus at the conclusion of the voyage Passepartout's triumph is complete. He has worked an incomparable miracle, causing a heart to beat in that chronometer of a man, Phileas Fogg. The marriage of Time and Weather has been consummated.

Few changes would be required to apply this analysis of *Around the World in Eighty Days* to *Gemini*. The twins Paul and Jean are to Time and Weather as Phileas Fogg and Passepartout. Paul is a man who views the heavens in an astronomical sense; he is rational, mathematical, and takes things to be totally predictable. Jean is joyfully accepting of the sky's infidelity, of sunshine and rain. Their story is that of the triumph of chronology over meteorology, of the intrusion of dawns and clouds into the clockwork of the heavens. Paul formulates the problem he must solve in these terms: "To find Jean. To bring him back to Bep. But even as I formulate this plan I see another, incomparably greater and more ambitious, looming behind it: to seize control of the troposphere itself, to rule the weather, to become master of the sun and the rain . . . to make myself the shepherd of the clouds and the winds." The journey is more the outward sign than the occasion of this metamorphosis.

Now is the time to say a word about the painter Urs Kraus's theory of "qualitative space." In kinetics objects are assumed to move in a perfect, uniform vacuum subject to no external force. This is obviously an abstraction, and the precise opposite would surely be closer to actual experience. Now, the precise opposite of a motion subject to no external force would be a motion occurring within the substance of the moving object itself, that is, a case of simultaneous *translation* and *alteration*.

This theory derives entirely from reflection upon the philosophy of Henri Bergson and is nothing more than an application to space of his analysis of the notion of time.[10] Instead of conceiving of time as a perfect, uniform vacuum in which every instant is identical to every other—a concept that is nothing more than space disguised as time for the purposes of abstract thought—Bergson imagined time as a concrete, qualitative duration, an irreducibly unique substance which for him was the stuff of life itself. In short, he assumed that time is inconceivable without change, or to put it more formally, alteration. It is remark-

able, incidentally, that the word *alteration*—a classical category if ever there was one, first put forward by Aristotle
at the very dawn of philosophical thinking and revived by
Octave Hamelin, an idealist philosopher and contemporary of Bergson—is cited so far as I know only once in all
of Bergson's work. Perhaps the impressionist in him re-
belled at this overly rational and eminently traditional notion. Bergson, who produced a philosophy of animal instinct and mystical intuition, was himself all intelligence
and reason. This contradiction compelled him to mask his
true intentions. Had he placed an Aristotelian category like
alteration at the center of his philosophy, he would have
risked disturbing the mask and revealing the great classical
rationalist underneath.

Transposed from time to space, the notion of alteration
turns every translation into an adventure, not to say a journey of initiation—all the more so when the traveler is a
person of the hereditary rather than the environmental
type.

I hope the reader will indulge me if I digress for a moment to talk about myself. Whenever I meet a great traveler—a reporter, explorer, or better yet a compatriot
whose profession obliges him to live in one country after
another—I am almost always surprised and even a little
scandalized to note how little living in such different environments and accumulating exotic experiences seems to
affect a person's personality. Apparently most people are
coated with an impermeable layer of varnish that protects
them from external influences. For them, translation is not
accompanied by alteration. I find this striking because I am
so completely different. Like a sponge or pumice, I soak
up the foreign environment and emerge from it utterly
transformed. For me, every important trip initiates profound changes. Alain Bosquet sensed this when he wrote

that in my case autobiology takes precedence over autobiography. I am a haruspex who reads past, present, and future by opening my belly and examining my own entrails.

Paul's pursuit of Jean is a journey of initiation to the extent that it alters his very substance and inexorably leads him to the Berlin Wall, where he suffers ritual mutilation. The trip was guided by Paul's relation to Jean even when his brother was at the other end of the earth, for in twins the struggle between heredity and environment is complicated by a third factor: the intertwin relationship.

A non-twin is simply a mass of heredity immersed in a certain environment. But twins move in an "intertwin space" that both unites and divides, a zone of variable dimension within which intense exchanges occur. This space—real but reduced to a minimum when the twin babies lie together in their crib in the fetal position—stretches and thins when one twin flees the other, yet it never breaks, not even when stretched to cover the entire world, whose cities, forests, oceans, mountains, and deserts take on new meaning when deciphered according to the code of twinship. Thus Venice, Djerba, Iceland, Nara, Canada, and Berlin all acquire special meaning as part of intertwin space, which incorporates places as small as a Japanese garden or as vast as a Canadian prairie in alternating expansions and contractions reminiscent of the systole and diastole of the heart. This alternation continues until the fleeing brother disappears forever and the surviving twin is left in sole possession of the intertwin space, his soul unfurled like a flag flapping in the wind. What has become of his brother? Is he vanished, lost, or dead? No. He has simply been absorbed by his twin thanks to this journey through qualitative space, this profound process of alteration and initiation, this conquest of the heavens with their weather by man with his time.

6

SOPHIA'S MISFORTUNES

Wisdom is an impure silence.
—Ibn al Houdaidah

*I*t is not difficult to imagine how a well-informed musicologist might have summed up the situation at the beginning of the nineteenth century: "Music has always been closely identified with the society destined to be known henceforth as the Old Regime, so recently swept away by the French Revolution and Napoleon's Empire. Music died with it. If you doubt this, listen to Haydn, Handel, and Mozart, and you will soon recognize them for what they are, three expressions of a paradise forever lost. No doubt we shall now be treated to revolutionary chants and martial hymns, but not a single note of true music will be composed on the ruins of what was once an exquisite world."

The argument is impeccable, its conclusions irrefutable. It was indeed true that in 1800 it was literally impossible to create music. And then suddenly there was Beethoven. With him the impossible became real, and in the same moment cast its possibility retroactively into the past.

What is Beethoven? Beethoven is Mozart's music into which by some unimaginable stroke of genius the roar of the revolutionary mob and the blare of the Grand Army's trumpets have been incorporated. To convince yourself of this, just listen to Mozart's overture *Bastien and Bastienne* followed by the beginning of Beethoven's *Eroica* symphony. The themes are the same. But Mozart's piece dates from 1768—the year in which the Countess du Barry replaced Madame de Pompadour in Louis XV's bed—and it was written by a twelve-year-old child who was then dazzling all the courts of Europe. Thirty years later, the mature Beethoven took this youthful theme and, in a paradox without precedent, charged it with all the upheavals that Europe had endured in the interim. One might even consider the theme in the abstract, forgetting the two composers and listening to it as if the music itself had lived and grown old between 1768 and 1804, exchanging the pink plumpness of childhood for the deeply lined face of a man who, though still young, has seen a great deal of battle.

What this example illustrates is that an element of unpredictability and even absurdity enters into all creation. It also offers a striking instance of static alteration, the phenomenon I previously described as the opposite of translation without alteration, symbol of abstract mathematics and physics. By alteration I mean qualitative, substantial, irreversible, undefinable change. It is noteworthy that in a world dominated by scientific logic, the word *alteration* almost always denotes a change for the worse, a diminution, decomposition, or degradation due to age as required by the third law of thermodynamics. This same science holds that in nature nothing is ever created or destroyed and that mechanical energy is *more noble* than thermal energy, even though heat along with light is one of the two attributes of the sun. The scientific world view is abstract, utilitarian, and quantitative; it is the vision of the engineer. But alteration can be positive as well as negative, as is shown by the ripening of fruits, the aging of wines, the slow maturation of wisdom, and the metamorphosis under pressure of history of *Bastien and Bastienne* into the *Eroica*. In a word, alteration can also be creation.

Creation, and beyond that genius and then wisdom. It was inevitable that this essay would touch on these dangerous subjects, which involve life's highest values and are rooted in our common past, a past that would be less obscure today if Western civilization had not turned its back on it in order to seek technical solutions to technical problems. We are terrorized by abstract knowledge, part experimental and part mathematical, and by a rationalization of our moral code. It all smells of regimentation, and with regimentation we may exist but we cannot live.

Let us try to see things more clearly, starting with wisdom. What have we made of the word wisdom—or *sagesse, sophia, sapientia, Weisheit?* In French *sagesse* means not only wisdom but also glum docility when applied to children and senile resignation when applied to the elderly. "Loose teeth, spineless wisdom," said Ambrose Bierce. Speaking of Sophie von Kühn, a fourteen-year-old girl dying of tuberculosis, Novalis said, "I am a philosopher because I love Sophie." Historically, this touching pun sounded the death knell of philosophy and wisdom as well as poor Sophie. For it was Romanticism that dug wisdom's grave.

For Socrates, Plato, and Aristotle, Sophia was the absolute best, the Sovereign Good. What exactly does that mean? A kind of knowledge that is also a rule of conduct: it is action identified with spirit, efficacious enlightenment. Conversely, the wicked action or crime can have no other source but ignorance, stupidity, or failure of the spirit. Stupidity and wickedness are identical in theory as well as practice. Ideas never entirely die out. Victor Hugo unexpectedly revived this old wisdom of the ancients, their identification of knowledge with morality, when he said, "To open a school is to close a prison"—a generous idea, which equates the fight against crime with the fight against illiteracy. Uttered in the middle of the nineteenth century, however, its anachronism was flagrant. For while it may be generous to view the murderer as an uneducated man, by doing so one inevitably turns the uneducated man into a potential murderer—a terrifying thought. It amounts to saying that an ignorant man is capable of anything, and that if a crime is committed anywhere, the police should look for the illiterate brute who committed it. It is obvious where such thinking leads. The truth is that belief in the ancient wisdom is inseparable from the most frightful sort of enlightened despotism. In any case, to grant the ignorant, uncultivated man the benefit of innocence is to consign him to animality. South Africa's white rulers achieve the ultimate in racism by subjecting blacks to an attenuated penal code from which the harshest penalties have been eliminated, as if negritude were a priori an extenuating circumstance. People even ascribe varying degrees of responsibility to animals depending on the supposed intelligence of the species. A dog that steals is punished but not a cow or pig that wanders into a field of crops.

Nevertheless, the wisdom of the ancients lived on in fairly robust health until the eve of the French Revolution.

To take only the greatest example, Spinoza (1632–77) identified clear and distinct ideas with action, while passion, which for him meant passivity plus emotion, was nothing more than a confused and mutilated idea. He quite naturally gave his great metaphysical treatise the title *Ethics*. In it we read that the sage is a man whose life is guided by reason (book 4, theorem 24). The absolutely virtuous action is one guided solely by reason. There follows an admirable series of precepts, not random observations but geometrical deductions from a set of first premises (*more geometrico*). There is nothing about which the wise man thinks less than death, for wisdom is not a meditation upon death but a meditation upon life. The wise man is freer when he obeys the common laws of the city of which he is a citizen than when he lives in solitude and obeys only himself. The joy we feel at the sight of our enemy's suffering is not pure but mixed with a secret sadness.[1]

No more complete fusion of true knowledge with just action is conceivable, and nothing would have shocked Spinoza more than the idea that knowledge of the truth neither increases nor diminishes our knowledge of how we ought to act. Yet this idea would take hold a hundred years later under the influence of Rousseau and Kant.

The first blow was struck by Rousseau's *Emile* (1762). Everyone is familiar with that book's hymn to the moral conscience, but what needs greater emphasis is the fact that the hymn goes hand in hand with a full-scale attack on speculative reason:

> Conscience! Conscience! Divine instinct, immortal and heavenly voice . . . without thee I feel nothing in me that raises me above the beasts except for the sad privilege of straying from error to error aided only by undisciplined understanding and unprincipled reason. Thank heaven we are now delivered from philosophy with all its terrifying

apparatus. We can be men without being scholars. Dispensed from the need to spend our lives in the study of morality, we have a surer and less costly guide through the vast maze of human opinion.

In short, morality is within reach of every man's brain. Instinct: the word evokes the animal. But Rousseau immediately qualifies it as divine and asserts that conscience is what gives man his likeness to God. Conscience is therefore both animal and divine. In all this man is just a little bit neglected, not to say condemned as a ratiocinator and abstractor of quintessences. Caught between bestiality and divinity, he is left with no responsibility beyond blind obedience to the injunctions of his animal–divine conscience. Nor was this the first or the last time that a parallel would be drawn between the animal and God in order to draw a contrast between both and man. The animal is mute and God is silent, but man possesses the power of speech. Later, Bergson would use animal instinct as a model for metaphysical knowledge.[2] First, however, it was necessary and sufficient to deny that metaphysical understanding can be achieved by any rational means.

This was Kant's contribution, and paradoxically it was Newton's creation of modern physics that led Kant to this conclusion. The "discovery" (or more accurately *invention*) of the law of universal gravitation, applicable to both the planets and the objects of everyday life,[3] was a prodigious triumph of empirical observation coupled with mathematical reasoning (the lark of experiment plus the horse of mathematics). According to Kant, this discovery proved that intelligence was totally incapable of attaining metaphysical knowledge. From this fabulous *plus* for rational understanding Kant deduced a radical *minus*. (In the next generation Auguste Comte took the opposite view, seeking in his *Positive Philosophy* to derive everything from science: understanding, politics, religion, and all the rest.)

If Kant is right, then morality must supplant wisdom as a guide to living and acting properly. According to Charles Seignobos, love was invented at the end of the eleventh century. Morality is of much more recent origin, for it was not invented until the end of the eighteenth century, more precisely in 1785, when Kant published his *Foundations of the Metaphysics of Morals.* Rousseau had laid the groundwork. The French Revolution was to begin four years later. In the very first lines of this brief work the philosopher of Königsberg (today Kaliningrad) defined morality: "Nothing in the universe—in fact, nothing whatsoever—can we possibly conceive as *absolutely* good except a *good will.*"[4] There it is. The supreme good, which all the philosophers of Greek and Latin antiquity and baroque Europe believed could be discovered through the highest efforts of the finest minds, was reduced to nothing more than the resolve to do good. What a miracle of shrinking and vulgarization! Only the good will is an absolute, for wisdom can promulgate only conditional imperatives. Its prescriptions inevitably assume a concrete desire, such as the desire to be happy, to avoid suffering, to see children and friends prosper, and so on. To men with an ambition nobler and more disinterested than happiness, Kant tells us, wisdom has nothing to say. All the secondary moral qualities—courage, judgment, lucidity, decisiveness—can serve evil ends, in which case the more they are developed, the more harmful they become. Only the good will is absolutely good, and the imbecile and illiterate possess neither more nor less of it than the most cultivated of men.

Actually, three kinds of degeneration have occurred. First, Newton's mathematical physics has become the model of all knowledge, with an authority bordering on despotism, not to say terrorism. Second, action and knowledge have been totally divorced. Action is henceforth to be based on categorical imperatives, as formal, unchallengeable, and opaque as military regulations. Third, as we saw earlier, education in the late eighteenth century lost its initiatory content and became merely a vehicle for imparting useful occupational information to children.

Defunct wisdom thus decomposed into mathematical and physical science, formal morality, and utilitarian information. "Blame Rousseau and blame Voltaire": was Gavroche right when he sang his accusatory ditty on the barricades of revolutionary Paris?

Surely we have better things to do than conduct a posthumous trial of the great men who built modern Western civilization. But the changes that have taken place warrant a moment's pondering. For twenty-five centuries Western man basked in the simple, unadorned sun of wisdom. One day that ardent, radiant heart broke into a thousand pieces. Its venerable debris lie at our feet, still warm and vital, but there is no point attempting to put them back together in order to restore what was. The least we can do, however, is pick up the pieces one by one, examine how they fit together, and look within ourselves for what remains of the immemorial institution of wisdom in its natural and untamed state.

Wisdom is temporal. Only contingent circumstances prevent me from learning physics, astronomy, or genetics in a matter of days or even hours. Given that these sciences are abstract constructs that can be fully mastered by memory and intelligence, the time required to absorb them is a purely technical matter and depends only on educational technique. There can be no doubt that computer-aided instruction will considerably reduce the time needed to master these subjects.

By contrast, when it comes to a living language, which is by definition deeply rooted in the realities of life, all I can hope to learn via accelerated methods is an emaciated residue of the real thing. In learning any language time inevitably plays a role. To fully assimilate a language one must immerse oneself in the environment in which it is spoken.

The fact that concrete knowledge invariably takes time to acquire is best expressed in Luke 2:52: "And Jesus increased in wisdom and in stature, and in favor with God and man."[5] There you have a process in which the time factor is not only absolutely essential but also irreducible. Wisdom is inseparable from stature and age. That explains the child-oriented connotations of the word *wisdom* in a language such as French, in which we speak of *enfants sages* (well-behaved children) and order the young to behave themselves by telling them to "be wise." For wisdom is living, almost biological knowledge; it is a matter of successful maturation, of full enjoyment of a mature body and spirit. For wisdom time is an inward duration, a question of living memory in which nothing is ever lost or forgotten, and not the uniform, abstract time of physics with its ballistic trajectories. Wisdom is alteration, maturation, change.

Strictly speaking, therefore, no adult can ever be wise. Adulthood is the period of stagnation that follows childhood, life disengaged from duration. Each moment is a grain of sand added to the child under construction. When the child stops incorporating the sand, it quickly buries him. Learning ceases to be an adventure. Implicit in this marking time is the disaster of old age. The senile are not to be pitied: they have merely become what they already were.

The best lives never reach the adult phase. Each new self is an additional treasure. Time exists exclusively in the predicate *temporary*. Hidden beneath the old man's mask is an astonished child.

Wisdom is intransmissible. Experience is a deceptive word. In French the word *expérience* has two meanings: it can mean an experiment, a test designed to confirm or deny a hypothesis, or it can mean knowledge accumulated over the years, which is to say, wisdom. English has the two words *experiment* and *experience,* and German, *Experiment* and *Erfahrung*.

Now, while the results of an experiment can easily be communicated, there is no way of enabling another person to profit from insight and experience gained over a lifetime. The terms in which such insight and experience are formulated are never adequate and merely cause the young to shrug their shoulders. They have no idea what to do with your advice, even if they are disposed to accept it. If people of experience often succumb to the temptation to give advice, it is because they confuse experience with experiment and think they can communicate the results. In reality, however, they are confusing two levels of knowledge, one profound, obscure, and intimately a part of heart, nerves, and genitals, the other abstract, cerebral, lightweight, and portable.

A look around is enough to convince us that large numbers of our contemporaries are unable to resign themselves to the death of wisdom, which is a blend of knowing and doing, and cling to one or another of its modern substitutes. Apparently, however, the decomposition of the ancient notion of the sovereign good has inexorably affected everything conceived subsequently in its image.

There can be no doubt that the Catholic religion in its glory days produced its own very powerful form of wisdom. Theology blossomed into a thousand subtleties, which in the realm of action admittedly took quite brutal forms. There was an odd contrast between the fine nuances of theological argumentation and the monotony of the bonfires and massacres to which subtle *distinguos* invariably led. But now that both theology and bonfires are relics of the past, the Catholic is left with nothing to which the mind can cling but the fairy tales of dogma, while the Church all but totally abstains from the exercise of temporal power. The most positive thing the Church can offer the believer is the moral comfort of belonging to a community. Reassuring as this bond may be, it is hardly the equivalent of either theological knowledge or moral teaching. It may even be the opposite.

Much the same can be said about yet another modern form of wisdom, Marxism. What is Marxism if not a *scientific* analysis of nineteenth-century Western society from which a program of political action has been deduced? The *Communist Manifesto* follows logically from *Capital,* and the communist takes to the streets with book in hand.

Nevertheless, it appears that Marxism has been no less afflicted by Sophia's misfortunes than Catholicism. Among Marxists, too, knowledge and action have dissolved into sentimental quietism. I hardly need point out that socialism and communism are opposed as the thesis and antithesis of a dialectical process, which is to say, as water and fire. Socialism may be defined as hypertrophy of the state, with its attendant bureaucratic dictatorship and its twin daughters Penury and Tyranny, whereas communism implies the withering away of the state. Hence one cannot go from one to the other by means of gradual and painless reform. It will take a violent revolution, another Red October, perhaps even another Katherinenburg. In short, socialism must be drenched in blood before communism can reign. Yet to make this point openly, even though it is consistent with Marxist doctrine and is borne out by every existing socialist regime, somehow impedes solidarity among workers. It is therefore strenuously denied by socialist leaders, who confuse the issue by passing themselves off as communists in order to avoid being killed, much as factory owners used to try to pass off their paternalism as socialism in order to fend off the real thing.

For the communist the essence of man resides not in the head or in the legs, but midway between the two, in the chest, in the heart. To be a communist (or for that matter a Catholic) is to belong to a large family, a family with its own jargon, holidays, quarrels, and dreams. The important thing is not to philosophize or carry placards through the streets but to rub elbows with other family members and keep up their good cheer. Anything that threatens to disrupt the warm good feeling of *Humanité*'s annual fair[6] is to be dismissed as "extreme left-wing provocation." A clear example of this was seen during the events of May 1968, when rebellious students tried to enlist the support of communist cells at the Renault plant near Paris. It turned out that there was a total lack of comprehension between the young intellectuals, who wanted to change the world, and the petty-bourgeois workers, who only wanted to change cars before vacation.

Religion and politics do perhaps yield a kind of wisdom. It is not, however, the authentically revolutionary wisdom that comes from creation and solitude but the homely, reassuring "wisdom" of the well-behaved child, the product of a process of regression, as shriveled as a head that has passed through the hands of a Jivaro headshrinker.

Creation and solitude are inseparable. The natural setting of biological—paternal and even more maternal—creation is the family and society. By contrast, intellectual and artistic creation, revolutionary by vocation, is appar-

ently doomed to take place in loveless, friendless surroundings. Great creators stand in fierce isolation, like col-
umns in a desert. Those who pretended to ignore this fate
were cruelly punished for it. Think of Johann Sebastian
Bach and his two wives and twenty children and of the
terrible swath cut through this family by the hand of death
during Bach's own lifetime. Less presumptuous, Leonardo
da Vinci adopted a child. After letting his father down in
the worst way, the boy died young in a bawdy house brawl
without knowing that he had lived his brief life in the presence of Leonardo da Vinci. The creator has ample reason
to bemoan his fate. Around him he sees communities,
congregations, and families, and he dreams. He imagines
a layman's monastery in which the finest minds of his time
would share their thoughts in freedom from material
cares. What power would radiate from such a community![7] More modestly, he looks around and sees seemingly
ideal couples: husband and wife, mother and son, friends
male and female, boyfriend and girlfriend, brother and sister. Occasionally he might indulge in a pleasantly melancholy game. He will take a relative or friend and alter that
person's image to suit himself, creating an ideal brother or
sister or friend, whom he will then marry in his imagination. What exquisite pleasure to live with such a person at
his side! What wealth! What inspiration!

But is it really so? The more deeply he becomes involved in his idyll, the heavier his invisible chains. Worse
yet, the cerebral ferment that is his reason for being slows
and, as winemakers say, "begins to throw a crust." His
mind surrenders, and he falls into a serene sleep.

Hence he tells himself that freedom, solitude, and creation are inseparable. When thy heart breaks from loneliness, thy mind laughs with freedom and thy brain engen-
ders the most surprising progeny. Thy works are desert

fruits that flourish only in arid climes. Hear not my supplications, O Lord! and if perchance I some day draw near an oasis with warm heart and welcoming body, please drive me away with swift kicks and send me back into the steppes I know so well, where the wind that blows is the cold, dry wind of pure ideas! For the ideal extinguishes the idea as water extinguishes a fire.

The great ancient wisdom is dead, and we must decide what we want to do about it, for no one has yet been able to adapt it to the modern world. At the very least we can keep in mind three or four truths to help guide our conduct. On the whole we have no choice but to put up with what the Jivaro headshrinker does to us; yet we must travel light, as though on foot, and sleep outdoors rather than in the vast, tepid dormitories maintained by the great spiritual families of man. Like plants that are soft and fragile in the plains but at higher altitudes, between harsh sky and barren earth, develop a variety smaller, sturdier, and more restrained but no less colorful or fragrant, we can fashion for ourselves a philosophy of scarcity, a sagacity of subsistence, a beggar's Baedeker.

Jean Cocteau was moving toward such a miniaturization of the ancient wisdom when he expressed the wish that our notion of genius be humanized, dedramatized, and brought back down to earth: "I very much like the nonchalant way in which Stendhal uses the word genius. He sees genius in a woman getting into a carriage, a woman who knows how to smile, or a man who lets his opponent win at cards."[8] After Stendhal others conceived of genius in a very different light. They confiscated the small amounts of it possessed by every man in order to bestow great quantities upon a few chosen individuals named

Beethoven, Balzac, Hugo, and Wagner. These beacons loomed high above a stupid, sterile, antipathetic mob— Flaubert's notorious "bourgeoisie." A sad and depressing view of the world, and dishonest to boot. One day a professional questioner stuck a microphone into my face and asked, "So you think you're a genius, do you?" Without hesitating I answered, "Yes, like everyone else," echoing the sentiments of Françoise Mallet-Joris, who in similar circumstances responded, "No, I do not believe in either banality or mediocrity."

Yes, everyone has genius, which is not one huge gem but a scintillating diamond dust scattered over all mankind. Genius is the most natural thing in the world, the most commonplace. It is present wherever anyone exists, acts, walks, smiles, or speaks in a unique, inimitable manner, thus evoking the infinite, which is to be found in every truly creative act. Hence it is solely up to us to recognize genius, and when we do recognize it, to celebrate its existence. For at this degree of modesty genius is doomed to nothingness by blindness, myopia, hypermetropia—that widespread malady whose symptom is failure to see what lies right under our noses—or mere distraction. Mozart's *Don Giovanni* cannot be ignored. It is easier to miss the magical moment when a bird encounters the sun's rays. Beauty is the world's most widely distributed good, but in thrall to quotidian needs our gaze fails to take it in. Fatigue casts a gray veil over the world, and it takes the authoritative intervention of a painter, sculptor, or architect to lift it.

We are constantly tempted to confine beauty to its own special preserve, to museums, libraries, palaces, and formal gardens far from everyday life, and to shut ourselves up along with it, much as we might drench ourselves in perfume so as to keep real odors away from our nostrils.

Certain people suffer from a terrible malformation of the heart and perversion of sexual desire: they distinguish between what is beautiful and what is loveable, desirable, or sexually stimulating.[9] This ghettoization of beauty is typical of a sick mind, possibly damaged by some act of aggression suffered in childhood. More often beauty is smothered by our trivial concerns. Fortunately this is not always the case. Let me tell you what makes me feel like a king. I'm in a crowded subway car at six in the evening, with hundreds of other men and women harassed, worn out, and drained by sordid, tedious, and ultimately insignificant worries. I have no fewer worries than anyone else, nor am I less tired, but somewhere in that compact mass of humanity that sways with every acceleration and deceleration of the train I have seen a beautiful face, and my gaze rests on it as it would on a bird on a branch in bloom. In that close, foul-smelling subway car I have found a tiny, living oasis. Secretly I feel pleasure. I feast my eyes upon it. Among the multitude of the poor I am as rich as Croesus.

But more is needed than the dedramatization of genius that Cocteau desired. We must proceed toward an atomization of the absolute. We must grant the wish of every person and thing that cries out—often in an imperceptible voice—to be recognized as absolute.

What is the absolute? Etymologically it is that which has no rapport with, no relation to anything else. Hence it is a negative term, which simply blocks the mind's spontaneous, alienating, scientific activity. For we are trained to weave a constant web of relations, in which we and all the people and things around us are caught up. Each object and each person is negated in itself so that it can be seen in relation to other objects and other persons, to extrinsic functions, uses, and values judged by standards set somewhere far from us or perhaps nowhere at all. Our gaze careens constantly from point to point, never lingering over anything and in the end seeing nothing.

In order to rediscover the absolute we have only to cut those ties and regard each face and each tree without reference to any other thing, as though it were the only thing that existed in the world, as though it were "useless yet indispensable," as Cocteau once said of poetry. When I drink a glass of water there is nothing to stop me from immersing myself in it totally, from plunging into its cool freshness, from enjoying the faint taste of the rocks over which it has flowed and feeling the cold serpent that wriggles its way down my esophagus while my fingers clutch the frosty surface of the glass. An apple—its weight in my hand, its polished skin, the crack it makes when I bite into it, the acid taste that steals over my palate—deserves a moment's rapt attention, an attentive and sensuous eternity.

Surely, though, it is in those most privileged of all places, the desert island and the walled garden, that the absolute—that flower of metaphysics—takes on its most exalted forms. The desert island as a geographical symbol of the absolute forms the conclusion of *Friday*. Crusoe becomes aware of this when the arrival of an English schooner offers him the opportunity to return to his native England twenty-eight years after his shipwreck. He refuses to go. He will never leave Speranza, the island of eternal youth, discovered at the end of a long and painful metamorphosis guided by the hand of Friday.

An island is a piece of land surrounded on all sides by water. This common definition already exhibits an affinity with the etymology of the word *absolute*. But one must distinguish between an island and a continent, which also fits the definition. The difference has to do first of all with size, but size introduces a more essential criterion. An is-

land's climate is subject to the influence of the sea throughout its entire extent, whereas a continent is large enough
to escape that influence, at least in part. England, for example, has a maritime climate and is therefore an island,
but Australia, with its extremes of weather in the center,
is a continent.

Thus the island, swept throughout by the ocean breeze,
is part of the sea's domain. And if land is memory, alteration, torment inflicted by time, the sea greets every storm
with the same elastic, unalterable surface. The sea does not
know how to grow old. A stone tells its own history, a
millennial tale embodied in every crack and eroded surface. The ocean wave is no older than the first day of creation.

The island, obedient to the sea's injunction, bathes in
eternity. The sea air effaces the differences between months
and drowns the seasons in uniformity. Ultimately an island has only one season: it is always summer. Rows of
palms sway gently in the salt breeze beneath cerulean
skies. Crusoe, a man who has become an island, fully
shares in these privileges. Eternal youth is his to enjoy.
Who would be so cruel as to imagine a Tahitian woman
elderly, toothless, and in her dotage? The island woman
remains unalterably fresh and desirable. If Crusoe refuses to leave Speranza, it is because he shudders at the
thought of succumbing to old age the moment he rejoins
society.

The garden is just the opposite. A continental creation,
it never escapes the round of the seasons. Fruits follow
flowers, both give way to the russet of autumn, and the
most perfect garden of all is the garden beneath the snow.
The man who resembles a garden ages well. He grows
long in the tooth, and every wrinkle embellishes his face.
The cemetery that he can see from his window if he hap-

pens to live in a presbytery is yet another garden. For the gardener the absolute does not encompass an infinite expanse of time but is compressed into one mystical moment.

I choose the garden. Mine is just under two hundred square feet, an ideal size, just big enough for me to take care of by myself without the help of a gardener. A square outline and old walls add to its perfection. But a garden is more than plane geometry. It has a third dimension, for it is the gardener's vocation to dig the earth and question the sky. To claim full possession of a garden one must do more than lay it out and rake it up. One must be intimate with the soil and gauge the course of the clouds.

The gardener also knows a fourth dimension: the metaphysical. Every summer morning, as I toast my bread and steep my tea by an open window through which I can smell the grass and hear the wind in the linden branches, I suddenly become aware that time has been compressed, that space has shrunk to those few square feet enclosed by a stone wall, and that a single living thing—my garden—flourishes in the exorbitant immobility of the absolute. The sun's first ray daubs the white trunk of a certain birch with pink, so that it glows like flesh amid the surrounding black fir. The earth, the sky, and the intervening chaos of vegetation assert their sovereignty. A warbler bends an old sweetbrier to the ground. Like a hairy, clenched fist a hedgehog sleeps in the shadow of the cosmos. Still damp from its nightly hunt, the cat comes toward me on silent feet. The present lingers on eternally in a divine improvidence and amnesia.

NOTES

Chapter 1: Born Under a Lucky Star

1. On the proper use of occupations: in January 1759, the French occupied Frankfurt. The Count de Thoranc, the king's lieutenant and a native of Grasse, moved into Goethe's parents' home and remained for two years. Little Wolfgang was ten. The nobleman from Provence taught him French and introduced him to the theater and painting. Yet the hostility of Goethe's father toward the occupying force never diminished, and Wolfgang was torn between the two men.

2. One day, as I was rereading *Madame Bovary* in the presence of my mother, I hit upon a sentence so beautiful in what Flaubert rightly calls its "henormity" that I could not prevent myself from reading it out loud. It is the sentence in which Homais says

of Emma Bovary that "she is a most resourceful woman, who would not be out of place in a subprefecture." I forgot that the woman in the room with me was the daughter of the pharmacist of Bligny-sur-Ouche. She pointed out that in that tiny village the city to which people referred as *the* city was not the prefecture, Dijon, but the much closer subprefecture, Beaune. So that for the people of Bligny it was—and perhaps still is—a mark of genuine urbanity to frequent the society of Beaune. But Flaubert's sarcastic caricature is evident in the fact that he has Homais say "subprefecture" instead of "Beaune."

3. See Robert Jaulin, *La Mort Sara,* published by Plon, which recounts real central African initiation ceremonies.

4. The most important work on the subject is René Zazzo's *Les Jumeaux, le couple et la personne.*

5. See the book *L'Attachement* in the Zethos series begun by René Zazzo.

6. Professor Léon Robin was famous around the Sorbonne for a comment that he never failed to make about this line in the *Monadology:* "Where the devil did Leibniz get the idea that people go in and out of windows?" Then, after a moment of ponderous silence, he would add, "Perhaps he meant glass doors."

7. Marcel Jouhandeau (1888–1979), novelist and essayist.

8. Frédéric Lange, author of the profound and enjoyable *Manger ou les jeux et les creux du plat,* published by Seuil, has called my attention to the humor in this formula. Is it really worth the trouble of writing out all those odd symbols to arrive at such a paltry result? The zero at the end of the equation is like the silly round mouth of a garbage disposal.

9. "Les Albums de Bécassine" were a series of picture books published in the 1920s and 1930s by Caumery, the pen name of Maurice Languereau, and illustrated by J.-P. Pichon—Trans.

10. Louis Pergaud (1882–1915), an elementary school teacher and poet with a profound grasp of the child's psychology.

11. Published in *Le Coq de Bruyère* (translated by Barbara Wright as *The Fetishist*).

12. This important book was oddly enough also published under another title: *Le Pur et l'impur.*

13. See especially Georges Snyders, *La Pédagogie en France aux XVIIe et XVIIIe siècles*, published by the Presses Universitaires de France.

14. Hugues Félicité Robert de Lamennais (1782–1854) was a priest who incurred the wrath of Rome for his defense of the French Revolution and his call for the separation of church and state. Ultimately he quit the Catholic Church and became active in republican politics. But Louis Napoleon's coup d'état in December 1851 ended that hope, too, and Lamennais died in despair—Trans.

Chapter 2: The Ogre

1. Charles Maurras (1868–1952) was a French writer and politician remembered as the founder of an antidemocratic, nationalist movement known by the name of its principal organ, the *Action française*—Trans.

2. The Croix-de-Feu was an extreme right-wing organization that achieved notoriety in the 1930s under the leadership of Colonel François de La Rocque—Trans.

3. Despite the name, the Radical-Socialist Party was neither radical nor socialist but pragmatic and centrist—Trans.

4. Maurice Leblanc (1864–1941) was the creator of the famous detective Arsène Lupin—Trans.

5. In those days wheat was transported to the farmyard in sheafs for threshing, and the chaff was used to line the floors of barns and stables, from which it emerged as manure. Today, manure has been replaced by chemical fertilizer, and the animals are kept in dry stables. No longer useful, the chaff is therefore ground up by the combine and returned to the earth.

6. Jean Wahl has since published a magisterial study.

7. At the time the prisons were filled with "collaborators." According to several accounts, the threat of a return of the Germans "coincided" with a marked improvement in their treatment. Human cowardice knows no limits.

8. Published in *Le Coq de Bruyère* (*The Fetishist*).

9. The writer Gyorgy Vladimov, much harassed by the Soviet government, had this to say in an interview published in *Le*

Monde on January 5, 1979: "No, I do not want to leave my country. I do not want to become an American writer or a French writer. I can only be a Russian writer. I was born here, I have lived here too long, I know Russian and the Russians, and I am not at all sure that I could live as a writer in the West. The novelist must live with his characters, he must share their fate. Of course those who live abroad are freer. They can write what they want and have access to whatever they want to read. But little by little they lose their tie to Russia. After two or three years they begin to think in a Western mode, like free men. And slowly what is unique about Russia vanishes from their memories. Of course I would like to see the world. But unless the prospect of return remains open, I cannot leave."

10. When these lines first appeared in France, they aroused righteous indignation on both the right and left. Yet they follow directly from my assumption that language and nationality are identical. In my view, anyone who speaks and writes French is French, and the better he speaks and writes it, the more French he is. Léopold Senghor, who is Senegalese by birth and breeding yet holds a doctorate in French grammar and writes admirable French poetry, is more French than most of the palefaces born on the banks of the Seine or the Loire. As for Robert Brasillach, I might have made the same point by saying that his judges wrote French less well than he did, although he was not a writer of the first rank—far from it. Furthermore, I am particularly fond of the word *métèque* (literally *metic,* used pejoratively in French as English uses *wog*), one of the last curse words in the language, if not the last. When it has disappeared—or, what comes to the same thing, lost its invective force—we will no longer have the means to sin verbally.

11. The *agrégation* is the highest competitive examination for teachers in France, leading to teaching either the last year of secondary school or university students—TRANS.

12. Claude Lanzmann is perhaps best known as the director of *Shoah,* a documentary film study of the Nazi extermination camps—TRANS.

13. Serge Rezvani (born 1928), an Iranian-born French novelist and playwright.

14. The Universum Film Aktiengesellschaft, or UFA, was a

leading German film studio which became a tool of Nazi propaganda—TRANS.

15. Hans Habe's *Christoph und sein Vater* was published by Desch in 1966.

16. See page 418 of the Folio paperback edition of *Le Roi des aulnes*.

17. This work has since been published in French under the title *Pas à pas avec Hitler* ("Step by Step with Hitler") by the Presses de la Cité.

18. Charles Perrault (1628–1703), the creator of the *Mother Goose Tales*.

19. The English verses here are translated directly from the author's French renderings of the German. In the American edition of *The Ogre,* the translation given of *The Erl-König* is by Walter Scott and obscures the point being made here—TRANS.

20. From this root I thought I had created a new word in *The Ogre: pedophore,* or bearer-transporter of children. I later learned that the Greek poet Meleager of Gadara writing in the first century B.C. used the word *pedophorus* specifically to refer to the wind, thus creating a bridge between *The Ogre* and *Gemini.*

21. Alphonse Daudet's admirable novel *Sapho* recounts an affair between Jean Gaussin, a very young Provençal newly arrived in Paris, and Sapho, a woman who is no longer young, a bit of an ogre, and quite fatal, whose body, bruised by a thousand affairs and breakups, closes around the young man like a trap. On the night they meet he takes her home, to the fifth floor of a student hotel where he is living. He carries her in his arms "like a child, for he was strong and well-built . . . and he ran up the first flight of stairs in a single bound." But the second flight proves longer, and by the third he is grunting like a housemover. The fourth flight is pure agony. Daudet should have ended his chapter there and trusted in his reader's intelligence. Alas, he felt obliged to add this clumsy comment: "Their entire story was told in that trip up the stairs in the dawn's depressing gray."

22. Published in French translation by Seuil.

23. From the Greek *kolaph,* for slap.

24. Marcel Déat, a French political figure of the 1930s who began as a socialist and ended as a fascist—TRANS.

Chapter 3: The Mythic Dimension

1. Gaston Bachelard (1884–1962), French philosopher. The books mentioned in the text are published in English translation by Beacon Press—TRANS.

2. Henri Petiot (1901–65), who wrote under the pen name Daniel-Rops, is best known for his novel *L'Ame obscure*. Maurice de Gandillac is a philosopher—TRANS.

3. Gilles Deleuze is a philosopher best known in the United States for his *Anti-Oedipus*, written with Felix Guattari—TRANS.

4. Alain Clément has more recently served as *Le Monde*'s United States correspondent—TRANS.

5. Louis de Saint-Just (1767–94) was along with Robespierre a leader of the Reign of Terror in the French Revolution—TRANS.

6. Pierre Ponson du Terrail (1829–71) was a popular nineteenth-century writer and creator of the character Rocambole. Saint-John Perse was the pen name of the diplomat and poet Alexis Léger (1887–1975), who won the Nobel Prize for literature in 1960.

7. Ubu was the creation of Alfred Jarry (1873–1907).

8. François Châtelet is a French philosopher whose works include *Platon*, published by Gallimard.

9. Michel Butor (born 1926) is a leading practitioner of the *nouveau roman*, or new novel.

10. Published by Knopf in 1943.

11. "I have just as many muscles as Hercules," wrote Paul Valéry. "It's just that they are smaller." That was his way of dealing with the problem of quantity and quality.

12. Entitled *Vendredi ou la vie sauvage* and published in the Folio Junior collection.

13. From the Latin *scrupulus*, meaning a small, pointed stone.

14. The Duke de La Rochefoucauld (1613–80) was the author of the famous *Maximes*—TRANS.

15. The noted anthropologist Claude Lévi-Strauss was for a time director of the Musée de l'Homme, Paris's museum of anthropology—TRANS.

16. Paul Bourget (1852–1935), René Bazin (1853–1932), and Delly, pseudonym of Marie Petitjean de La Rosière (1875–1947) and his brother Frédéric (1876–1949), were all French writers of a rather conventional stamp.

17. Victor Cherbuliez (1829–99), French writer.

18. Jacques Bénigne Bossuet (1627–1704), France's most illustrious literary ecclesiastic.

19. Léon Bloy (1846–1917), writer and author of a journal entitled *Le Mendiant ingrat* ("The Ungrateful Beggar").

20. Jean Cocteau (1889–1963), poet and writer.

Chapter 4: Friday

1. From pages 106 and 108 of the 1955 Oxford edition, edited by Rae Blanchard; spelling modernized—TRANS.

2. This is, however, the theme of Saint-John Perse's admirable *Images à Crusoé.*

3. Roland Jaccard, *L'Exil intérieur: Schizoïdie et civilisation,* published by Presses Universitaires de France.

4. As a child, though, I was much impressed by Benjamin Rabier's vehemently anticolonialist picture book, *Le Fond du sac* (1921).

5. Montesquieu (1689–1755) wrote among other things a satire of European society entitled *Lettres persanes*—TRANS.

Chapter 5: The Meteors, or Gemini

1. The same idea is contained in the original sense of the French verb *acharner.* Breeders of hunting birds and dogs "les acharnaient," or fed them raw meat, in order to foster in them a taste for blood and enthusiasm for the hunt.

2. A third famous escaped convict in French literature deserves a study of his own: Molière's Tartuffe.

3. My students at the University of Paris VII called my attention to the *phoric* aspects of Valjean's character. It is in carrying a bucket of water that this chaste man comes to know Cosette. He experiences the fullness of possession while carrying her in his arms. And finally, he saves her fiancé Marius by carrying him through the sewers of Paris.

4. Monstrous as this sentence may be, it does shed a new light on the psychology of the normal couple and as such is an excellent example of the way in which studying exceptional cases can add to our understanding of ordinary ones. I recently asked a friend of mine, the very image of the perfect husband and father,

if he was ever tempted to cheat on his wife. After a moment's thought he answered: "No, of course not. In fact I would find it rather disgusting to sleep with somebody I didn't know." Is there not a certain affinity between this supernormal view and the apparently pathological attitude of the twin? Both reflect an endogamic instinct, a horror of sex with strangers, that exists in everyone.

5. When asked about sexual relations with her sister, one twin hit upon this lovely formula: "At night things used to happen, but in the daytime we never talked about them."

6. I have always found it surprising that no one protests against the violently reactionary spirit of Molière's *Bourgeois Gentilhomme,* a ferocious satire of a commoner who dares to trespass upon the domain of culture, which the aristocracy regards as its private preserve.

7. The theme of absolute language is broached repeatedly: in the exchanges between the mentally retarded, the babbling of babies, the conversations of Adam and Eve, the rhythms that retarded Franz takes from the Jacquard loom and the fireworks, the twins' cryptophasia, Koussek's pentecostal logos, old Méline's mumbo-jumbo, and finally the cosmic ear imputed to Paul after his amputation.

8. Jules Barbey d'Aurevilly (1808–89) and Maurice Barrès (1862–1923), French writers.

9. See "Le Voyage à Hammamet" in *Voyages,* a special issue of *La Nouvelle Revue Française* published in October 1974.

10. Chiefly in the *Essai sur les données immédiates de la conscience.*

Chapter 6: Sophia's Misfortunes

1. These few lines would suffice to make Spinoza the anti-Pascal par excellence. Everything else simply heightens the contrast.

2. "There are things for which intelligence may search forever but that it will never find unaided. Those things instinct will find, but on its own it will never look for them"—Henri Bergson, *L'Evolution créatrice.*

3. The law of universal gravitation states that two bodies will

attract each other with a force directly proportional to the product of their mass and inversely proportional to the square of the distance between them.

4. Brendan Liddell's translation—TRANS.

5. This simple sentence contains two words whose ambiguity is precious. *Hēlikia* means both age and stature, and *charis*, or favor, is sometimes translated as *grace*, a word that combines physical (choreographic) charm with divine benediction.

6. *Humanité* is the newspaper of the French Communist Party, and it holds a fair for party members and others each year outside Paris—TRANS.

7. In this connection see Hermann Hesse's novel *Magister Ludi: The Glass Bead Game*. That brain power alone is not enough is illustrated in the end by the hero's tender and ironic drowning.

8. Jean Cocteau, *Le Foyer des artistes*, published by Plon.

9. Gide on Proust: "He answered that first of all what attracts him is almost never beauty and that in his judgment it has little to do with desire." See André Gide, *Journal*, p. 694 of the Gallimard edition.